Practical Advice from
Thirteen Experts Who've
Walked in Your Shoes

Living a
Covenant
Marriage

Edited by Douglas E. Brinley and Daniel K Judd

DESERET
BOOK

SALT LAKE CITY, UTAH

Library of Congress Cataloging-in-Publication Data

Living a covenant marriage : practical advice from thirteen experts who've walked in your shoes / [edited by] Douglas E. Brinley, Daniel K Judd.
    p.   cm.
    Includes bibliographical references and index.
    ISBN 1-59038-278-1 (hardbound : alk. paper)
    1. Marriage—Religious aspects—Church of Jesus Christ of Latter-day Saints.   2. Church of Jesus Christ of Latter-day Saints—Doctrines.   3. Spouses—Religious life.   I. Brinley, Douglas E. II. Judd, Daniel K
BX8641.H64 2004
248.8'44'088289332—dc22   2003027512

Printed in the United States of America   72076
Publishers Printing, Salt Lake City, UT

10   9   8   7   6   5   4   3   2   1

Contents

Preface

A decade ago, we asked a number of marriage counselors and family life educators whom we knew and respected to write a chapter for a Deseret Book publication entitled *Eternal Companions*. The assignment we gave to each author was to "write a chapter on what you do or recommend to Latter-day Saint couples to resolve marital problems and enrich their marriages." That particular volume contained wise and practical counsel to help husbands and wives strengthen their marriages.

Now Deseret Book's director of publishing has asked us to do it again. Marriage and family problems certainly have not disappeared. In fact, President Gordon B. Hinckley indicated that his greatest concern as Church president was the disintegration of marriages and families worldwide. Early in his tenure as president, he said: "I am concerned about family life in the Church. We have wonderful people, but we have too many whose families are falling apart. It is a matter of serious concern. I think it is my most serious concern."[1]

That statement has proven to be prophetic, not only with an increase in the dissolution of marriage but with the springing up of alternatives to marriage ("civil unions" for gay and lesbian couples, for example). To be sure, the challenges to marital stability and spousal harmony have not lessened in the intervening years. The present volume is our attempt to provide some perspective and suggestions for couples to divorce-proof, as well as enrich, their marriages.

We asked a few of the previous authors and some new contributors to share their best counsel on marriage from a gospel perspective.

Elder Bruce C. Hafen, a member of the First Quorum of Seventy, begins the volume with an excellent article adapted from his conference address on covenant (versus contract) marriage. Each of the remaining contributors is either a teacher in an educational or professional setting or is a marriage counselor in private practice with extensive experience working with Latter-day Saint couples.

The book is written for couples, rather than a professional audience, thus avoiding the technical jargon that often gets in the way of simple, powerful gospel principles that can change the course of marriage for the better. The practical counsel and insights will help husbands and wives improve their own perspectives and practice of gospel principles, which in turn will aid them in one of the greatest adventures of mortality—marriage and family relations.

Our thanks to Cory Maxwell at Deseret Book, whose encouragement motivated us to produce a book that will inspire and strengthen married couples in their quest for a "celestial marriage." We appreciate the efforts and professional assistance of Chris Schoebinger and Jay Parry of Deseret Book, who helped make this volume more readable and professional in its presentation.

Note

1. "Pres. Hinckley Notes His 85th Birthday, Reminisces about Life," *Church News,* 24 June 1995, 6.

1

Covenant Marriage

Elder Bruce C. Hafen

Some time ago I watched a new bride and groom, Tracy and Tom, emerge from a sacred temple.[1] They laughed and held hands as family and friends gathered to take pictures. I saw happiness and promise in their faces as they greeted their reception guests, who celebrated publicly the creation of a new family. I wondered that night how long it would be until these two faced the opposition that tests every marriage. Only then would they discover whether their marriage was based on a *contract* or a *covenant*.

Another bride sighed blissfully on her wedding day, "Mom, I'm at the end of all my troubles!" "Yes," replied her mother, "but which end?"

When troubles come, the parties to a *contractual* marriage seek happiness by walking away. They marry to obtain benefits and will stay only as long as they're receiving what they bargained for. But when troubles come to a *covenant* marriage, the husband and wife work them though. They marry to give and to grow, bound by the covenants to each other, to the community, and to God. *Contract* companions each give 50 percent; *covenant* companions each give 100 percent.[2]

Marriage is by nature a covenant, not just a private contract one may cancel at will. Jesus taught about contractual attitudes when he described the "hireling" who performs his conditional promise of care only when he receives something in return. When the hireling "seeth the wolf coming," he "leaveth the sheep, and fleeth . . . because he . . . careth not for the sheep." By contrast the Savior said, "I am the

1

good shepherd, . . . and I lay down my life for the sheep" (John 10:12–15). Many people today marry as hirelings. And when the wolf comes, they flee. This idea is wrong. It curses the earth, turning parents' hearts away from their children and from each other.

Before their marriage, Tom and Tracy received an eternal perspective on covenants and wolves. They learned through the story of Adam and Eve about life's purpose and how to return to God's presence through obedience and the Atonement. Christ's life is the story of giving the Atonement. The life of Adam and Eve is the story of receiving the Atonement, which empowered them to overcome their separation from God and all opposition until they were eternally "at one" with the Lord and with each other (see D&C 2).

Without the Fall, Lehi taught, Adam and Eve would never have known opposition: "And they would have had no children; wherefore they would have remained in a state of innocence, having no joy, for they knew no misery" (2 Nephi 2:23). Astute parents will see a little connection here—no children, no misery! But left in the garden, they could never know joy. So the Lord taught them they would live and bear children in sorrow, sweat, and thorns.

Still, the ground was cursed *for their sake* (see Moses 4:23): Their path of affliction also led to the joy of both redemption and comprehension (see Moses 5:11). That is why the husband and wife in a covenant marriage sustain and lift each other when the wolf comes. If Tom and Tracy had understood all this, perhaps they would have walked more slowly from the gardenlike temple grounds, like Adam and Eve, arm in arm, into a harsh and lonely world.

And yet, marrying and raising children *can* yield the most valuable religious experiences of their lives. Covenant marriage requires a total leap of faith: they must keep their covenants without knowing what risks that may require of them. They must surrender unconditionally, obeying God and sacrificing for each other. Then they will discover what Alma called "incomprehensible joy" (Alma 28:8).

Of course, some have no opportunity to marry. And some

divorces are unavoidable. But the Lord will ultimately compensate those faithful ones who are denied mortal fulfillment.

Every marriage is tested repeatedly by three kinds of wolves. The first wolf is natural adversity. After asking God for years to give them a first child, David and Fran had a baby with a serious heart defect. Following a three-week struggle, they buried their newborn son. Like Adam and Eve before them, they mourned together, brokenhearted, in faith before the Lord (see Moses 5:27).

Second, the wolf of their own imperfections will test them. One woman told me through her tears how her husband's constant criticism finally destroyed not only their marriage but her entire sense of self-worth. He first complained about her cooking and housecleaning, and then about how she used her time, how she talked, looked, and reasoned. Eventually she felt utterly inept and dysfunctional. My heart ached for her, and for him.

Contrast her with a young woman who had little self-confidence when she first married. Then her husband found so much to praise in her that she gradually began to believe she was a good person and that her opinions mattered. His belief in her rekindled her innate self-worth.

The third wolf is the excessive individualism that has spawned today's contractual attitudes. A seven-year-old girl came home from school crying, "Mom, don't I belong to you? Our teacher said today that nobody *belongs* to anybody—children don't belong to parents, husbands don't belong to wives. I am *yours*, aren't I, Mom?" Her mother held her close and whispered, "Of course you're mine—and I'm yours, too." Surely marriage partners must respect one another's individual identity, and family members are neither slaves nor inanimate objects. But this teacher's fear, shared today by many, is that the bonds of kinship and marriage are not valuable ties that bind, but are instead sheer bondage. Ours is the age of the waning of belonging.

The adversary has long cultivated this overemphasis on personal autonomy, and now he feverishly exploits it. Our deepest God-given instinct is to run to the arms of those who need us and sustain us. But he drives us away from each other today with wedges of distrust and suspicion. He exaggerates the need for having space, getting out, and being left alone. Some people believe him—and then they wonder why they feel left alone. And despite admirable exceptions, children in America's growing number of single-parent families are clearly more at risk than children in two-parent families.[3] Further, the rates of divorce and births outside marriage are now so high that we may be witnessing "the collapse of marriage."[4]

Many people even wonder these days what marriage is. Should we prohibit same-sex marriage? Should we make divorce more difficult to obtain? Some say these questions are not society's business, because marriage is a private contract. But as the modern prophets recently proclaimed, "marriage . . . is ordained of God."[5] Even secular marriage was historically a three-party covenant among a man, a woman, and the state. Society has a huge interest in the outcome and the offspring of every marriage. So the public nature of marriage distinguishes it from all other relationships. Guests come to weddings because, as Wendell Berry said, sweethearts "say their vows to the community as much as to one another," giving themselves not only to each other, but also to the common good "as no *contract* could ever join them."[6]

When we observe the covenants we make at the altar of sacrifice, we discover hidden reservoirs of strength. I once said in exasperation to my wife, Marie, "The Lord placed Adam and Eve on the earth as full-grown people. Why couldn't he have done that with this boy of ours, the one with the freckles and the unruly hair?" She replied, "The Lord gave us that child to make Christians out of us."

One night Marie exhausted herself for hours encouraging that child to finish a school assignment to build his own diorama of a Native American village on a cookie sheet. It was a test no hireling would have endured. At first he fought her efforts, but by bedtime, I saw him set "his" diorama proudly on a counter. He started for his bed, then turned around, raced back across the room, and hugged his

4

mother, grinning with his fourth-grade teeth. Later I asked Marie in complete awe, "How did you do it?" She said, "I just made up my mind that I couldn't leave him, no matter what." Then she added, "*I didn't know I had it in me.*" She discovered deep internal wellsprings of compassion because of her strength to lay down her life for her sheep, even an hour at a time.

Now I return to Tom and Tracy, who discovered wellsprings of their own. Their second baby threatened to come too early to live. They might have made a hireling's convenient choice and gone on with their lives, letting a miscarriage occur. But because they tried "to observe their covenants by sacrifice" (D&C 97:8), active, energetic Tracy lay almost motionless at home for five weeks, then in a hospital bed for another five. Tom was with her virtually every hour when he was not working or sleeping. They prayed their child to earth. Then the baby required eleven more weeks in the hospital. But she is here, and she is theirs.

One night as Tracy waited patiently upon the Lord in the hospital, she sensed that perhaps her willingness to sacrifice herself for her baby was in some small way like the Good Shepherd's sacrifice for her. She said, "I had expected that trying to give so much would be really difficult, but somehow this felt more like a privilege." As many other parents in Zion have done, she and Tom gave their hearts to God by giving them to their child. In the process, they learned that theirs is a covenant marriage, one that binds them to each other and to the Lord.

May we restore the concept of marriage as a covenant, even "the new and everlasting covenant of marriage" (D&C 131:2). And when the wolf comes, may we be as shepherds, not hirelings, willing to lay down our lives a day at a time, for the sheep of our covenant. Then, like Adam and Eve, we will have joy (see 2 Nephi 2:25).

Notes

1. This chapter has been adapted from an address given by Elder Bruce C. Hafen at the 166th Semiannual General Conference, 5 October 1996. See "Covenant Marriage," *Ensign*, November 1996, 26–28.

2. See Bruce C. Hafen and Marie K. Hafen, *The Belonging Heart* (Salt Lake City: Deseret Book, 1994), 257–65; Pitirim Sorokin, *Society, Culture and Personality,* 2nd ed. (New York: Cooper Square Publishers, 1962), 99–107.
3. See Barbara Dafoe Whitehead, "Dan Quayle Was Right," *Atlantic Monthly,* April 1993, 47.
4. Maggie Gallagher, *The Abolition of Marriage* (Washington, D. C.: Regnery Publishing, 1996), 4–5.
5. "The Family: A Proclamation to the World," *Ensign,* November 1995, 102.
6. See Wendell Berry, *Sex, Economy, Freedom and Community* (New York: Pantheon Books, 1993), 137–38; emphasis added.

2

Gospel-Based Marital Therapy, Part 1: The Foundation

Douglas E. Brinley

I have always felt that bibliotherapy—resolving personal and family issues through good literature—can generate ideas and solutions for us to function more effectively as individuals and spouses. This is especially true when we read inspirational material such as scripture, conference talks, articles from Church magazines, and a variety of uplifting publications and periodicals. I want to share a few excerpts from some favorite readings that influenced me to be a better husband and a more softhearted father. These five quotes happen to come from the sermons or writings of prophets, seers, and revelators.

Excerpt #1. Many years ago Elder Boyd K. Packer delivered a classic address at Brigham Young University and then later in general conference.[1] In it, he said:

> We seem to be developing an epidemic of "counselitis" which drains spiritual strength from the Church. . . .
>
> That, some may assume, is not serious. It is very serious! . . .
>
> We have become very anxious over the amount of counseling that we seem to need in the Church. Our members are becoming dependent. . . .
>
> *If we are not careful, we can lose the power of individual revelation.* . . .
>
> Spiritual independence and self-reliance is a sustaining power in the Church. If we rob the members of that, how can they get revelation for themselves? How will they know there is a prophet of God? How can they get answers to prayers? How can they know for *sure* for themselves? . . .

There may be a time when deep-seated emotional problems need more help than can be given by the family, the bishop, or the stake president. . . .[2]

. . . Ultimately it is the member who must solve [his or her problems]. . . .

If you find a case where professional help is justified, be very careful.

There are some spiritually destructive techniques used in the field of counseling. . . . Solve problems in the Lord's way.

Some counselors want to delve deeper than is emotionally or spiritually healthy. They sometimes want to draw out and analyze and take apart and dissect.

While a certain amount of catharsis may be healthy, over-much of it can be degenerating. It is seldom as easy to put something back together as it is to take it apart.

By probing too deeply, or talking endlessly about some problems, we can foolishly cause the very thing we are trying to prevent. . . .

We live in a day when the adversary stresses on every hand the philosophy of instant gratification. We seem to demand *instant* everything, including instant solutions to our problems.

We are indoctrinated that somehow we should always be instantly emotionally comfortable. When that is not so, some become anxious—and all too frequently seek relief from counseling, from analysis, and even from medication.

It was meant to be that life would be a challenge. To suffer some anxiety, some depression, some disappointment, even some failure is normal.

Teach our members that if they have a good, miserable day once in a while, or several in a row, to stand steady and face them. Things will straighten out.

There is great purpose in our struggle in life.[3]

I thought this was wise counsel back in the 1970s and even more so today. We live in a day when it is fashionable for people to have a "personal therapist." Someone will say, "My therapist thinks I should . . ." or "My analyst says I need to be more. . . ." Of course we appreciate receiving information and ideas from experienced, competent people. For example, when we suffer a serious malady we want a doctor who has extensive experience outside of a textbook. We want a surgeon who has repeatedly performed an operation similar to what we need. Likewise, therapists and other health professionals can be helpful with complex issues such as depression, schizophrenia, personality disorders, addictions, and so forth, because they have experience in treating organic malfunctions and destructive psychological behavior that is beyond the scope of most of us. There is no need to invent the wheel again when serious complications exist, or to deny that they exist.[4]

On the other hand, Latter-day Saints have an abundance of gospel resources to resolve marital problems, resources besides the medical or mental health model. We understand the gospel of Jesus Christ, the plan of salvation, which orients us to the purposes of mortality and aids us in dealing with life's challenges and trials. We have each other. As spouses, we are to be therapists for one another.

We knew before we left our premortal home that we would be going through experiences that would help develop our mental, emotional, physical, spiritual, and social character. Growth in physical and emotional attributes comes through confronting and overcoming challenges that are inherent in our fallen natures. Through our experiences here in a telestial environment where Satan resides, we are learning how to qualify for exaltation and life eternal. As couples we are apprenticing in a divinely ordained curriculum that has as its objective the goal of preparing and refining us for life as exalted beings. Such graduate work will require our very best effort; it was not meant to be easy. Marriage and parenthood experiences are perhaps the toughest of all challenges we face in this estate.

Sometimes as couples we just need to step back and review the "big picture," the divine purposes inherent in our first-time experience with marriage and family. This is our initial adventure into marriage, procreation, and parenthood. Though we were brothers and sisters to each other in the premortal life, and sons and daughters to God, in our first estate we were never husbands or wives, fathers or mothers. Following the resurrection we will no longer be subject to death. Divorce will be unknown. So mortality is our time to learn how to be capable, loving spouses and parents. Gospel principles provide us with the conceptual model, while priesthood power unites a couple and family in an eternal relationship. We ought to be able to resolve marital difficulties because we understand the purpose of marriage as a preparation for a relationship of eternal duration. Our entire theology is geared to help us succeed as married companions. A gospel-based therapy, therefore, should be our first line of defense in building a solid, stable companionship.

My thoughts on the value of looking at marriage from the perspective of a gospel-based therapy were generated in a personal conversation years ago with Carlfred Broderick, a well-known Latter-day Saint who trained professional marriage counselors at a prestigious California university. His graduate curriculum for his students was, of course, secular in nature rather than gospel-oriented. On one occasion he commented to me, "Doug, we're not saving very many, are we." It was not a question but an observation based on a great deal of experience with counseling techniques, observing and intervening with couples, teaching communication skills to graduate students and clients, and using the theories and research of psychologists in an attempt to help troubled couples. Yet the low success rate in keeping marriages intact was disturbing to him. His comment has come back to me over the years as I have met people who spent thousands of dollars and countless hours in marital "therapy," to no avail.[5] The secular approach fails so many. And there is nothing more disconcerting to a counselor than to lose his clients to divorce or separation—or to see

10

them remain in a marriage that is detrimental to their character without being able to change it.

Excerpt #2. President Joseph Fielding Smith was the Church president when I was a young married husband and father. He made this observation:

> If all mankind would live in strict obedience to the gospel, and in that love which *is begotten by the Spirit of the Lord,* all marriages would be eternal, divorce would be unknown. Divorce is not part of the gospel plan and has been introduced because of the *hardness of heart and unbelief of the people....*
>
> There *never could be a divorce* in this Church *if* the husband and wife were keeping the commandments of God....
>
> When divorce comes to those who are married in the temple, it has come because they have *violated the covenants and the obligations* they have taken upon themselves to be true to each other, true to God, true to the Church. If they will continue to live in that faithfulness, if they will have love in their hearts for each other, respect each other's rights and not one attempt to take an advantage unduly of the other but have the proper consideration, *there will be no failures....*
>
> Now I realize that there are some cases where a wife needs to have a separation, perhaps a husband should have a separation, but *always* because of a violation, a serious *violation of the covenants* that have been made....
>
> Marriage according to the law of the Church is the most holy and sacred ordinance. It will bring to the husband and the wife, if they abide in their covenants, the fulness of exaltation in the kingdom of God. When that covenant is broken, it will bring *eternal misery to the guilty party,* for we will all have to answer for our deeds done while in the flesh. It is an ordinance that cannot be trifled with, and the covenants made in the temple cannot be broken without dire punishment to the one who is guilty.[6]

President Smith's comments persuaded me years ago that divorce and marital problems were mostly spiritual problems and that spiritual penalties exist for violating marriage covenants. We tend to ignore such comments in a day when divorce is easily accepted. He suggested that couples who live the gospel on a daily basis will find happiness through righteous living because they will have the Spirit of the Lord with them, thus eliminating the need for relief through divorce. He boldly stated that divorce is typically the result of transgression, unfaithfulness to covenants, a failure to look to God and the plan of salvation for solutions, and a lack of understanding of the doctrinal importance of marriage in the eternal plan.

I think one of his most important statements, however, is this one:

> If a man or a woman who has been sealed in the temple for time and eternity should sin and lose the right to receive the exaltation in the celestial kingdom, he or she could not retard the progress of the injured companion who had been faithful. Everyone will be judged according to his works, and there would be no justice in condemning the innocent for the sin of the guilty.[7]

This quote gives those who are mostly innocent in a breakup of a temple marriage some relief from guilt, particularly when they know they did all in their power to keep the marriage together.

Excerpt #3. President Ezra Taft Benson said:

> The . . . family has serious problems. Divorce is epidemic. The incidence of delinquency is on the rise. The answer is *not more marriage counselors or social workers.* The answer lies in a husband and wife *taking their marriage covenant seriously,* realizing that they both have a . . . responsibility to make their marriage a happy one.[8]

President Benson saw the increase in divorce statistics as a failure on the part of spouses to live their marriage covenants. His primary solution to the deterioration of marriage and the family was not to encourage those involved to seek outside help; rather, he encouraged a man and a wife to be faithful to their covenants with Heavenly Father.

Excerpt #4. President Gordon B. Hinckley taught:

Why all of these broken homes? What happens to marriages that begin with sincere love and a desire to be loyal and faithful and true one to another?

There is no simple answer. I acknowledge that. But it appears to me that there are some obvious reasons that account for a very high percentage of these problems. I say this out of experience in dealing with such tragedies. I find *selfishness* to be the root cause of most of it.

I am satisfied that a happy marriage is not so much a matter of romance as it is an anxious concern for the comfort and well-being of one's companion.

Selfishness so often is the basis of money problems, which are a very serious and real factor affecting the stability of family life. Selfishness is at the root of adultery, the breaking of solemn and sacred covenants to satisfy selfish lust. Selfishness is the antithesis of love. It is a cankering expression of greed. It destroys self-discipline. It obliterates loyalty. It tears up sacred covenants. It afflicts both men and women.

Too many who come to marriage have been coddled and spoiled and somehow led to feel that everything must be precisely right at all times, that life is a series of entertainments, that appetites are to be satisfied without regard to principle. How tragic the consequences of such hollow and unreasonable thinking! . . .

There is a remedy for all of this. *It is not found in divorce.* It is found in the gospel of the Son of God. He it was who said, "What therefore God hath joined together, let not man put asunder" (Matt. 19:6). The remedy for most marriage stress is not in divorce. *It is in repentance.* It is not in separation. It is in simple integrity that leads a man to square up his shoulders and meet his obligations. It is found in the Golden Rule.[9]

President Hinckley echoed President Spencer W. Kimball's view that "every divorce is the result of selfishness on the part of one or the other or both parties to a marriage contract."[10]

Excerpt #5. President Gordon B. Hinckley said:

> If every man in this church who has been ordained to the Melchizedek Priesthood were to qualify himself to hold a temple recommend, and then were to go to the house of the Lord and renew his covenants in solemnity before God and witnesses, we would be a better people. There would be little or no infidelity among us. Divorce would almost entirely disappear. So much of heartache and heartbreak would be avoided. There would be a greater measure of peace and love and happiness in our homes. There would be fewer weeping wives and weeping children. There would be a greater measure of appreciation and of mutual respect among us. And I am confident the Lord would smile with greater favor upon us.[11]

A man must hold the Melchizedek Priesthood in order to marry in the temple. This level of priesthood involves an "oath and covenant" (D&C 84:39; see vv. 33–41) that he will be faithful to his ministry. A man who possesses this authority of God represents the Savior among men and women on the earth. He should do what the Lord would do if He were in the man's place. If a man held this priesthood, how would he treat a daughter of God, especially his spouse? How would such a man treat children who were given to him by God to rear in His behalf? Such a man should and would be an example of the same traits that Jesus manifested—traits we even refer to as "Christlike" traits.

Therapy through the Gospel

From these five excerpts, the following principles stand out:

1. Marriage between a man and woman is ordained of God and was intended by Deity to be an eternal companionship.

2. Divorce is not part of the gospel plan but comes about because of serious violations of marriage covenants and individual disobedience and transgression. Divorce is not pleasing to God. We do not want to disappoint the Father, the presiding authority in the universe; his Son, Jesus Christ; or the Holy Ghost.

3. The solution to marital problems is to honor personal temple covenants and live gospel principles on a daily basis so our hearts remain softened and we then conform our behavior to our gospel understanding.

4. When *both* marriage partners are loyal to each other, keep their covenants, and seek each other's welfare, they have the Spirit of the Lord in their lives. That Spirit then unites their hearts and souls in an everlasting tie.

5. Obvious solutions to marital stress lie in repentance, forgiveness, personal integrity, living the Golden Rule, keeping personal covenants, honoring priesthood obligations, and speaking together with respect and love as two Christlike people who are going through the experience of marriage for their first time in all eternity. Patience with each other should be a mandatory attribute because we must learn how to be spouses and parents from each other and our children. We have never been in these roles before!

6. A man must hold the Melchizedek Priesthood to marry in the temple. With that authority, he represents Christ to his spouse, children, and fellow mortals. He can perform miracles, if need be, and he has the stewardship to bring himself and his family back into the presence of God.

My thesis, therefore, is that a "gospel-based" therapy is an effective and powerful way to eliminate and correct most marital problems. In fact, in most cases (but not all), I believe it is far superior to methods involving only the philosophies of the secular world. To put it another way, knowing and understanding the doctrine of our Father's plan of salvation provides us with the most powerful incentives to do our best as married partners. That is one of the principal messages of the apostles and prophets in "The Family: A Proclamation to the World,"[12] where they categorically state that "happiness in family life *is most likely* to be achieved when founded upon the teachings of the Lord Jesus Christ."[13] All this is not to say that we can't learn from the research and thoughts of good people outside the Church—but we can more accurately understand their value when we understand the plan of salvation.

Here is my point: *Long-term positive changes in behavior take place when both spouses understand and live in harmony with the truths of the restored gospel of Jesus Christ.*

At first glance, such a premise may appear obvious to most Church members. And, at least intellectually, I think most members agree. But my experience is that when individual Church members or couples are confronted by serious marital difficulties, many are quick to run to secular counselors for help. They seek those trained in the philosophies and theories of men while resisting solutions within the gospel framework. It is as if they think the principles of the gospel have little power to resolve serious marital problems. I say this because almost daily I receive phone calls from Church members seeking a marriage counselor. My first reaction to their call is this: "Why are you looking outside the gospel plan for help? Isn't it obvious that the first line of defense is what you *already know?* You learned the solutions in Primary, in Sunday School. The problem is that it takes two people to make a great marriage. One can sabotage the relationship. Most likely, one or both parties have lost the Spirit of the Lord. If you need help, start with yourselves, then if necessary you have a bishop or stake president. That is the Lord's program."

Perhaps they just want to shift the responsibility for solving their problems to someone else. It was President Harold B. Lee who reminded us:

Teach those who are having problems to go to the father of the ward, their bishop, for counsel. *No psychiatrist in the world, no marriage counselor,* can give to those who are faithful members of the Church the counsel from one any better than the bishop of the ward. Now, you bishops don't hesitate to say, marriage is the law of God, and is ordained by him and man and wife are not without each other in the Lord, as the apostle Paul declared.[14]

If the bishop or stake president feels that your problems are beyond his ability to deal with (and a person will not repent and apologize—see D&C 6:9), he may refer the person or couple to an appropriate agency such as LDS Family Services.

I have pondered why even faithful Saints, when a serious marital problem surfaces, are quick to look for answers outside the gospel framework when they *already know* the answers. Perhaps it is a familiarity issue. We have attended Church for so many years, had multiple lessons on the Godhead, think we have an understanding of the apostasy and restoration, first principles of the gospel, the Joseph Smith story, and so forth. We have been through the scriptures every four years in Gospel Doctrine classes. We know the gospel principles well from Primary on. Yet when we face a serious marriage problem, we conclude that the gospel is deficient. The reasoning must go like this:

"Since I already know the gospel (I regularly raise my hand in Gospel Doctrine class), if my spouse and I are not getting along, the solution to our problems must lie elsewhere. We need to see a professional counselor, one who knows something we don't teach in the Church curricula. Perhaps there is a communication skill that *my spouse* doesn't know about yet. My knowledge of the First Vision is not helping *my wife* eliminate her stubborn streak, nor does reading Helaman change *her* spending habits. (I didn't see anything in the Book of Mormon about money issues, either.) How does Lehi's counsel to his sons change *my wife's* dominating attitude? Although I love

17

scriptural classes, I don't see how the challenges of marriage in modern times are covered there."

We assume that *because we can conceptualize and articulate basic doctrines of the Church, we are living them.*

This inability to view gospel principles as solutions to mortal challenges is not a new phenomenon. There have always been those who didn't "get it," even when it was "plainly manifest unto them" (D&C 93:31), so we ought not to be surprised that the same problem exists today despite our literacy level.

Consider these points: If the gospel of Jesus Christ (as restored in our dispensation) has not the power to solve marital problems, then honestly, how useful and practical is it? If its principles are only good for Sabbath worship, have we not been duped? What *was* the plan of salvation we sustained in the premortal life? Did we think it through when it was presented to us at that time? Did the Father and Son really know what they were doing when they asked us to sustain the plan? Were we so intimidated in their presence that we did not examine it carefully enough to see if it covered every conceivable problem that mortality could throw at us? Did Satan think it through better than we did?

Of course these questions do not really identify the problem. Consider this: If there are truths in the philosophies of men that can solve marital problems more effectively than can gospel principles, then wouldn't those same truths and philosophies *be* part of the gospel? Is the wisdom of man more effective in resolving marital problems than the wisdom of Heavenly Father? Can mortal men and women really come up with better solutions to marital problems than the Father of us all? Can we conclude that if marriage is at the heart of the plan of salvation—as it is—then the gospel must contain the *very keys* to marital happiness?

Incidentally, this matter of people not "getting it" is not just a recent occurrence.[15] The people of Noah's day didn't "get it" either before the flood waters took them; the Jaredite civilization ended in a disaster after such a magnificent beginning with Jared and his brother, friends, and families. The Nephites failed to follow through on the foundation laid by Lehi and Nephi and later prophets. They blamed the Lamanites for their troubles when at times the Lamanites were more righteous than they were!

Look First to Gospel Principles

A personal experience illustrates the importance of first turning to gospel principles to resolve marital problems. Years ago, after my graduate work, I was reassigned to teach at the Institute of Religion in Ogden, Utah, where I taught marriage classes to single students, most of whom were sure *their* marriages would be filled with never-ending bliss.

Meanwhile, I taught a six- or eight-week course in a number of stakes around the area. There I knew I would find real challenges to family stability and solidarity. After the first night of class, I would inevitably receive a phone call: "Brother Brinley, I think our problems are a little more complex than what you can cover in a class setting. We were wondering if we could come and see you privately." I agreed to do so, but before I could hang up the caller would shock me by saying: "Oh, by the way, if you can't fix us, I'm afraid this is it. You are our last hope. We've been to a number of counselors before, and if it doesn't help this time, I think we will give up. We're making one last attempt to hold this together." Apparently, they wanted a quick fix, a miracle worker.

I admit those phone calls drove me to my knees. "Heavenly Father," I pleaded earnestly, "what theory that I learned in graduate school should I use to help this particular couple? They are threatening divorce, and if I can't help them they might end their marriage." I took their phone calls very seriously. (When you visit with troubled couples, you walk on sacred ground in those precious moments together. You realize that what you do or say, or don't do or say, may influence a couple to break their temple covenants—a scary proposition!) I did not want to fail them. I sought divine help. The inspiration came clearly:

"Get the Saints to live the gospel." "Well, that's too simple," I thought to myself. "These are Church members in serious trouble. They already know the gospel. They are active Church members." I protested, "But what about my graduate training? What about all the theories I learned there?" "Get the Saints to live the gospel" was the unmistakable answer.

That has been my personal charge over the years: to help couples resolve marital problems by applying the principles of the gospel—not as a professional counselor and client, but as friends getting our heads together to see what gospel principles will best apply to their situation. Similar to what a bishop might do, I remind them of their potential as sons and daughters of God, of the importance of marriage in the Father's plan, and their covenant with him. If they expect to remain married in the next life, I tell them, it is important that they bring their lives into harmony with the principles of the gospel. They have agency and can do as they please. But if they want to continue as a married couple after the Resurrection, I remind them, it will require humility, repentance, forgiveness—a genuine conversion to the principles of the gospel of Jesus Christ.

These couples have learned that with a return to fundamental gospel principles they could receive inspiration, even revelation on how to solve almost any specific marital problem.

We Are Influenced by a Gentile Culture

Perhaps another factor operates here too. We live and grow up in a secular world. We live in the dispensation of the gospel to the "Gentiles" (see D&C 45:25, 28, 30; JS–H 1:41). America was discovered and settled by latter-day Christians, who are modern Gentiles. They inhabit and govern in the land in which we live. We are educated and trained in their secular curriculum. We identify with them in many ways (see D&C 109:60). We are part of their social system and structure. We study and obtain degrees in the philosophies of their best thinkers. We are enamored of their advanced degrees, their research methods, their statistics. We trust their findings, their conclusions, their logic to guide our lives. Because we believe the light of Christ inspires men to explore and investigate areas of science, medicine, psychology, and philosophy, it is natural for us to rely on their intellectual contributions past and present.

We realize that great thinkers and good people exist outside the Church. Our own scriptures counsel us to search "out of the best books words of wisdom" (D&C 88:118). But the gentile curriculum is growing more and more secular. Religion is trivialized. Ethics has replaced doctrine. As my colleague Robert L. Millet has written: "Ethics is not necessarily righteousness. The very word *ethics* has come to connote socially acceptable standards based on current consensus, as opposed to absolute truths based on God's eternal laws. Ethics is too often to virtue and righteousness what theology is to religion—a pale and wimpy substitute."[16]

The mention of God in our society is becoming an embarrassment to many. "Why," they ask, "do we need faith in God when we can solve our own problems through technology, modern medicine, and inventions that reduce pain and make life more comfortable? Why do we need faith in a Supreme Being when our free enterprise system delivers more laborsaving devices and medical miracles preserve longevity? Why wait for God to bless us when we have credit cards and can have what we want now?" How easy it has become to rely on the "arm of flesh." "If everyone had a Ph.D.," some would advocate, "we would finally have peace on earth." Sadly, we live in a time when prophets and apostles—and those who believe in revelation, scripture, resurrection, miracles, and faith in an invisible God—are ridiculed as "right-wing" religious fanatics. And this in a land founded by religious adherents seeking freedom to worship.

As Latter-day Saints, How Are We Doing?

Now let's look at the Latter-day Saints, custodians of the Restoration. How are we doing living in the middle of this gentile culture? In the midst of unprecedented political freedom, economic prosperity, leisure time, and shopping malls, are our priorities right? Are we focused on building a righteous people, a Zion people, as is our charge from the Doctrine and Covenants? (See the topic *Zion* in the index to the Doctrine and Covenants for a multitude of references.) Do we understand that without strong and stable marriages and family relations, we cannot fulfill our charge to take the gospel to the world, perfect the Saints, and redeem the dead? Are we obedient to the teachings of the Lord and his servants, or are we "doing our own thing," participating in the spiritual drifting of the gentiles? Do we gather our families together on Monday nights to share the truths of the gospel and to build solid family relationships? Or are we caught up in the inventions and technological marvels of our day to the exclusion of and ignoring of our divine mandate? Have we come to the point where we too are guilty of what the Lord told Joseph Smith: "They draw near to me with their lips, but their hearts are far from me, . . . having a form of godliness, but they deny the power thereof" (JS–H 1:19)?

Living prophets tell us of our spiritual condition. President Gordon B. Hinckley explained the need for the 1995 Proclamation: "Why do we have this proclamation on the family now? Because the family is under attack. All across the world families are falling apart. The place to begin to improve society is in the home. . . . We are trying to make the world better by making the family stronger."[17] This is not Isaiah or Lehi speaking to us from the dust. It is the Lord's present-day prophet—a living prophet—speaking to us in our day in rather ominous tones. We are not yet sanctified! It is a call to Latter-day Saints to come to attention spiritually and check our marriage relations.

Husband, does your wife enjoy being married to you? Are you meeting her personal needs? Is she trying desperately to send you messages that you are not receiving or that you are ignoring because you are the family "head" and you think you are to make all the decisions?

Wife, does your husband wish he had not made the offer he did years ago? Does he regard you as his greatest treasure? Are you an even better sweetheart to him than you were when you married him? Are you living up to the covenant you made to be his helpmeet? Are you meeting his needs as your husband and the father of your children?

I believe that an assessment of our present state of marital happiness reveals that too many of us are embarrassing the Lord and his prophets because of the levels of divorce, abuse, and marriage problems that exist. Our divorce rate, unfortunately, is hardly dropping into the single digits where it belongs. That women and children are suffering physical and mental abuse by men holding the priesthood is inexcusable given our theology and emphasis on eternal marriage and parenthood. When couples fail to live their covenants, it is both a serious spiritual failure and a negative contribution to social stability. To be worthy of the appellation "Saints," we cannot be routinely violating marriage covenants. If we do, there will be serious spiritual penalties. Broken marriages should be and must be extremely rare among us. Divorce, offensive to God, the Author of marriage, is the cause of much heartache and pain in the lives of men, women, and children. Elder L. Tom Perry condemned abusive men who contribute to divorce statistics:

> I stand before you today to accuse many of the husbands and fathers who are within the sound of my voice and throughout the world of failing in your two major God-given responsibilities. The reason for most of the problems we find in the world today must be laid at your door. Divorce, infidelity, dishonesty, the use of drugs, deterioration of family life, loss of identity, instability and unhappiness have resulted from the lack of your leadership in the home.[18]

Theological and Doctrinal Foundations

The ultimate goal of Latter-day Saints is to attain exaltation—to live in the family unit for all time, the kind of life our Heavenly Parents live. As their children, we are passing through a divine curriculum to reach eternal life. Elder Dallin H. Oaks gave this perspective: "Our theology begins with heavenly parents. Our highest aspiration is to be like them. Under the merciful plan of the Father, all of this is possible through the atonement of the Only Begotten of the Father, our Lord and Savior, Jesus Christ. As earthly parents we participate in the gospel plan by providing mortal bodies for the spirit children of God. The fulness of eternal salvation is a family matter."[19]

I have a friend who taught marriage seminars to parents with children in "wilderness therapy." During a break in a seminar, a mother approached him and asked, "What would you recommend as the best book to build a great marriage?" My friend handed her a Triple Combination (Book of Mormon, Doctrine and Covenants, and Pearl of Great Price).

"Oh," she said, "I know about that. I mean something useful, something practical." He again picked up the volume of scriptures to show her.

"No," she said, "what I mean is, you professionals read all this good professional literature. What is the best book on the latest research and material to make a happy marriage? What do you personally recommend other married couples read?"

When he reached a third time for the Triple Combination, she walked away muttering.

I have found that many of the Saints are much like this lady. They see a need for scriptures on the Sabbath, a need to train missionaries in scripture before they serve missions. In the case of a major marital difficulty, however, we think the scriptures are deficient in relevant answers!

Pop psychology suggests marital problems are best solved by (1) increasing the *amount of communication* between husband and wife; (2) couples developing *more effective communication skills;* and (3) partners becoming *better listeners.* Let's discuss these points.

Amount of Communication—a Key?

Positive communication is an important aspect of marital relations. Couples who are hesitant to exchange personal ideas and feelings will find it difficult to enrich and strengthen their relationship. Obviously we can all improve in our attentiveness and willingness to share ideas and feelings with our spouse and children more effectively. There is little question that we can improve the quantity and quality of communication between family members. However, communication works best between those who are already friends. Trying to increase the *amount of communication* between two people *who don't like each other* (like most couples who come to counseling) does little to resolve issues. In fact, pushing for more verbal interaction between contentious individuals usually causes more negative emotions, defensiveness, and further intransigence as each remains angry, belligerent, and adamant in his or her views. As an extreme example, placing the Israeli prime minister and the leader of the Palestinians in the same room with the charge to resolve Middle East tensions will not likely bring a cessation of hostilities. Why? Because when people are upset and angry, they are blind to any position but their own. It is difficult for any of us, when angry, to see another's side to an issue. Instead, we become more entrenched, more convinced, more committed to our own position.

The same principle holds among contentious married couples. A husband or wife argues his or her side of an issue convinced that if the spouse would only pause long enough to really listen to what he or she is saying, peace would be restored. However, their emotional state prevents the openness that could lead to a change of opinion.

Is the problem between political leaders or unhappily married couples a lack of communication skills? An inability to articulate views? No, that is *not* the problem. The political leader would not be where he or she is, nor would the couple have married in the first instance, had they been deficient in communication skills. The point is this: when people are happy, they communicate adequately. When there is an interest in listening, human beings listen attentively. Communication, an exchange of ideas and understanding, functions best when both parties have soft hearts and respect each other enough to consider options besides their own.

Is It Then a Skill Issue?

Let's consider skills. A skill is something that we gain greater proficiency in as we repeat the action. Athletic skills, musical talent, operating computers, using software, throwing darts, hammering nails, and even changing diapers are improved by practice. But we don't normally practice communication skills. We don't practice saying to ourselves, "Honey, I love you," only to critique ourselves on how it sounded. We don't rehearse a phrase until we "get it right" just to impress a spouse, do we? We don't practice putting our arm around a child. We either feel like putting it there or we don't.

I'm not saying that communication skills aren't essential. What I am saying is that by the time we reach adulthood and are capable of marriage, most people *already know how to carry out the basic functions of communication or they would not find a marriage partner.* We don't take courses, classes, or use practice sessions to learn how to express positive feelings. If we feel love for a spouse or child, we naturally reach out to them in affectionate ways. And even if we are quite clumsy in early attempts (our noses touch before our lips do), we do not take offense. Practicing saying things to a spouse or children even seems a little manipulative.[20]

On the other hand, we do need information on how to be better sweethearts and meet each other's needs more effectively. Such information comes to us as we learn from each other in a positive environment.

Rather than looking at marriage as a skill issue, let's consider it as a heart matter. *Most adults communicate quite well with other adults when their hearts are soft and they respect one another.* Have you noticed that prophets and scriptures don't approach marriage and family

26

problems from a "skills" perspective? In most cases, these are "attitude matters" rather than "skill issues."

Think about our experience in Church settings. In Relief Society, do they ever pair sisters in exercises to listen or paraphrase back to each other to improve their listening or communication skills? Do we split men into teams in priesthood meetings to practice "I" statements?[21] Have you ever attended a Church lesson that required you to practice saying things until you could say them more perfectly or correctly? Church lesson manuals and scriptures do not use such an approach. Can you imagine a daughter coming to you and saying, "Dad, Mom, my fiancé is so frustrating. I don't understand much of what he says half the time. Sometimes he doesn't speak to me for a day or so. I have a hard time comprehending what he says. But," she goes on to tell you, "I can hardly wait for our marriage next month in the temple." No doubt, as parents, you would sit this young lady down for a long talk. Have you observed that people do not complain about communication skills *before* they marry? If the communication just wasn't there, they typically wouldn't get married. We generally marry someone we can comfortably share both heart and soul with. Most young couples tell me, "Jim and I have talked about everything. We have stayed up late some nights, and I think I know how he feels about most things. I can't think of anything we have not discussed about our hopes and dreams."

The Issue Is a Heart Problem

The Lord stresses the "heart" approach. He seems more interested in our "heart condition" than our skill level.[22] Communication skills are not mentioned in the scriptures, but there are many references to heart matters.

If we find ourselves not communicating in positive ways *after* marriage, it is not because during the honeymoon we suddenly lost our ability to share with each other. The reason people have difficulty with communication after marriage is not because of lack of ability or skill.

The problem, instead, is that we throw off our newlywed status and begin to find fault with each other. We become each other's critic. The issue then becomes this: We don't feel like sharing our very being, our inner self, our deep-down-inside-where-we-live feelings with someone *who is critical of us.* We can't enrich marriage when a spouse is domineering, always right, temperamental, certain they came from the "true family," smothering, sarcastic, critical of their spouse's ideas, or consistently negative.

We can communicate well before marriage because our hearts are soft at that point in time. We are trying to impress someone to marry us. We are usually on our best behavior. We can actually hide negative personality traits while dating and courting because we realize that no one would marry us if we are grumpy. We hide deficiencies before marriage—even marginal mental deficiencies can be hid.

The bottom line is that most of us know how to communicate adequately before we marry, even though we haven't taken classes, read books, or gone to therapy.

Hearts Come in Two Kinds

Soft-hearted people communicate well with each other. A soft heart is a humble heart, a meek and charitable heart. Hearts, though, can also be hard. A hard heart is one that is proud, defensive, critical, insensitive. Hearts are softened by doctrinal and eternal perspectives, an understanding of the "big picture," the plan of salvation. A hard heart comes from a worldly or secular view ("get it while you can") and becomes further hardened through selfishness and pride, as we see in the "natural man" of King Benjamin's sermon (see Mosiah 3:19). When hearts are soft we use our agency to behave in charitable, kind ways, and we use our communication abilities in positive and uplifting ways (as we did when we were dating). When hearts are hardened, we hesitate to share ideas and thoughts for fear of ridicule or being put down. Then two individuals remain at a superficial level of communication because that level is less threatening. But a superficial level of communication does not build positive emotions—feelings of love—between spouses.

If you found someone to marry you, you already have good evidence that you can be soft-hearted.[23] The fact that someone wanted to marry you in the first place is the best evidence you have that you possess adequate communication skills to succeed. If you were able to convince a member of the opposite sex to marry you, you must have had sufficient communication skills at one time. Both of you were satisfied that you could talk with ease on a variety of important subjects. You felt comfortable exchanging personal ideas and feelings in that premarital setting.

Professional Counseling

Who would go to a secular counselor to hear that their prayers must be more effective, that personal faith in God must increase, that scriptures should be read more intently, that humility is lacking, that pride and selfishness are the destructive factors in one's relationship, that continued church activity, more effective family home evenings, and meaningful interviews with children must take place? Who would pay money for that information? Professional counselors use a non-gospel, nonreligious approach to resolve marital problems because that is what they learned in their university training. A professional counselor uses psychological theories centered most often in behavioral and cognitive approaches. They share ideas and theories from scholars who have studied the family. That approach may be helpful, but a gospel-based approach ought to be even more powerful. How specific doctrines provide couples with power to resolve marital problems is the subject of the next chapter.

Notes

1. Boyd K. Packer, "Solving Emotional Problems in the Lord's Own Way," general conference, April 1978 (see *Ensign*, May 1978, 91–95). "Self-Reliance" was given at Brigham Young University in March 1975 (see *BYU Speeches of the Year*, 1975, 343–60).

2. Individuals who suffer symptoms of bipolar disorder, schizophrenia, addiction, or serious mental disorders need more help than simple bibliotherapy. They often require medication and competent medical attention.

3. Boyd K. Packer, "Solving Emotional Problems in the Lord's Own Way," *Ensign*, May 1978, 91–93.

4. It hasn't been that long ago when people suffering from depression were thought to be unfaithful, or not fully "living the gospel." "You need to pray more, read the scriptures more, and do more religious works" was the counsel many lay people gave. Please know that there are serious psychiatric disorders that are physiological in nature. It is not my intent to discourage psychological help when needed.

5. By the time people decide to "invest" in counseling services, it is usually a "last resort." They have exhausted all their "free" services, including friends and family members who, of course, generally take their side in any marital feud.

6. Joseph Fielding Smith, *Doctrines of Salvation,* comp. Bruce R. McConkie, 3 vols. (Salt Lake City: Bookcraft, 1954–56), 2:80–84.

7. Ibid., 2:177.

8. Ezra Taft Benson, "America at the Crossroads," *New Era,* July 1978, 38; emphasis added.

9. Gordon B. Hinckley, "What God Hath Joined Together," *Ensign,* May 1991, 73–74; emphasis added.

10. Spencer W. Kimball, *Marriage* (Salt Lake City: Deseret Book, 1978), 42.

11. Gordon B. Hinckley, "Of Missions, Temples, and Stewardship," *Ensign,* November 1995, 53.

12. "The Family: A Proclamation to the World" lists nine suggestions to strengthen marriage: faith, prayer, repentance, forgiveness, respect, love, compassion, work, and wholesome recreational activities. Note that communication was not one of the nine.

13. "The Family: A Proclamation to the World," *Ensign,* November 1995, 102; emphasis added.

14. Harold B. Lee, "President Harold B. Lee's General Priesthood Address," *Ensign,* January 1974, 100; emphasis added.

15. The Jews missed the Savior's coming though they were ostensibly looking for a Messiah (see Jacob 4:14). Modern Christians are so rooted to the Bible that they miss its message—you must have living prophets; they therefore fail to see the need for continuing revelation. The Christian world thinks God is some kind of three-in-one mystery and yet considers Latter-day Saints non-Christian! The Book of Mormon recounts the visit of Jesus Christ to this land after his resurrection, but few Christians who claim interest in Jesus care to find out if the story is true. Examples of people not "getting it" throughout history abound.

16. Robert L. Millet, "Divine Deterrent to Creeping Relativism," *Religion C 234,*

LDS Marriage and Family Relations, Student Manual (Dubuque, Iowa: Kendall/Hunt Publishing Company, 1998), 27.

17. Gordon B. Hinckley, "Inspirational Thoughts," *Ensign*, August 1997, 5.

18. L. Tom Perry, "Father—Your Role, Your Responsibility," *Ensign*, November 1977, 62.

19. Dallin H. Oaks, "Apostasy and Restoration," *Ensign*, May 1995, 87.

20. Lawyers, teachers, missionaries, and salespersons may practice closing arguments and techniques, concepts, or lessons. But normally spouses and parents don't practice expressing love to each other. They learn that through social experiences and dating practices and after marriage.

21. An "I" statement requires an individual to own his or her thoughts and feelings and take responsibility; it prevents one person from speaking on behalf of the other person when not authorized to do so. "You" statements can be accusatory. Sticking with your own feelings—"I feel," or "I think"—is less likely to create negative feelings in the other party.

22. The word *heart* is used 790 times in the Old Testament and 168 in the New Testament. The Book of Mormon contains 453 references to *heart*, the Doctrine and Covenants, 196. The Pearl of Great Price uses the word 28 times.

23. This is not to suggest single people are hard-hearted. It is simply the idea that to impress someone sufficiently that they want to marry for eternity requires an ability to converse at several different levels of communication, including superficial, personal, and validating.

3

Gospel-Based Marital Therapy, Part 2: Doctrines and Principles

Douglas E. Brinley

President Boyd K. Packer emphasized that understanding doctrine was the foundation for changes in behavior. "True doctrine, *understood*," he said, "*changes attitudes and behavior*. The study of the doctrines of the gospel *will improve behavior quicker than a study of behavior* [read: psychology] *will improve behavior*. . . . That is why we stress so forcefully the study of the doctrines of the gospel."[1] In a later address he repeated the same theme: "I have long believed that the study of the doctrines of the gospel will improve behavior quicker than talking about behavior will improve behavior."[2]

In this chapter I will be more specific in explaining how doctrine changes behavior, and I will provide examples of doctrines that turn hard hearts to soft ones in positive, marriage-enriching ways.

Here is one example of the connection between doctrine and behavior:

> Once we accept the truth of the doctrine that *we are the children of God,* that realization *changes us.* Thereafter *we cannot willingly injure another or transgress against him.* That simple, profound doctrine has a very practical value. It brings a feeling of self-worth, of dignity, of self-respect. Then self-pity and depression fade away. We then can yield to self-discipline and to the discipline of a loving Father and accept even the very hard lessons in life.
>
> The gospel is *good medicine.*[3]

Here is a simple diagram showing the relationship between doctrine and behavior:

Understanding Doctrine → *Soft Heart* → *Christlike Behavior* → *Happy Marriage*

The Book of Mormon is full of this doctrine-heart-behavior model. Here are two examples:

1. *Mosiah 5:2.* After teaching doctrine concerning the future Messiah, King Benjamin sought the reaction of his people concerning his message. They responded: "We *believe all the words which thou hast spoken unto us* [doctrine]; and also, we know of their surety and truth, because of the Spirit of the Lord Omnipotent, which has wrought a mighty change in us, *or in our hearts,* that we have *no more disposition to do evil, but to do good continually*" (Mosiah 5:2; emphasis added).

Note the connection between doctrine, "heart condition," and behavior change. Learning the doctrine of a coming Messiah softened the hearts of Benjamin's people to such an extent that they made a behavioral commitment: "We have no more disposition to do evil, but to do good continually." What bishop or stake president, to say nothing of a husband or wife, would not like to see this outcome? What spouse or child would not benefit from such a behavioral commitment by a spouse or parent?

2. *Alma 5:11–13.* Alma, converted by the preaching of doctrine by Abinadi, taught his followers doctrine at the waters of Mormon. Alma's son reflected on the experience of his father:

> Behold, I can tell you—did not my father Alma believe in the words which were delivered by the mouth of Abinadi? . . .
>
> And according to his faith there was a mighty change wrought in his heart. Behold I say unto you that this is all true.
>
> And behold, *he preached the word* [doctrine] unto your fathers, and *a mighty change was also wrought in their hearts,*

and they humbled themselves and put their trust in the true and living God. And behold, *they were faithful until the end; therefore they were saved* (Alma 5:11–13; emphasis added).

What spouse or child would not like to witness that resolve in the heart of their companion or parents?

Below are a few doctrines that have power in their conceptualization to influence marriage and family life for the better. This list of doctrines is not exhaustive, nor is it presented in any particular order of importance. Some I'll explain more in detail; with others I hope the application will be obvious. My hope is that as you read a principle or doctrine, the Spirit will enlarge and enlighten your mind and help you see its specific application in your marriage.

Doctrine/Principle 1: In Marriage We Covenant with Each Member of the Godhead

We perform most ordinances of the gospel in the name of Jesus Christ. There are, however, three exceptions: baptism, marriage, and the sealing of children to parents. These specific ordinances use the names of all three members of the Godhead. At baptism, we covenant as individuals to accept and conform our lives to the principles and laws of the gospel. Baptism is the covenant of salvation. It is the gate to the celestial kingdom, where the Godhead presides.

When we are confirmed, each new member is commissioned to seek inspiration and direction from our heavenly monitor, the Holy Ghost.

In marriage, a couple enters the patriarchal order, and each covenants with the entire Godhead to live worthily, as sweethearts, to obtain the highest degree of glory in the celestial kingdom. It seems to me that each member of the Godhead has an interest in our success as marriage partners. Here are some thoughts about why this is so.

First, Heavenly Father

Our Father is interested in and cares about our marital success because:

1. It is his plan of salvation that has us leave our premortal home, come to earth, obtain a physical body, and then marry (if we can) and experience for ourselves similar joys (and sorrows) to those he experiences through marriage and parenthood. (He even "loans" some of his children to us on which to practice!)

2. As a literal Parent, he deeply desires the happiness of each of his children, just as earthly parents care about their own. Happiness cannot be achieved alone; it requires both male and female in a marital union. Happiness comes as we learn together how to serve each other and our offspring. It also comes as we work together to resist evil and embrace good. Satan tests us through temptation and sophistry. After Adam and Eve partook of the fruit, the Father said to Jehovah, "Behold, the man is become as one of us to know good and evil" (Moses 4:28). God isn't God because he doesn't know what evil is. He knows what it is better than anyone else, but he has learned to choose only good. That is a lesson we are all learning in this estate.

3. Our Heavenly Father is married (only Latter-day Saints understand this), and he wants us to experience the same joy that comes to him in marriage and parenthood experiences. As mortals, we have similar desires for our own mature offspring. The Father said to Jehovah, "It was not good that the man should be alone; wherefore, I will make an help meet for him" (Moses 3:18).

4. God's work and glory consists in his children gaining spiritual maturity and attaining a state of exaltation. By definition, exaltation is a state of marriage for eternity.

Application: A couple who fail at marriage are not only disappointing each other, but Heavenly Father, whose plan of salvation we are seeking to follow. To prove to God that we are unable to live the very plan he ordained to exalt us brings anguish to his soul and ours! (Of course, divorce is not permanent failure; another marriage with a sealing is possible.) It is especially sad if we cannot succeed in marriage in a day of an abundance of laborsaving devices, medical miracles, access to education, literature, the Internet, television, books, and living prophets. Don't disappoint Heavenly Father!

Second, Jesus Christ

The Savior has an interest in our marital success because:

1. His atonement allows us to repent and be forgiven of our sins, to sanctify our lives so as to be worthy of a celestial inheritance. The Savior's life and labor to bring about an atonement and resurrection provided a way for us to live in family units as exalted beings. If we fail in marriage, much of his life's work and ministry would be wasted.

2. His resurrection provides us an immortal soul—body and spirit together forever.

3. In the resurrection we remain male or female. Because we no longer die, the way is open for an eternal marriage relationship.

4. The Savior's teachings and examples prepare us to live as celestial beings if we acquire Christlike attributes.

Application: Without the Savior's atonement and resurrection, we could not live with the eternal blessing of a physical body joined to our spirit, and therefore marriage and procreation in the eternities would be impossible. Don't disappoint the Savior!

Third, the Holy Ghost

The Holy Ghost has a deep interest in our marital success because:

1. At baptism this member of the Godhead is assigned by the Father and the Son to help us. He encourages us to be faithful in our lives and stewardships. He prompts and inspires us to become more perfect, more godlike, and to repent of our sins. As a celestial monitor, he counsels with us to help us make proper choices throughout our lives, including our search for a compatible spouse.

2. He is aware of our foreordinations from the premortal life, and his divine tutelage prepares us for them.

3. He communicates to us that which will help us improve as spouses and parents.

4. He inspires us to live in conformity with gospel principles so that we may qualify for eternal life. Don't disappoint the Holy Ghost!

Application: The entire Godhead is interested in our success and supports us in our righteous efforts to live the gospel. We, by proper use of agency, appropriate ordinances, and keeping covenants, can attain exaltation and eternal life. We do not want to disappoint any member of the Godhead. To do so would result in restrictions on our eternal progression.

Doctrine/Principle 2: The Temple Gives Us a Model for Strengthening Marriages

The temple model includes at least six components that greatly strengthen marriages. I have provided only a basic outline below, with a brief commentary, and invite those who have been endowed in the temple to consider each of the six elements more fully.

1. Worthiness	*2. Instruction*	*3. Covenants*
Recommend	Endowment	Endowment
D&C 97:15–17	Creation	Power
Initiatory	Fall	
ordinances	Atonement	
	Moses 1–4	
	Abraham 4–5	

4. Ceremony	*5. Practice*	*6. Repentance*
Sealing	Background	"I'm sorry."
	Habits	"I will do better."
	Character	
	Temperament	

The first element of the temple model is *worthiness,* an essential requirement to enter the house of the Lord. It is "measured" by an interview with priesthood leaders, who then may issue a recommend (see D&C 97:15–17 concerning the need for a recommend). We must be clean and prepared (which includes receiving preliminary ordinances) before we can gain admittance back to Deity. We are then prepared for divine *instruction,* the *endowment.* The basic principles of temple worship and the endowment are found in the records of Moses and Abraham: the creation of the earth, the creation of Adam and Eve, the fall of our first parents, and the Atonement, which restores what was lost in the Fall. We must comprehend our fallen natures and understand the purposes of mortality and the need for a Redeemer. We also learn, as did Moses, that Satan exists (see Moses 4:1–4). We *covenant* with God, who has the power to bring us back to his presence as we overcome the spiritual and physical deaths brought by Adam and Eve. Covenants provide mortals with the power to live righteously in a fallen world. God doesn't break covenants, so when we tie ourselves to him by covenant, we become eligible to attain the blessings associated with the covenant through our obedience to the laws of the gospel and their provisions. We are then prepared for the marriage *ceremony,* the *sealing* of the blessings of Abraham (Elias) upon us through the sealing power (Elijah) and priesthood keys restored in the Kirtland Temple (see D&C 110).

Following the ceremony (and reception), we begin our married life as sweethearts. We begin our apprenticeship together, *practicing* the principles of the gospel. We learn much more about each other after marriage—habits, background, character, and temperament, along with mortal strengths and flaws that come to light. We make mistakes and misjudgments of each other, and we need the gospel of *repentance* (see D&C 6:9). When we freely apologize and forgive each other as married couples, profound lessons of life and relationships help us build character. Our marriage covenants are made with the assumption that neither one is perfect, but we accept each other's strengths and weaknesses and commit to learn from each other how to become a spouse and a parent. We want to please each other as we move together through the mortal life cycle.

Reviewing this sequence periodically as we attend the temple allows us to keep these principles always before us. Our attendance at the temple reminds us of our eternal potential to be eternal companions.

Application: We usually attend the temple as adults when we are going on a mission or getting married. When we understand the instruction therein and tie ourselves to God by covenants, we gain the incentive and power to live in harmony with our newfound knowledge about life and companionship. We realize our potential is to live together as exalted beings. We learn that we are happiest when we have a healthy marriage. We want a partner who loves us and to whom we are sealed as sweethearts by the sealing power of the priesthood. We desire the highest degree of eternal glory (see D&C 131:1–4), where married couples reside. We know that we can gain exaltation only if we like each other! We clearly see that we are apprenticing in a program of marriage and family life designed to prepare us to live as exalted beings in the celestial kingdom.

Doctrine/Principle 3: Understanding Marriage and Family in the Plan of Salvation Can Strengthen Our Desire to Succeed

Let's consider a few principles that have been revealed in this latter-day dispensation concerning marriage and family life:

1. We were never married before this life. Marriage was not open to us as the spirit children of our Heavenly Parents.

2. Procreation was not open to us in that premortal sphere. The power to generate life requires the union of our spirit body with a body of a different kind of element. We enjoy that privilege now, lose it when we die and return to our spirit body, and regain the power to generate life again when (and if) we are resurrected to the highest degree of glory (see D&C 131:1–4; 132:19–20).

3. Satan's damnation lies in his inability to have a physical body, to marry, and to be a parent himself; he will forever be limited to a spirit body and therefore he is permanently impotent and unable to marry.

4. A temple marriage unites us with the promise of eternal companionship.

Application #1: We cannot attain the highest heaven alone. We must be married to a compatible and loving spouse. We therefore should choose a marriage partner wisely and carefully. We learn through the experiences of living together to cherish each other as we grow in character attributes that make us more lovable as we mature. Our willingness to be patient, kind, and Christlike in character grows as we experience the sweetness of marriage.

Application #2: We must be eligible and worthy of marriage. The selection of a spouse is one of the most important decisions we make in this life. Before we get married, we need sufficient time together (and apart) to evaluate important issues relative to personality, temperament, ambition, spirituality, testimony, work ethic, in-laws, money management skills, attitudes, a desire to enrich marriage, and so forth. When we feel a high level of compatibility, we seek heavenly approval, and then we are prepared for the ordinances available in the temple.

Doctrine/Principle 4: Prayer Is a Key to Success in Marriage

In the home, there are three categories of prayer: individual, couple, and family. As the children of Heavenly Father, we have a right to pray directly to him. We seek his help because of his wisdom and experience. We seek counsel, wisdom, and blessings. There are no marital problems he cannot help us resolve. An individual prayer as a spouse might contain a plea such as this: "Heavenly Father, I appreciate the opportunity to come to the earth through noble parents and now to be an adult son (or daughter), married, and enjoying the privilege of parenthood. Please help me to do my best in these stewardships. I pray that my spouse will be forgiving and love me in spite of my weaknesses and imperfections. Help me to do my best in my marriage relationship."

A couple prayer, kneeling together, might contain these elements:

"Heavenly Father, we are grateful for the chance to be sweethearts in this mortal probation. We know we must be patient and kind and loving with each other. Help us to forgive one another, to be kind and gentle with each other, to remember charity. We are so blessed we found each other and are now sealed in an eternal companionship. Help us to learn the lessons we came here to learn through our marriage and parenting experiences. We want to be worthy of thy presence, and we pray that we will do our best to love each other and stay close to each other and thee. We promise to live the principles of the gospel to the best of our abilities."

A family prayer might include this plea: "Heavenly Father, we are thankful to be a family. Please help us to live together in love, to appreciate the talents and abilities of each member of our family. Help our children to know that we love them, that we cherish the chance to help them to grow to adulthood, to love and respect the principles of the gospel, to be good citizens of the kingdom, to be worthy of thy Spirit, to be true latter-day Saints. Help us as parents to set a good example for them, to lead them as thou would have us lead them. We appreciate this privilege to labor together and we pray for inspiration to be kind in daily associations. Help each of us to be happy as we serve each other. Help us to be worthy of remaining an eternal family."

For marriage companions struggling with serious challenges, their couple prayer might be even more fervent: "Heavenly Father, thou knowest of our struggles together. Please help us to be humble, to be kind and patient with each other, to regain that love that we enjoyed at the beginning of our marriage. We need help and inspiration to do better. We know that our hearts must be softened to better serve each other. We want to do better. We know we can do better. We know that we must do better. Renew in our hearts the desire to love and bless each other."

Application: God, our Father, can help us to do our best in marriage if we approach him in prayer with humility and a desire to be better companions. When we become upset with each other we often stop having couple prayer. Never stop praying as a couple; it is one of the most important prayers you offer because prayer is a window into the soul of your spouse. As long as one soul is pure and wants to do what is right, the heart of his or her companion can be softened through prayer.

Doctrine/Principle 5: Degrees of Glory

We learn from the Lord's revelations and instructions through Joseph Smith that only those who obtain the highest degree of glory will continue marriage and parenthood:

> In the celestial glory there are three heavens or degrees;
>
> And in order to obtain the highest, a man must enter into this order of the priesthood [meaning the new and everlasting covenant of marriage];
>
> And if he does not, he cannot obtain it.
>
> He may enter into the other, but that is the end of his kingdom; he cannot have an increase (D&C 131:1–4).

Joseph Smith taught this principle on another occasion:

> Except a man and his wife enter into an everlasting covenant and be married for eternity, while in this probation, by the power and authority of the Holy Priesthood, they will cease to increase when they die; that is, they will not have any children after the resurrection. But those who are married by the power and authority of the priesthood in this life, and continue without committing the sin against the Holy Ghost, will continue to increase and have children in the celestial glory.[4]

Application: Exaltation is open only to those who love each other, marry properly, live righteously, keep their covenants, and qualify for the highest degree in the celestial kingdom. And, by definition, exaltation is the only state in the eternities that will allow continuing marriage and parenthood.

Doctrine/Principle 6: Satan's Damnation Involves No Physical Body, No Marriage, No Parenthood

Because he rejected the Father's plan in premortality, Satan will never obtain a body of physical elements. Without that body as a counterpart to a spirit body, he can never, ever, be a husband or father. His greatest efforts, no doubt, are to prevent us from participating in marriage and parenthood. Joseph Fielding Smith taught:

Some will gain celestial bodies with all the powers of exaltation and eternal increase. . . .

In both of these (lower) kingdoms there will be changes in the bodies and limitations. They will not have the power of increase, neither the power or nature to live as husbands and wives, for this will be denied them and they cannot increase. . . .

Some of the functions in the celestial body will not appear in the terrestrial body, neither in the telestial body, and the power of procreation will be removed.[5]

Orson Pratt gave this powerful insight:

Could wicked and malicious beings, who have irradicated every feeling of love from their bosoms, be permitted to propagate their species, the offspring would partake of all the evil, wicked, and malicious nature of their parents. . . . It is for this reason that God will not permit the fallen angels to multiply; it is for this reason that God has ordained marriages for the righteous only; it is for this reason that God will put a final stop to the multiplication of the wicked after this life; it is for this reason that none but those who have kept the celestial law will be permitted to multiply after the resurrection; . . . for they alone are prepared to beget and bring forth [spirit] offspring.[6]

Application: Two of Satan's greatest victories come when we (1) fail to marry in the temple and (2) fail to live so that we can remain eternal companions. His goal is to destroy marriages and prevent us from gaining eternal life.

Doctrine/Principle 7: The Scriptures Help Us in Our Understandings about Marriage

Each volume in the standard works helps us understand the plan of salvation more completely. What is the value of these books to a married couple?

1. *The Book of Mormon.* This record, like all the standard works, was written to "bring us to Christ." It begins with the story of a family with many challenges. Two of Lehi and Sariah's children made poor choices that brought devastating results. We do not want to rear a Laman or a Lemuel in our homes. We see how extensive the damage can be to succeeding generations when family members make poor choices. We see and feel the need to be better parents ourselves, to instruct and instill in the hearts of our children a love for the gospel.

This ancient record contains a rare scriptural example of a wife complaining against her husband (and the resolution to the problem). We see how a Christlike priesthood leader treated a discouraged wife (see 1 Nephi 5:1–8). From this text we learn what happens when civilizations fail to live the principles of the gospel. We see the same processes taking place today and wonder about the fate of our own nation in these latter days.

2. *The Doctrine and Covenants.* This scriptural volume is the only standard work given originally in English. It is the Lord's word to the Latter-day Saints. It records the establishment of the Church in this last dispensation and emphasizes the importance of ordinances and covenants. It contains revelations pertaining to marriage and family relations (see D&C 49:15–17; 131:1–4; 132:15–20).

3. *The Pearl of Great Price.* This volume prepares us for temple worship through presenting portions of the "endowments" of Moses

and Abraham. Some of the basic elements of temple instruction are given, with additional information in chapters 6 through 8 of the book of Moses about the dispensations of Enoch and Noah. The book of Abraham is the oldest account we have of some of the truths included in the endowment.

4. *The Old Testament.* This record introduces us to the creation of the earth, including man and woman, and the need for a Savior and Redeemer following the fall of Adam and Eve. This record emphasizes the importance of Abraham and the covenant God established with him and his posterity throughout time and eternity. Portions of this covenant are sealed upon those who marry in the temple. The dispensations of the gospel given to Adam, Enoch, Noah, Abraham, and Moses, together with other prophets of ancient Israel who saw our day, are open to study and investigation. We learn that people who fail to keep their covenants, who reject the word of living prophets, do not prosper spiritually.

5. *The New Testament.* The earthly ministry of Jesus Christ among mortals, including his genealogy, the miracle of his birth, and his teachings and those of his apostles, are given down to the time of John's revelation.

Application: The standard works are doctrinal repositories of the gospel of Jesus Christ. When we read them on a regular basis, the doctrines are renewed in our minds and we are able to maintain an eternal perspective. When we understand doctrine, as President Packer indicated, we desire to conform to gospel laws and ordinances.

Doctrine/Principle 8: The Counsel of Living Prophets Helps Us in Marriage

God uses prophets to counsel, teach, and warn his children of the dangers that exist in the society in which they live. Prophets and apostles teach us what God would have us know and do in our own day. "Watchmen on the tower" ensure that we understand the gospel and encourage us to live its principles (see D&C 112:30–33). Scripture comes through the prophets, there being no "Book of Christ." Modern prophets counsel us on the importance of marriage and family life and the dangers of broken marriages. Here is an excerpt from President Gordon B. Hinckley concerning the resolution of marital issues:

There must be recognition on the part of both husband and wife of the solemnity and sanctity of marriage and of the God-given design behind it.

There must be a willingness to overlook small faults, to forgive, and then to forget.

There must be a holding of one's tongue. Temper is a vicious and corrosive thing that destroys affection and casts out love.

There must be self-discipline that constrains against abuse of wife and children and self. There must be the Spirit of God, invited and worked for, nurtured and strengthened. There must be recognition of the fact that each is a child of God—father, mother, son, and daughter, each with a divine birthright—and also recognition of the fact that when we offend one of these, we offend our Father in Heaven.

There may be now and again a legitimate cause for divorce. I am not one to say that it is never justified. But I say without hesitation that this plague among us, which seems to be growing everywhere, is not of God, but rather is the work of the adversary of righteousness and peace and truth.

You need not be his victims. You can rise above his wiles and entreaties. Get rid of the titillating entertainment, the pornography that leads to evil desires and reprehensible activity. Wives, look upon your husbands as your precious companions and live worthy of that association. Husbands, see in your wives your most valued asset in time or eternity, each a daughter of God, a partner with whom you can walk hand in hand, through sunshine and storm, through all the perils and triumphs of life. Parents, see in your children sons and daughters of your Father in Heaven, who will hold you accountable for them. Stand together as their guardians, their protectors, their guides, their anchors.

The strength of the nations lies in the homes of the people. God is the designer of the family. He intended that the greatest of happiness, the most satisfying aspects of life, the deepest joys should come in our associations together and our concerns one for another as fathers and mothers and children.[7]

Application: Living prophets teach us simple keys to keep our marriages and families functioning properly. We learn from their counsel the reasons for marital conflict, which usually include selfishness and pride, twin plagues that destroy marriages and family life. We learn from these leaders how to avoid the pitfalls that ruin marital relations.

Doctrine/Principle 9: Living Prophets Have Given Us an Inspired Proclamation on the Family

Occasionally there is an issue of such importance that the Lord brings it to our attention through a proclamation, thus formalizing vital principles. We live in a day when marriage and family relations are in jeopardy because birth control and antibiotics make it possible for people to live together without pregnancy or many diseases. People justify living together without marriage, contrary to gospel principles. The proclamation on the family, issued by the First Presidency and the Quorum of the Twelve, outlines the position of the Church on a variety of marriage and family issues, seeking to combat the threat to the family by those choosing to live below acceptable standards of decency and morality.[8] Trial marriages, premarital sex, and adultery are offensive to God and decent people everywhere. Prophets state the Lord's position on marriage and family life and give counsel on personal performance. "Successful marriages and families

47

are established and maintained on principles of faith, prayer, repentance, forgiveness, respect, love, compassion, work and wholesome recreational activities," says this document. The proclamation mentions the following nine elements that contribute to a successful marriage:

Faith. The proclamation does not specify "faith in the Lord Jesus Christ," as does the first principle of the gospel. However, without him, there is no possibility of eternal marriage. It is important that each companion has faith in Jesus Christ; but they also must have faith in their spouse, faith that the partner has the same goals and desires for eternal life and exaltation. If a spouse were married to a nonbeliever, for example, or to a less-active spouse, it would be difficult to have faith or confidence that exaltation was within their potential.

Prayer. I have already discussed the privilege we have to commune directly with God, our Father. Our marriage covenant is with him, and we seek his counsel and blessings.

Repentance. We are mortal, fallen beings. We sin. We make mistakes. We err. We need forgiveness from God, from each other, and from our children. Normally, repentance in marriage occurs when we offer genuine apologies to those we offend. Sincere and genuine repentance enables the relationship to be whole again.

Forgiveness. "I, the Lord, will forgive whom I will forgive, but of you it is required to forgive all men" (D&C 64:10). To forgive others is a divine attribute. It is our responsibility to accept the sincere repentance of others, especially of a spouse or child.

Respect. Males and females are different in many ways. We think differently; we act and react differently. Hoorah! (How would you like to be married to a clone of you?) We learn to respect and appreciate each other's opinions, feelings, and desires as our lives intermingle.

Love. This term surely includes affection—emotional and physical intimacy. Affectionate expressions are part of the marriage relationship and strengthen one another. We share our male or female attributes in a unique oneness. We express affection regularly as sweethearts

48

and lovers. We enjoy sentiments of love and endearment and joyful intimacy. We marry with the idea that we will come to know the heart and soul of another in intimate and confidential ways known only to the two in the marriage.

Compassion. We hurt when our spouse and children hurt. We rejoice at their successes. Our hearts are softened for those of our own household. We realize that children are children and they make mistakes. (We made them ourselves in the past.) We have compassion on them as we see them make their way from innocence to adulthood.

Work. This term must include employment and earning income, along with a work ethic. Bills are ever-present, and expenses must be met. Children need chores and meaningful assignments in the family. The Lord rebuked early Church leaders because their children lacked a work ethic: "I, the Lord, am not well pleased with the inhabitants of Zion, for there are idlers among them; and their children are also growing up in wickedness; they also seek not earnestly the riches of eternity, but their eyes are full of greediness" (D&C 68:31).

Wholesome recreational activities. "Families who play together stay together" states the old adage. As a couple or family, getting away from phones and responsibilities, playing together at the park, picnicking, vacationing, or just being together on a variety of occasions helps children appreciate parents as their moms and dads labor to build relationships with them. We need, on occasion, to get out of our "work clothes" and play together in informal settings.

Application: These nine suggestions strengthen marriage and family relations. The proclamation also presents the Church's position to a world quickly losing the vision of marriage as worldly substitutes replace the time-honored definition of family. The chilling prospect spoken of by President Spencer W. Kimball has now taken on a prophetic ring: "Many of the social restraints which in the past have helped to reinforce and to shore up the family are dissolving and disappearing. The time will come when only those who believe deeply and actively in the family will be able to preserve their families in the midst of the gathering evil around us."[9]

Doctrine/Principle 10: Your Spouse Is Your Therapist

Marriage is based on the proposition that we love each other enough to want to spend our lives together here and hereafter. It is a joint venture. When I learn what my wife would like of me, I can, as a free agent, use my talents and abilities to seek to meet those expectations. As she recognizes my efforts to serve her and her wants, she returns the favor by using her feminine traits and talents to bless me as her husband. I then respond even more completely to her needs, and she reciprocates, and we become a mutual admiration society. Marriage is a commitment that assumes that as we share our lives we can solve a myriad of challenges. The rule must be this: A problem for one is a problem for both. Though we are independent beings, our marriage makes us interdependent. Marriage requires a sense of oneness, a sharing of life—good and bad. We counsel together. As married sweethearts we resolve marital tensions together.

Application: The Lord designed marriage so husbands and wives can help each other deal with the inevitable problems in mortality. We mentor each other. A husband learns how to be a husband from his wife. How can a woman learn to be a wife and mother if it is not from her husband and children teaching her and providing her feedback? Marriage is both a profound commitment and a covenant wherein we can learn much from each other.

Doctrine/Principle 11: The Life Cycle Teaches Us to Prepare for Eternity

Birth is a stunning miracle. Death reminds us of our fragile natures. We all witness the good and bad marriages of loved ones and friends. We observe people in our wards who struggle to maintain a semblance of marriage. We observe those with loving families and those who labor under difficult circumstances or have health issues.

As young men serve missions they mingle with ward or branch families and observe those who have strong, solid marriage and family relationships and those who do not. They want to imitate good ones. They learn of the damage that divorce brings.

We all see marriages we thought were stable, only to see them disintegrate. We see people struggle to hold their marriages together, and we are forced to examine our own lives to see what we are doing to enrich our marriage. We learn much by observing the joys and sorrows of those who do or do not live by the principles of the gospel.

Application: We are witnesses to the heartbreak and joy that come to people who have either broken temple covenants or who have preserved wonderful relationships. We observe people using agency improperly and know of the misery it causes and the broken hearts that result from carelessness. We learn vicariously by observing others in success or failure.

Doctrine/Principle 12: Many Publications Teach and Inspire Us in Doctrinal Understanding

We live in a time when information is readily available. The Church publishes magazines reviewing doctrines and containing articles on marriage and parenting issues. The Internet can help us research any topic we care about enough to search or investigate. We can read the positive and negative experiences of others. Inspiring stories of sacrifice and effort come in printed form both in and outside the Church. Our hearts are softened as we read of the misfortunes of those who lose a spouse to cancer, accident, or disease. We read of children who lose one or both parents and yet rise above an expected mediocrity to become lights and pillars in the community and kingdom. Movies present gripping drama and tell tragic stories of those whose lives have been destroyed by careless spouses or rebellious children. We live in an informational era that can help us in every aspect of marriage and family living.

Application: We have access to sufficient bibliotherapy to learn how to function more effectively in our marriage and parenting roles. We have manuals, scriptures, volumes, videos, and other media to encourage us to do well in carrying out our responsibilities. We have little excuse for failing in marriage and parenting responsibilities. The Church's Internet Web site is a wonderful source of help to enrich and stabilize marriage and families.

Doctrine/Principle 13: We Have Personal Access to Counseling and Priesthood Blessings

Each person in the Church has a bishop, a stake president, and home teachers. Each woman in the Church has visiting teachers and a Relief Society president to whom she can turn. We are surrounded by wise men and women with ideas on how to function more effectively in our family callings. Relief Society meetings help women be more effective spouses and homemakers, while men attend priesthood meetings to learn to be more effective husbands and fathers.

We have parents, siblings, and extended family around us. Often our prayers are answered through other people. We need the society of Saints in our ward and stake, along with the counsel and wisdom of good friends. Family home evenings and family councils are opportunities to gather as families and discuss discrepancies that need our attention.

Application: The Lord organized his church so that each member has an ecclesiastical leader with whom he or she can counsel on difficult issues.

Doctrine/Principle 14: Church Meetings and Instruction Can Help Us in Marriage

The Church encourages each member to attend meetings where discussions on ways to apply gospel principles in our lives are accessible. We study and discuss the standard works and their principles to see their application. We have classes on marriage and family relations and family history. We have priesthood and Relief Society manuals to study the counsel of prophets. We share experiences with peers that strengthen us. We come to realize that others face similar problems relative to children, teenagers, married children, and empty nests.

Application: We attend sacrament, Sunday School, priesthood, and Relief Society meetings weekly or more often. In a lay church, we hear, share, and prepare lessons and talks on subject matter that strengthens our lives as sweethearts and companions.

Doctrine/Principle 15: Patriarchal Blessings Can Help Us Have Perspective

The Lord, through an ordained patriarch, gives a personal revelation to each worthy adult Church member. This blessing is recorded, and a copy of the blessing is given to each recipient. Through revelation, a patriarch voices divine counsel, inspiration, warnings, reproof, and an inkling as to the part the blessing's recipient will play in the dispensation drama. We learn from this special blessing that the Lord knows us individually and has blessings in store if we are faithful. Promises pertaining to exaltation are extended to us, based on our faithfulness. Patriarchal blessings assure us that God is aware of our lives, our desires, our goals, and our weaknesses (see Ether 12:27).

Application: I recommend you memorize your spouse's patriarchal blessing at least once in your married lifetime. You ought to know what divinely appointed opportunities and callings may come to your spouse so you can be supportive of his or her Church assignments. Memorizing your own blessing will also yield valuable fruit. A patriarchal blessing is a personal witness that our Father loves us and wants us to succeed in our earthly ministry. This blessing provides each of us with an anchor in life that ties us to our Heavenly Father.

Doctrine/Principle 16: Contemplating the Final Judgment Can Help Us in Our Family Relationships

Perhaps a scenario like this will take place in the future.

A wife might be asked the following question: "How did you enjoy being married to your husband?" For some, the response could be, "Whew, am I glad that's over! That was not enjoyable for me."

Perhaps children might be asked, "Tell me about your father." Some will answer by saying, "I really did not like my father. He was so temperamental, so impatient. He was abusive to me and my brothers and sisters. It was not enjoyable for us to be around him." If those answers were given about you, do you think you would qualify for an eternal marriage and more children?

A husband may be asked to share his feelings about his wife. Suppose he answers, "I really didn't enjoy being married to her. She was such a domineering person. She always had to be right, she was not interested in intimate contact with me, and she spent money unwisely. She did not like motherhood."

Suppose children are asked, "Tell me about your mother." They might respond, "My mother was seldom home. She was gone most of the time. I usually came home to an empty house, and when she was home she was not easy to get along with. She was not a good friend. She was upset most of the time. I spent a lot of time at my friend's place."

For us to be married forever, a wife's response would ideally sound something like this: "My husband was the greatest man I knew in mortality. He loved me, and he was kind to me and to our children. Our children loved their father; he was terrific. He taught them how to fish, to play, to work hard, and to live the gospel. I loved him dearly because of the way he treated me and our children."

How wonderful it would be if your children could say something like this: "My dad was my hero. I loved spending time with him. He was patient with me and even when I made mistakes, he was kind and loving. He taught me the gospel and inspired me to serve a mission.

He gave me blessings and counseled with me frequently. I wanted to be just like him."

A husband's response would ideally sound like this: "My wife was a saint to live with. She was the kindest, sweetest woman I ever knew. She loved me. She loved the children. She gave her life for their welfare and happiness. I was honored to be her husband."

The children might say something similar to this: "My mom was the sweetest soul I ever knew. She made many sacrifices for us. She took time for us; she cooked; she taught. I learned to pray at her knee. She loved the scriptures and taught me why they were so important. She was a great blessing to all of us children. She was a wonderful mother."

If a positive response is not given about you by your spouse and children, perhaps you should reevaluate your thinking about an eternal marriage and family relationship. Elder Robert D. Hales explained the concept:

> As taught in this scripture [D&C 132:19], an eternal bond doesn't just happen as a result of sealing covenants we make in the temple. How we conduct ourselves in this life will determine what we will be in all the eternities to come. To receive the blessings of the sealing that our Heavenly Father has given to us, we have to keep the commandments and conduct ourselves in such a way that *our families will want to live with us in the eternities.* . . . The Lord clearly declares, "Thou shalt love thy wife with all thy heart, and shalt cleave unto her and none else" (D&C 42:22).[10]

A temple marriage is not sufficient by itself. We have members who think that because they married in the temple, they will be together regardless of whether or not they liked each other in mortality. How silly! Why would those who didn't like their spouse in this life suddenly like them in the resurrection?

Application: Family members don't want to live "forever" with someone they did not love in this life. However, because this is the first time we marry or become parents, we make mistakes of varying degrees of seriousness. The atonement covers every sin except the unpardonable one. Repentance is always open to us. We do our best in marriage and parenting, given our backgrounds and personalities. Miracles can occur through the atonement and the Lord's Spirit when we genuinely repent and forgive. What may look hopeless at one point in time can be turned into blessings in the long run. The atonement is infinite and covers every conceivable mortal failure even if it takes until the next life to make things completely right and whole again.

Summary

Gospel doctrine and principles give us power to align our behavior with celestial requirements. Doctrines soften hearts and cause individuals and couples to bring their behavior into conformity with eternal principles. When we understand (1) that mortality is a brief time to marry and rear children, (2) that priesthood keys allow us to be sealed together as companions and family, and (3) that we must repent and live the principles of the gospel and honor covenants, then we place ourselves on the path to eternal life. We want to take advantage of the atonement of Jesus Christ in order to qualify for the ultimate goal—eternal life as a family in the kingdom of God. Only those who develop relationships of love and mutual devotion, where righteousness, gospel principles, and ordinances and covenants are first and foremost in their lives (and this probationary time is our time to do so), will remain together forever as eternal companions.

Notes

1. Boyd K. Packer, "Little Children," *Ensign,* November 1986, 17; emphasis added.
2. Boyd K. Packer, "Washed Clean," *Ensign,* May 1997, 9.
3. Boyd K. Packer, *Let Not Your Hearts Be Troubled* (Salt Lake City: Bookcraft, 1991), 1–2; emphasis added.

4. Joseph Smith, *Teachings of the Prophet Joseph Smith,* sel. Joseph Fielding Smith (Salt Lake City: Deseret Book, 1976), 300–301.
5. Joseph Fielding Smith, *Doctrines of Salvation,* comp. Bruce R. McConkie, 3 vols. (Salt Lake City: Bookcraft, 1954–56), 2:287–88.
6. Orson Pratt, in *The Seer,* January 1853, 156–57.
7. Gordon B. Hinckley, "What God Hath Joined Together," *Ensign,* May 1991, 74.
8. "The Family: A Proclamation to the World," *Ensign,* November 1995, 102.
9. Spencer W. Kimball, "Families Can Be Eternal," *Ensign,* November 1980, 4.
10. Robert D. Hales, "The Eternal Family," *Ensign,* November 1996, 65; emphasis added.

4

Jesus Christ, the Sure Foundation

Daniel K Judd

A marriage in crisis is one of the most difficult situations an individual or couple can face. Whether because of the strain placed on husband and wife, the anxiety experienced by the couple's children, family, and friends, or the responsibility placed upon those who are asked to help, marital conflict and the threat of divorce are almost always a heavy burden to bear. Though divorce may be authorized in some unique circumstances (see Matthew 19:3–9; 1 Corinthians 7:10–16), perhaps the pain, sorrow, anger, guilt, fear, confusion, apathy, and desperation that typically accompany the breaking of the marital covenant explain why we read in scripture that the Lord "hateth" divorce (see Malachi 2:16).[1]

While there are many theories, therapies, theorists, and therapists that offer good counsel for those who are facing such challenges, the central message of this chapter is that it is only through Jesus Christ that a wounded couple (and family) can honestly and completely heal. President Howard W. Hunter taught: "I am aware that life presents many challenges, but with the help of the Lord, we need not fear. If our lives and our faith are centered on Jesus Christ and his restored gospel, nothing can ever go permanently wrong. On the other hand, if our lives are not centered on the Savior and his teachings, no other success can ever be permanently right."[2]

On another occasion Elder Hunter made a similar statement specifically about marriages and families: "Whatever Jesus lays his hands upon lives. If Jesus lays his hands upon a marriage, it lives. If he is allowed to lay his hands on the family, it lives."[3]

Some time ago I met with a woman whose husband had recently confronted her by bluntly stating that he did not love her, had never loved her, and that their marriage had been a mistake from the beginning. She was devastated. While she knew that their marriage wasn't what either of them had envisioned before they were married, she believed that they were making progress and that divorce wasn't even an option to be considered. My initial conversation with her occurred just hours after her husband had communicated his feelings and his intentions. Not only was she experiencing a hurt she described as coming from "deep within" her soul, but she was having thoughts of taking her own life. As I reflected on it later, her situation reminded me of the sister Saints mentioned in the Book of Mormon whose unfaithful husbands were rebuked by the prophet Jacob:

"Ye have broken the hearts of your tender wives, and lost the confidence of your children, because of your bad examples before them; and the sobbings of their hearts ascend up to God against you" (Jacob 2:35).

After talking with her at length, providing counsel, and making the necessary arrangements to ensure that she wouldn't end her life, I began my attempts to contact her husband. As anyone who has worked with couples in conflict knows, there are usually two sides to the story.

Though he was certainly a good man, I found the husband to be resolute in his decision to divorce. He believed he had made a mistake in marrying his wife and had convinced himself that by divorcing her he was simply making right a wrong choice he had made years before. He reminded me that our theology allows for divorce, and that even though I was his priesthood leader, the decision to divorce was his choice to make. He too was in much pain and voiced what I am confident were, at least in part, legitimate concerns about his wife's shortcomings and sins. From the very beginning of our conversation it was very apparent that he did not have "ears to hear" (Matthew 11:15) any counsel I had for him regarding what he could do to reconcile. Perhaps all of us are guilty of being unwilling to heed counsel from time to time, but this brother's response to my words reminded me of the following accusation of the Savior:

"For this people's heart is waxed gross, and their ears are dull of hearing, and their eyes they have closed; lest at any time they should see with their eyes, and hear with their ears, and should understand with their heart, and should be converted, and I should heal them" (Matthew 13:15).

I was convinced that this marriage should not end and could be healed, but there was nothing that I or anyone else could say or do that appeared to have any influence on him. He was willing to deal with any consequence that came to him, his wife, or their children as a result of his decision to divorce. Though I understand this man's right to exercise his agency, in my judgment he was exercising his right to choose in a way that would hurt him and his family. As the Lord states in the Doctrine and Covenants, "Behold, here is the agency of man, and here is the condemnation of man; because that which was from the beginning is plainly manifest unto them, and they receive not the light" (D&C 93:31).

Even though I was able to meet with this couple on several occasions and was later joined in my efforts by a faithful and competent marriage and family therapist, they later divorced. This decision has had and will yet have temporal, spiritual, and eternal consequences for each of them, for their children, for all who know and love them.

Though, as mentioned earlier, divorce can in some unique circumstances be a personal choice sanctioned by the Savior and his servants, it appears from scripture and the writings of latter-day prophets that the decision to divorce has solemn consequences and should not be taken lightly. President Gordon B. Hinckley has stated: "There may be now and again a legitimate cause for divorce. I am not one to say that it is never justified. But I say without hesitation that this plague among us, which seems to be growing everywhere, is not of God, but rather is the work of the adversary of righteousness and peace and truth."[4]

When the Savior was questioned by the Pharisees, "Is it lawful for a man to put away [divorce] his wife for every cause?" He answered: "Have ye not read, that he which made them at the beginning made them male and female, and said, For this cause shall a man leave father and mother, and shall cleave to his wife: and they twain shall be one flesh? Wherefore they are no more twain, but one flesh. What therefore God hath joined together, let not man put asunder" (Matthew 19:3–6). Clearly, divorce isn't a part of the Lord's plan, but because of the hardness of heart of either one or both spouses, the Lord in his mercy has not forbidden the practice. While an adulterous spouse is one of the legitimate justifications for divorce mentioned in scripture, Elder James E. Faust has provided additional insight:

> What, then, might be "just cause" for breaking the covenants of marriage? Over a lifetime of dealing with human problems, I have struggled to understand what might be considered "just cause" for breaking of covenants. I confess I do not claim the wisdom nor authority to definitely state what is "just cause." Only the parties to the marriage can determine this. They must bear the responsibility for the train of consequences which inevitably follow if these covenants are not honored. In my opinion, "just cause" should be nothing less serious than a prolonged and apparently irredeemable relationship which is destructive of a person's dignity as a human being.

Elder Faust continued by identifying reasons for divorce that are not legitimate:

> At the same time, I have strong feelings about what is not provocation for breaking the sacred covenants of marriage. Surely it is not simply "mental distress," nor "personality differences," nor "having grown apart," nor having "fallen out

of love." This is especially so where there are children. Enduring divine counsel comes from Paul: "Husbands, love your wives, even as Christ also loved the church, and gave himself for it" (Eph. 5:25).[5]

Likening the words of scripture unto my own life, I often ask myself the question when working with couples like the one I described above, "What could I have done more?" (Jacob 5:41), as well as what more could these troubled couples have done early on and what can other couples be doing now to prevent such a tragedy from happening in their marriages. While realizing that decisions concerning marriage and divorce should be left up to the individuals involved, what can those of us who are trying to help do to assist? And more importantly, what can those of us who are married or who hope to be married do to ensure that we do not have a similar experience?

Christ As the Foundation

Many books (including the one you are reading), essays, and addresses on marriage provide various "steps" or "principles" the reader can follow to strengthen his or her marital relationship. While such *laws* for marital success exist, the heart and soul of any strategy for a successful marriage must have the *Lawgiver*—Christ—at its center. The Savior has taught: "Behold, *I am the law*, and the light. Look unto me, and endure to the end, and ye shall live; for unto him that endureth to the end will I give eternal life" (3 Nephi 15:9; emphasis added).

One week from the time I first met with the sister I described in the first part of the chapter, I was scheduled to meet with her in my office. I had scheduled a couple of hours, anticipating that this session would go like many I had experienced before and that it would take some time to begin to address the multitude of issues involved. As I went into the waiting room to greet her, I was astounded. No longer did she look as I had seen her look the week before. She radiated a strength and a peace that I hadn't anticipated. Within my own mind I concluded that her husband must have returned and they were in the process of reconciling their differences.

After we were in my office I asked the question (confident that I knew the answer), "Has your husband returned?" She explained that her husband had not returned and the situation was probably worse than it had been the previous week. She went on to tell me that even though it looked like there wasn't much hope for their marriage, she was feeling much better. She also said that though she continued to feel the deep hurt she had described earlier, she no longer had feelings of suicide and could sense that while she had a long road ahead of her, in the end everything would be okay. After discussing some of the details of what was happening with her, her husband, and the children, I asked her to explain to me how it was that she was apparently doing so well in the face of very difficult circumstances. Was she being honest about how she felt? Was she masking what was really happening? Was she in denial? She responded to my questions by explaining to me that even though she hadn't analyzed why she was doing so much better, she had just read an article in the waiting room, awaiting our appointment, that seemed to explain what was happening. She then read to me the following passage from a general conference address by Elder Russell M. Nelson of the Quorum of the Twelve Apostles:

> Years ago when Sister Nelson and I had several teenaged daughters, we took our family on a vacation far away from telephones and boyfriends. We went on a raft trip down the Colorado River through the Grand Canyon. As we started our journey, we had no idea how dangerous this trip could be.
>
> The first day was beautiful. But on the second day, when we approached Horn Creek rapids and saw that precipitous drop ahead, I was terrified. Floating on a rubber raft, our precious family was about to plunge over a waterfall! Instinctively I put one arm around my wife and the other around our youngest daughter. To protect them, I tried to hold them

close to me. But as we reached the precipice, the bended raft became a giant sling and shot me into the air. I landed into the roiling rapids of the river. I had a hard time coming up. Each time I tried to find air, I hit the underside of the raft. My family couldn't see me, but I could hear them shouting, "Daddy! Where's Daddy?"

I finally found the side of the raft and rose to the surface. The family pulled my nearly drowned body out of the water.

The sister continued by reading the doctrinal and personal application Elder Nelson was attempting to teach by relating his story:

> Brothers and sisters, I nearly lost my life learning a lesson that I now give to you. As we go through life, even through very rough waters, a father's instinctive impulse to cling tightly to his wife or to his children may not be the best way to accomplish his objective. Instead, if he will lovingly cling to the Savior and the iron rod of the gospel, his family will want to cling to him and to the Savior.
>
> This lesson is surely not limited to fathers. Regardless of gender, marital status, or age, individuals can choose to link themselves directly to the Savior, hold fast to the rod of His truth, and lead by the light of that truth. By so doing, they become examples of righteousness to whom others will want to cling.[6]

After reading the words of Elder Nelson, this sister then explained to me how his article articulated something she believed the Lord, through the Holy Ghost, had taught her during the week. She had come to the realization that the focus of her life, which before her marriage had been centered in and built upon the foundation of Jesus Christ, had shifted from the Savior to her husband. After several years of marriage, when her husband communicated his intention to divorce, her life no longer had a foundation and she felt as if she was in a free fall that would surely be followed by a heartbreaking and soul-shattering crash. We read together from the Book of Mormon the words of Helaman to his sons Nephi and Lehi:

> And now, my sons, remember, remember that it is upon the rock of our Redeemer, who is Christ, the Son of God, that ye must build your foundation; that when the devil shall send forth his mighty winds, yea, his shafts in the whirlwind, yea, when all his hail and his mighty storm shall beat upon you, it shall have no power over you to drag you down to the gulf of misery and endless wo, because of the rock upon which ye are built, which is a sure foundation, a foundation whereon if men build they cannot fall (Helaman 5:12).

This sister had appropriately married her husband and had taken his name upon her, but in doing so had allowed her relationship with her husband to eclipse the prior covenants she had made with her Heavenly Father at baptism. These covenants are articulated in the sacrament prayer:

> O God, the Eternal Father, we ask thee in the name of thy Son, Jesus Christ, to bless and sanctify this bread to the souls of all those who partake of it; that they may eat in remembrance of the body of thy Son, and witness unto thee, O God, the Eternal Father, *that they are willing to take upon them the name of thy Son,* and *always remember him,* and *keep his commandments* which he hath given them, that they may always have his Spirit to be with them. Amen (Moroni 4:3; emphasis added).

Even though only a few days had passed since her husband had announced his intention to file for divorce, she discovered that renewing her covenants and reestablishing her relationship with Heavenly Father and Jesus Christ would allow the Holy Ghost to comfort her and guide her through the difficult and dark days of divorce. While there were many well-meaning friends and family members who were giving her counsel concerning what she should do, she remembered the words of Nephi:

> And now, behold, my beloved brethren, I suppose that ye ponder somewhat in your hearts concerning that which ye should do after ye have *entered in by the way.* . . .
>
> . . . Wherefore, I said unto you, *feast upon the words* of Christ; for behold, *the words of Christ will tell you all things what ye should do.*
>
> Wherefore, now after I have spoken these words, *if ye cannot understand them it will be because ye ask not,* neither do ye knock; wherefore, ye are not brought into the light, but must perish in the dark.
>
> For behold, again I say unto you that if ye will enter in by the way, and *receive the Holy Ghost, it will show unto you all things what ye should do* (2 Nephi 32:1, 3–5; emphasis added).

This sister began to "feast upon the words of Christ" (verse 3), searching (not just reading) the scriptures and the conference reports for specific counsel from the Lord concerning what he and his servants would have her do. She also began to offer specific, meaningful prayers petitioning the Lord for guidance. Most importantly, she began to listen for and receive counsel from the Holy Ghost concerning "all things what [she] should do" (verse 5). I often counsel people, as I did this sister, to make sure they always have paper and pencil with them to record the promptings of the Holy Ghost as inspiration comes. Alma records that as he "heard these words he *wrote them down* that he might have them" (Mosiah 26:33; emphasis added).

As she returned to Christ she began to experience what the Book of Mormon missionary Amulek described when he promised the once-faithful Zoramites that if they would again come to Christ, "*immediately* shall the great plan of redemption be brought about unto you" (Alma 34:31; emphasis added). While she and her children continue to struggle with the consequences of divorce, Christ is once again her foundation and she has the assurance described in the following words of the Savior: "For the mountains [or spouses] shall depart and the hills be removed, but my kindness shall not depart from thee, neither shall the covenant of my peace be removed, saith the Lord that hath mercy on thee" (3 Nephi 22:10).

All of us, whether we be married or single, would be greatly blessed if we were to evaluate our lives and honestly determine if Jesus Christ is "the rock upon which [our lives] are built" (Helaman 5:12). My experience is that many of us have allowed the adversary to lull us into a sense of well-being that becomes our reason for not taking the gospel and our covenants seriously. It's too bad that it often takes a tragedy to awaken us to the reality of just how vital Christ and his gospel are to us and our families. The Lord warned the early Saints of this same tendency, but he also promised compassion and mercy:

> Behold, I say unto you, there were jarrings, and contentions, and envyings, and strifes, and lustful and covetous desires among them; therefore by these things they polluted their inheritances.
>
> They were slow to hearken unto the voice of the Lord their God; therefore, the Lord their God is slow to hearken unto their prayers, to answer them in the day of their trouble.
>
> In the day of their peace they esteemed lightly my counsel; but, in the day of their trouble, of necessity they feel after me.
>
> Verily I say unto you, notwithstanding their sins, my bowels are filled with compassion towards them. I will not utterly cast them off; and in the day of wrath I will remember mercy (D&C 101:6–9).

Even though the following words from President Harold B. Lee were originally given to men serving as bishops, the principle taught is applicable to all: "Most men do not set priorities to guide them in allocating their time, and most men forget that the first priority should be to maintain their own spiritual and physical strength. Then comes their family, then the Church, and then their professions—and all need time."[7]

The Family Is Central to the Creator's Plan

Some of the questions that arise with a discussion about putting God first in our lives involve the relative significance of family and Church. Haven't we learned that it's the family that is central to God's plan? Aren't Christ, the gospel, and the Church here to strengthen the family? Shouldn't the family come first? At the same time, haven't we made covenants to sacrifice whatever is required to build the Church and the kingdom?

Elder M. Russell Ballard has stated that the Church has been placed on earth as a "scaffolding that helps support and strengthen the family."[8] A scaffolding is a temporary support structure used by builders and others to construct, remodel, or clean a building; that support structure is then removed upon completion of the project. Though eternal and "central to the Creator's plan for the eternal destiny of His children,"[9] the family organization in and of itself cannot save or exalt individuals or families. Whether we bear the name of Judd, Farnsworth, Seegmiller, or Sullivan, our family, though sacred and essential, cannot save us. The scriptures plainly and repetitively teach "that there shall be no other name given nor any other way nor means whereby salvation can come unto the children of men, only in and through the name of Christ, the Lord Omnipotent" (Mosiah 3:17). King Benjamin taught his people:

> And now, because of the covenant which ye have made ye shall be called the children of Christ, his sons, and his daughters; for behold, this day he hath spiritually begotten you; for ye say that your hearts are changed through faith on his name; therefore, ye are born of him and have become his sons and his daughters.
>
> And under this head ye are made free, and there is no

other head whereby ye can be made free. There is no other name given whereby salvation cometh; therefore, I would that ye should take upon you the name of Christ, all you that have entered into the covenant with God that ye should be obedient unto the end of your lives (Mosiah 5:7–8; see also Alma 38:9).

The Savior taught: "He that loveth father or mother more than me is not worthy of me: and he that loveth son or daughter more than me is not worthy of me. And he that taketh not his cross, and followeth after me, is not worthy of me. He that findeth his life shall lose it: and he that loseth his life for my sake shall find it" (Matthew 10:37–39). The moment we reverse the intended order of the commandments to (1) "love the Lord thy God" and to (2) "love thy neighbour" (Matthew 22:37, 39), we are going against the divine order given by God. The family is central to God's plan, but Christ and his gospel must be the foundation for our lives—individually, maritally, and as a family.

Sometimes when we talk about our relationship with God and Christ having preeminence over spouse and family, there is the possibility of a serious, and sometimes fatal, misunderstanding. Most of us have known people who have allowed their Church membership or calling to become their justification for not embracing their family responsibilities. I have often wondered if Zeniff's overzealousness had any influence on his son Noah's living the life he did (see Mosiah 7:21; 9:3). The apostle Paul warns of having "a zeal of God, but not according to knowledge" (Romans 10:2), the Book of Mormon prophet Jacob warns of "looking beyond the mark" (Jacob 4:14), and the Savior warns of "omitt[ing] the weightier matters of the law" (Matthew 23:23) in favor of doctrines, principles, practices, and people who are of less importance.

There are only two whom the Lord has commanded me to love "with all my heart"—my God and my wife. In the Doctrine and Covenants, the Lord stated, "Thou shalt love thy wife with all thy heart, and shalt cleave unto her and none else" (D&C 42:22), and in the gospel of Matthew we read the Lord's command with which we are familiar: "Thou shalt love the Lord thy God with all thy heart, and with all thy soul, and with all thy mind. This is the first and great commandment. And the second is like unto it, Thou shalt love thy neighbour as thyself. On these two commandments hang all the law and the prophets" (Matthew 22:37–40).

President Ezra Taft Benson said: "When we put God first, all other things fall into their proper place or drop out of our lives. Our love of the Lord will govern the claims for our affection, the demands on our time, the interests we pursue, and the order of our priorities. We should put God ahead of *everyone else* in our lives."[10]

While it is easy to misinterpret and also rationalize what it means to put God first, sometimes family responsibilities take precedence over Church duties, and other times the Lord asks us to leave our family for a time and fulfill our responsibilities in the Church. In 1830, Thomas B. Marsh was called to leave his family "for a little time" (D&C 31:6) and serve a mission. The Lord gave Brother Marsh the following counsel in response to his concerns over the welfare of his family:

> Lift up your heart and rejoice, for the hour of your mission is come; and your tongue shall be loosed, and you shall declare glad tidings of great joy unto this generation. . . .
>
> Therefore, thrust in your sickle with all your soul, and your sins are forgiven you, and you shall be laden with sheaves upon your back, for the laborer is worthy of his hire. Wherefore, your family shall live.
>
> Behold, verily I say unto you, go from them only for a little time, and declare my word, and I will prepare a place for them (D&C 31:3, 5–6).

Elder Jeffrey R. Holland provided a powerful description of the challenge we face when we try to identify what the Lord would have us do when family and Church responsibilities appear to conflict. He quoted a sister who told him how difficult it was to find quality time with her husband, who was a bishop. It seemed "uncanny," she said, that a ward emergency always seemed to occur just at the moment he and she were about to go out together. Finally they agreed to "guarantee" a date night once a week. But their very first date night the telephone rang just as they were about to leave.

"This is a test," I smiled at him. The telephone kept ringing. "Remember our agreement. Remember our date. Remember me. Let the phone ring." In the end I wasn't smiling.

My poor husband looked trapped between me and a ringing telephone. I really did know that his highest loyalty was to me, and I knew he wanted that evening as much as I did. But he seemed paralyzed by the sound of that telephone. "I'd better at least check," he said with sad eyes. "It is probably nothing at all."

"If you do, our date is ruined," I cried. "I just know it."

The bishop promised he'd be right back, but it didn't happen. Finally she got out of the car, went into the house, and went to bed. He apologized the next morning, and she accepted, but she continued to be troubled.

Some time later a sister in the ward spoke privately with the bishop's wife. This sister said that she had been feeling overloaded and unhappy with her life. Her husband was gone a lot, working full time and attending school full time. Her small children were "demanding, noisy, and exhausting."

Then she met another man who brought some new excitement into her life. As the relationship with this other man deepened, she said,

My rationalization persuaded me to think I could walk away from my husband, my children, my temple covenants, and my Church and find happiness with a stranger. . . .

The plan was set; the time for my escape was agreed upon. Yet, as if in a last gasp of sanity, my conscience told me to call your husband, my bishop.

I say "conscience," but I know that was a spiritual prompting directly from heaven. Almost against my will, I called. The telephone rang and rang and rang. Such was the state of my mind that I actually thought, "If the bishop doesn't answer, that will be a sign I should go through with my plan." . . . I was about to hang up and walk straight into destruction when suddenly I heard your husband's voice. It penetrated my soul like lightning. Suddenly I heard myself sobbing, saying, "Bishop, is that you? I am in trouble. I need help." Your husband came with help, and I am safe today because he answered that telephone.

Then she said to the bishop's wife: "I don't know you well, but I wish to thank you for supporting your husband in his calling. I don't know what the cost for such service has been to you or to your children, but if on a difficult day there is a particularly personal cost, please know how eternally grateful I will be for the sacrifice people like you make to help rescue people like me."[11]

Elder Holland follows this story by reminding us that "nine times out of ten I would have been right alongside that wife telling her husband *not* to answer that telephone"[12]—but he indicates that when we follow the Spirit sometimes we must make a quick change in our priorities.

I would expect that most husbands and wives would be grateful if their spouses would put God first in their lives. In my experience, the real problems come when a spouse puts his or her own desires before both God and spouse—in a word, selfishness. Some individuals interpret the scriptural phrase "Thou shalt love thy neighbour as thyself" to mean that we must first "love ourselves" before we can love others. While the Lord certainly wants us to know that "the worth of souls is great in the sight of God" (D&C 18:10) and to have a healthy sense of who we are, the kind of "self-love" God would have us experience can come only by putting him first. Consider the words of Ammon to his brother Aaron, after Aaron had expressed a concern over Ammon's apparent boasting:

"I do not boast in my own strength, nor in my own wisdom; but behold, my joy is full, yea, my heart is brim with joy, and I will rejoice in my God. Yea, I know that I am nothing; as to my strength I am weak; therefore I will not boast of myself, but I will boast of my God, for in his strength I can do all things" (Alma 26:11–12).

Conclusion

The Lord has plainly taught that "it is not good that the man should be alone" (Genesis 2:18), and that marriage between a man and a woman is central to the Lord's plan for each of us. In order for us to enter the highest degree of the celestial kingdom, "a man [and a woman] must enter into this order of the priesthood [meaning the new and everlasting covenant of marriage]" (D&C 131:2; latter brackets in the original). Those of us who are faithful and not privileged to marry in this life will certainly be blessed to do so in the next. While "celestial marriage is the crowning gospel ordinance,"[13] it is also absolutely essential to know, to remember, and to act upon the doctrinal truth "that there shall be no other name given nor any other way nor means whereby salvation can come unto the children of men, only in and through the name of Christ, the Lord Omnipotent" (Mosiah 3:17). The love of God is essential if we are to truly love our spouse and family. We must remember the Savior's answer in response to the question, "Which is the great commandment in the law?" (Matthew 22:36):

"Thou shalt love the Lord thy God with all thy heart, and with all thy soul, and with all thy mind. This is the first and great commandment. And the second is like unto it, Thou shalt love thy neighbour as thyself. On these two commandments hang all the law and the prophets" (Matthew 22:37–40).

Elder Henry B. Eyring has said:

Keeping the first commandment always leads to keeping the second, because to love the Father and the Son is to serve those they love. In prayers for guidance, They send the Holy Ghost to tell us how to help others and to feel at least a part of God's love. So in that service, our love of God increases and the keeping of the second great commandment leads us back to the first, in an ascending circle.[14]

While many of our leaders have counseled fathers that the most important thing they can do for their children is to "love their mother,"[15] perhaps we could also add that the most important thing one spouse could do for the other is to love God by placing Christ at the center of their lives.

Notes

1. The King James Version (KJV) of the Bible uses the phrase "putting away" to designate divorce. Many other versions, including the New International Version (NIV), simply state, "I hate divorce, says the Lord God of Israel."
2. Howard W. Hunter, *The Teachings of Howard W. Hunter*, ed. Clyde J. Williams (Salt Lake City: Bookcraft, 1997), 40.
3. Howard W. Hunter, "Reading the Scriptures," *Ensign*, November 1979, 65.
4. Gordon B. Hinckley, "What God Hath Joined Together," *Ensign*, May 1991, 74.
5. James E. Faust, "Father, Come Home," *Ensign*, May 1993, 36–37.
6. Russell M. Nelson, "Set in Order Thy House," *Ensign*, November 2001, 69.
7. Harold B. Lee, *The Teachings of Harold B. Lee*, ed. Clyde J. Williams (Salt Lake City: Bookcraft, 1996), 615.
8. M. Russell Ballard, "Feasting at the Lord's Table," *Ensign*, May 1996, 81.
9. "The Family: A Proclamation to the World," *Ensign*, November 1995, 102.
10. Ezra Taft Benson, "The Great Commandment—Love the Lord," *Ensign*, May 1988, 4; emphasis in original.
11. Jeffrey R. Holland, "Called to Serve," *Ensign*, November 2002, 37–38.
12. Ibid., 38; emphasis in original.
13. Howard W. Hunter, *The Teachings of Howard W. Hunter*, ed. Clyde J. Williams (Salt Lake City: Bookcraft, 1997), 132.
14. Henry B. Eyring, *Because He First Loved Us* (Salt Lake City: Deseret Book, 2002), ix.

15. This statement has been made by several leaders of the Church. For example, see Howard W. Hunter, "Being a Righteous Husband and Father," *Ensign*, November 1994, 50; David O. McKay, as quoted by Gordon B. Hinckley, "Reach Out in Love and Kindness," *Ensign*, November 1982, 77; and, most recently, Russell M. Nelson, "Endure and Be Lifted Up," *Ensign*, May 1997, 71.

5

Keeping Marital Love Alive

Marleen S. Williams

Many young couples see their wedding day as the culminating event in their search for marital happiness. I recently asked a group of young women how they envisioned their marriages. Surprisingly, many focused on the wedding day. They shared their dreams of how the wedding party would be attired, what food would be served, where the reception would be held, and how the wedding dress would look! They had not thought beyond the romance of those exciting events. They also assumed that as long as they married the "right person," they were assured an easy path to marital bliss throughout their married life. Just as graduation from college or training is only the beginning rather than the completion of a career, the wedding is a commencement of a new adventure rather than the final goal. This process that begins with marriage involves personal struggle, growth, mutual negotiation, and the development of new skills and awareness. It is not a stagnant process!

The concept of eternal development and progression implies change. Marriage partners may not always change and grow at the same rate or uniformly in the same areas. This makes adjustments necessary. The Lord has decreed, however, that the process of learning how to be married and how to be in a loving relationship is necessary in order to fulfill the measure of our creation and obtain eternal life (see D&C 49:15–17). Growing in love rather than growing apart requires attention and effort by both spouses. The process refines us and requires us to look more closely at our own motivations, desires, and beliefs and bring them in line with eternal principles. What keeps love alive throughout the challenges of that process? This chapter focuses on five ideas that have been observed from counseling couples: (1) valuing and respecting differences, (2) developing emotional intimacy, (3) seeing the good in your spouse, (4) accepting accountability instead of assigning blame, and (5) serving one another.

Valuing and Respecting Differences

There is a saying that "Love is the very painful realization that other people are real." An individual may enter marriage with the belief, "If my spouse truly loves me, he or she will always think what I think, want what I want, and feel what I feel. Then I will know I have married the 'right' person." Those with such an attitude find it easy to believe that any differences are a betrayal of that love or a sign of incompatibility. They may even believe that they must compel their spouse into becoming a replica of themselves in order to be compatible. In reality, all marriages have differences. People enter marriage having different genetic backgrounds, childhood experiences, family dynamics, traditions, and ideas. When you understand another person through the lens of his or her own life experience and history, you will find it easier to interpret that person's behavior accurately and to learn how to accommodate differences.

Mary and Sam* frequently argued over how to spend Sunday evenings. Mary believed that the "right" thing to do was to visit their parents, who lived close by. As a child, she had enjoyed Sunday visits to her grandparents' homes and believed this would strengthen family ties. Sam wanted to spend Sunday evenings playing games and reading with the children, as his family had always done. He believed this was the best way to get close to their children. Both claimed the higher moral ground and demanded that if the other really understood the gospel, he or she would agree. Both believed

---

* All names used in the examples are fictional. Stories are examples of principles learned from counseling couples but do not represent real cases.

that giving in meant they were neither loved nor validated. Each held onto their own view in the hope that the other would give in first as a sign of love. When they were finally able to empathetically discuss the different ideas and memories they had learned as children, they realized their differences were not an obstacle but an opportunity. They each brought something unique from their family of origin to the family they were now creating. When they realized they could honor both perspectives without feeling betrayed or unloved, they worked out a compromise.

Worldly philosophies often seek "self-fulfillment" at the expense of relationships. An attitude of entitlement can lead people to believe that they must always have their opinions validated and their views accepted as right in order to have their needs met in relationships. When there is little empathy and tolerance for differences, divorce is often seen as the solution to end the frustration. Without the ability to value and respect differences, the person ends up either alone or in another marriage with just another set of differences and frustrations. Yet it is often the subtle differences between individuals that attracted them to each other in the first place.

Max was drawn to Anna's outgoing personality. He was more quiet and private, but appreciated the way she could smoothly enter social situations. Although he had less need for social interaction than Anna, he realized that he could learn and benefit from this quality in her. Anna appreciated the quiet stability and predictability of Max. She liked his independent strength and organizational skills. She saw this as a complement to her more spontaneous personality. Rather than competing or trying to change each other, they both recognized the gift the other brought to the relationship. Their differences became an asset to the relationship.

Developing Emotional Intimacy

Closely related to the capacity to value differences is the development of emotional intimacy. Emotional intimacy is the ability to honestly share real thoughts, feelings, and experiences without fear of reprisal, ridicule, or rejection. It is to truly "know and be known" by another (see 1 Corinthians 13:12). Paul teaches that this kind of closeness with another is dependent on the pure love of Christ. Even when two people do not experience things in the same way, treating a spouse's self-disclosure with dignity, sensitivity, and kindness can open the door to greater trust and confidence in the relationship. More fulfilling physical intimacy is often facilitated in a marriage by the trust, communication, and openness that are part of emotional intimacy.

Dennis was sexually abused as a young boy. In adolescence he struggled with a sexual addiction as he tried to understand what had happened to him as a child. He feared rejection and being close to others. Through counseling, work with his bishop, and spiritual effort on his part, he was able to overcome his addiction and to faithfully serve a mission. He still worried, however, that if any LDS woman were to discover his past struggles, she would reject him and refuse marriage to him. When he started dating Amanda, he liked that he could easily talk with her. They were able to share many hopes, dreams, and values together. As the relationship deepened to love, Dennis finally felt courageous enough to risk telling Amanda about the painful events of his childhood. He shared with her his journey to recover his own spiritual well-being. Amanda responded with charity and compassion rather than rejection. For the first time, Dennis believed that Amanda could still really love him even when she truly knew him. He and Amanda married. He reports that because of her capacity for charity and emotional intimacy, he feels unconditionally loved and accepted for the first time.

Living closely with another person in a marriage relationship provides a ringside seat to their struggles, sensitivities, and shortcomings. It is important to protect sensitive material about one's spouse from ridicule by others. Making jokes about issues that are sensitive to a companion is a sure method of shutting down emotional intimacy. Likewise, sensitive material that has been disclosed in the relationship should never be used as "ammunition" in an argument.

Sometimes couples use sensitive information as part of a hurtful attack in the name of "honesty." Hostility and criticism in the name of "honesty" may just be an excuse to discharge anger at the expense of emotional intimacy. There is a connection between the ability to love and the ability to bridle passions (or intense emotions) (see Alma 38:12). Sometimes it is necessary to put one's own emotions "on hold" temporarily in order to respond empathetically to another. Self-discipline and self-restraint are not the same as shutting down open communication "for the sake of peace." Honest communication and feedback can occur with sensitivity and kindness rather than criticism and attack.

Matt is sometimes annoyed at Cindy because she never had the opportunity to learn how to cook interesting and nutritious food. Cindy is self-conscious about this and gets defensive whenever the issue comes up. Matt knows he could "really get at her" by venting his annoyance and criticizing her cooking, but he is more interested in giving useful feedback that might help her to improve the family's diet. He never makes public jokes about her cooking, and he praises dishes he does like. He is open with positive requests, however. When Matt states requests in a noncritical manner, it becomes easier for Cindy to respond nondefensively. Instead of "you" criticisms ("You should learn how to cook better"), he uses "I" requests ("I like it when you fix a lot of vegetables. I feel healthier and appreciate your efforts to help me stay healthy."). He also shares in cooking some of their favorite dishes.

Change may sometimes occur slowly. Being patient with human imperfections is necessary. Perfectionism can interfere with emotional intimacy. A spiritual quest for wholeness, growth, and eternal perfection is different from a frantic drive for an absolutely flawless performance. The Book of Mormon teaches us that "men are, that they might have joy" (2 Nephi 2:25). Wholeness, growth, and righteous personal development in one's spiritual, physical, and social life lead to joy. Perfectionism, however, is strongly associated with depression, anxiety, fear, and frustration. Christ's admonition to be perfect (see Matthew 5:48) is not a command to immediately possess all possible skills and good qualities without ever making a mistake. It is a command to enter into a covenant process that involves repentance, change, and growth. This process is also dependent on the Atonement, which makes repentance possible. Christ is the only one who ever lived a perfect life. But even he "continued from grace to grace, until he received a fulness" (D&C 93:13).

President Joseph Fielding Smith further clarified this concept by saying: "Salvation does not come all at once; we are commanded to be perfect even as our Father in heaven is perfect. It will take us ages to accomplish this end, for there will be greater progress beyond the grave, and it will be there that the faithful will overcome all things, and receive all things, even the fulness of the Father's glory."[1]

We are promised that if we continue faithfully in that process, we will eventually become perfected through Christ (see 2 Nephi 31:16–21; D&C 67:13).

Perfectionists experience excessive shame in making mistakes. They believe that people are only of value if they are performing well. Perfectionists believe that people must excel and perform well in all areas of their lives or they are inadequate and unworthy. We learn from the scriptures that "all have not every gift given unto them" (D&C 46:11). We are all given weaknesses to teach us compassion and humility (see 1 Corinthians 1:27–30; 2 Corinthians 12:10; Ether 12:27). When you demand instant perfection from yourself or your spouse, it becomes difficult to disclose and share problems and struggles in the marriage. There is then no way to provide support for each other in overcoming challenges. When you can openly discuss weaknesses and struggles without fear of rejection or ridicule, however, you can create a "safe place" in the relationship. This facilitates the kind of self-examination that is necessary for growth.

Seeing the Good in Your Spouse

A third capacity is the willingness to see the good in your spouse. In troubled marriages, individuals are often quick to jump to the most condemning, negative explanations for a spouse's behavior. Most behaviors can be explained in multiple ways.

> Russell keeps forgetting to take out the garbage cans on Saturday mornings. His wife, Michelle, has many options for explaining his behavior: (1) he is lazy; (2) he is just doing this to annoy or get back at her; (3) he is tired because they are usually up late on Friday nights; (4) he has a lot on his mind because he is working hard and is distracted; (5) he is busy thinking about planning family activities he would enjoy on Saturday. How she chooses to conceptualize the problem will influence how she responds to Russell.

Sometimes "seeing the good" requires a process called "thought disputation," which is an active effort to generate alternative explanations for your spouse's behavior. Evidence can then be checked to explore which explanation is most likely to interpret the event accurately. This allows you to dispute an initial negative interpretation by exploring plausible positive interpretations. Checking for evidence to support each interpretation allows for a more thorough search for the truth. A basic principle to remember is that the most kindly and charitable interpretation is also likely to be the most accurate.

> Michelle thinks more carefully about why Russell keeps forgetting to take out the garbage cans. Her initial reaction is

that he is just lazy. When she thinks about this explanation, she remembers that he works very hard at the office and always helps the children with school projects. This evidence refutes the explanation of laziness.

Her next theory is that he is trying to get back at her or annoy her. She has not seen him do this in other relationships, nor can she identify any unresolved conflicts that might contribute to this motive. She also remembers the many considerate things he does for her. As she thinks more carefully, she becomes more aware that he works very hard throughout the week. Saturday is the only day he has to relax. Taking out the garbage is simply an unpleasant chore that is easy to forget. When he is finally able to get away from duties and responsibilities at work, he is just more likely to be thinking about family recreation.

She then realizes that Russell's actions are not a personal affront to her, and she then feels less angry and hurt. Changing her interpretation allows her to deal with the problem charitably and, therefore, she is less personally offended. She can now explore solutions to the problem with Russell while still seeing the good in him.

When multiple explanations are available, choosing with compassion and generosity will strengthen the goodwill in the marriage. It is also helpful to verbally communicate good intentions to your spouse. Being able to recognize and affirm those good intentions strengthens correct understanding between partners.

Shortly after their marriage, Kent and Sue realized they had differences in their needs for orderliness. Sue became very irritated when Kent followed her around and cleaned up after her. She interpreted his behavior as a criticism of her housekeeping and felt threatened and hurt. When she tearfully confronted him with what she perceived as his displeasure with her, he was genuinely surprised. He explained that he recognized how much she hated housework and that he honestly desired to lighten her responsibilities. He further explained that because he enjoyed cleaning, he saw this as a way he could show his love for her. Being able to believe his good intentions and trust the sincerity of his love eliminated her irritation with his behavior.

Accepting Responsibility Instead of Assigning Blame

When couples disagree, they often waste time and emotional energy trying to attach blame to each other. Each believes the other is the cause of the dispute and that convincing the spouse of his or her guilt will then solve the problem. They may also believe that nothing can change unless their spouse changes first. The argument goes back and forth like a Ping-Pong game but nothing ever really changes.

Wife: You are mean. You are mad all the time.

Husband: I only get mad because of what you do. You are so controlling. You are always telling me what to do.

Wife: I only do that because you are so selfish. I can't get you to do anything I want you to do. You don't give me enough time and attention.

Husband: I only do that because you are such a nag. You nag and try to control me so much that I have to get away from you to have any peace.

Wife: I only nag because I have to in order to try to get you to stop being so mad all the time. You won't listen unless I nag.

In this dialogue, neither the husband nor the wife is willing to accept responsibility for their own need to grow because neither will let go of what they cannot change in the other. It remains a battle of who must change first. Neither partner will accept the challenge to grow independently of what their spouse chooses to do.

It is a common human problem not to take responsibility for those things we do. Learning how to be responsible for one's self while providing support for the growth of one's spouse is a process that takes some maturity and time to develop. It is not easily learned. Understanding the psychological concept of interpersonal boundaries can help individuals take responsibility for their own growth. Boundaries help us to determine who "owns" what and is therefore responsible. If you can differentiate who "owns" feelings, attitudes, and behaviors, it is then easier to know to whom a particular problem belongs. If you think of a boundary as a property line, it is easier to understand the concept.

Sally had a large old tree in her backyard. Some of the branches went over the fence into her neighbor's yard. Instead of discussing the annoying branches with Sally or even just trimming the branches that came across the fence, the neighbor went over while Sally was gone, cut down the tree, and cut it into firewood, which was then distributed around the neighborhood.

When Sally returned, the neighbor told her, "We knew you would be so happy to see the tree gone. We've solved your problem for you. The tree had grown so big we thought you would appreciate having it gone. We think your yard looks much better now, and you have more space to plant a garden. We distributed the firewood and told the neighbors it was from you."

Sally did not appreciate losing the tree. She enjoyed how it shaded her home in the hot summers. Cutting down the tree was not the solution she would have chosen. She loved the tree—but more importantly, she owned the tree. She would have gladly trimmed the branches that crossed into her neighbor's yard. When the neighbor went into Sally's property without her permission and cut down her tree, the neighbor clearly violated Sally's boundaries.

If we know who "owns" which problem, we know who it is that bears the responsibility for change. Understanding this concept is the beginning of personal power. If we can courageously and lovingly look at and "own" our personal areas of needed growth, we become empowered to have a different experience. We no longer experience ourselves as victims of another's behavior. We become the architects of our own personal development rather than waiting for someone else to change. We can stop blaming another for our own lack of progress, even if they refuse to change. We reclaim our own agency when we allow for the agency of others. We cannot dictate the behaviors of others, but no one can take away our freedom to choose how we will respond to those behaviors.

In the example given earlier of the couple's argument, the wife sees herself as a helpless victim who must nag and control in an attempt to change her husband. Her husband sees himself as being forced to get angry and withdraw in order to assert his independence. Neither has yet realized that they cannot force the other to change. Neither has yet realized the power he or she can possess by recognizing they are still free to choose to grow and progress. If both are willing to do this, their energy can be spent on finding real solutions to problems rather than wasting time and energy on deciding who is to blame.

Taking responsibility requires both love and faith. When we are willing to examine our own lives, we become aware of the universal need for the atonement. This gives us a greater love and appreciation for the Savior. As we struggle with our own weaknesses, we develop empathy for how hard it is to change behavior, and we become less angry with our spouse for not being able to change as quickly as we want him or her to change. When we acknowledge our own dependence upon the atonement, we realize how much Christ loves us. Christ did not wait to love us until we were perfect or had fully developed our ability to love him. He loved us first and was willing to show that love by suffering in Gethsemane and dying on the cross for our sins, infirmities, and weaknesses (see 1 John 4:19). By drawing close to Christ, we build our own spiritual and emotional reserves and have more love to give to our spouse. We then can give love instead of just focusing on our own "needs." Ironically, it is often our own capacity to love that makes us more lovable to others.

Serving One Another

Love requires the ability to stretch and extend oneself in the service of another's growth and well-being. When we love another, we can experience service as a gift we freely choose to give rather than as a chore or burden that is demanded. When we are willing to sacrifice in order to provide dependable, consistent service in our concern for the life, welfare, and feelings of each other, love can be kept alive even through difficult challenges.

When Nathan and Sheri married, they had hopes of a peaceful, happy life together. Over the years they experienced many difficult problems—a child with chronic health problems, financial setbacks, employment struggles, loss of their home, and other challenges. Rather than blaming one another and complaining, they worked hard to lift each other's spirits. Each helped the other when burdens became heavy. Neither "kept score" of whose "turn" it was to serve. Thoughtful surprises were frequent—a card, a small gift, or extra help when needed but not asked for. After many years, Nathan asked Sheri, "We have been through so much. Are you ever sorry that you married me? I haven't given you all that you had hoped for when we first married." Sheri thoughtfully responded, "You have given me much more. Without these experiences that we have been through together, I would have never known for myself the depth of my own capacity to love and be loved. Knowing this is worth everything to me."

87

Some individuals fear service because it feels like subservience or subjugation. They may fear a loss of power if they submit to the needs of another. The Lord's plan for relationships does not include any form of dictatorship. Power in marriage cannot be handled except upon principles of righteousness (see D&C 121:36–42). Real power comes from service that is done in a spirit of love, kindness, gentleness, and meekness. This kind of service can bind another to us insomuch that they choose to be in the relationship "without compulsory means" (D&C 121:46). They are in the relationship because they desire to be there and choose it freely, not because they are forced or compelled. In this kind of a relationship, no one need fear submission to the other.

Paul's admonition to wives to "submit yourselves unto your . . . husbands" (Ephesians 5:22) has sometimes erroneously been used as justification for unrighteous dominion in marriage. A more careful reading of the surrounding verses, however, makes it clear that the command is to *submit to love* rather than domination. Husbands are commanded to "love [their] wives, even as Christ also loved the church, and gave himself for it" (Ephesians 5:25).

Submitting to love involves allowing our hearts to be vulnerable. When we submit to love, we release our heart to the other and take the risk to love and be loved. We become tenderhearted and gentle with our spouse. Service is no longer experienced as subjugation or a burden. It is a gift of love. When love is shown and expressed by consistent, dependable service to one another, no one need fear vulnerability and subjugation. We then prove the truth of the old adage that says, "We love those whom we serve."

Some worldly philosophies suggest that sacrifice and service to another cause us to lose our own identity. President Spencer W. Kimball gave wise counsel for how service can strengthen identity rather than diminish it. He stated, "There is great security in spirituality, and we cannot have spirituality without service!" Then he elaborated on that truth:

So often, our acts of service consist of simple encouragement or of giving mundane help with mundane tasks, but
what glorious consequences can flow from mundane acts and
from small but deliberate deeds! . . .

. . . In the midst of the miracle of serving, there is the
promise of Jesus, that by losing ourselves, we find ourselves.
(See Matt. 10:39.)

Not only do we "find" ourselves in terms of acknowledging guidance in our lives, but the more we serve our fellow-
men in appropriate ways, the more substance there is to our
souls. . . . Indeed, it is easier to "find" ourselves because there
is so much more of us to find![2]

A marriage need not be perfect and without challenges to be one
of great joy and peace. Peace does not come from a lack of problems,
disruptions, and difficulties, but from knowing that one's life is in
harmony with the will of God (see John 14:27; 16:33). When our
hearts are troubled, problems can bring us to our knees in prayer. We
can then learn how to find peace and solutions to our problems. It is
through these challenges that we are brought to God for instruction
on how to become a celestial companion. This process can give us
access to the Comforter, who can reassure us when we are on the right
path. If we continue in this process, we are promised a fullness of joy.

"The secret of a happy marriage is to serve God and each other,"
President Ezra Taft Benson said. "The goal of marriage is unity and
oneness, as well as self-development. Paradoxically, the more we serve
one another, the greater is our spiritual and emotional growth."[3]

Notes

1. Joseph Fielding Smith, *Doctrines of Salvation*, comp. Bruce R. McConkie, 3 vols.
   (Salt Lake City: Bookcraft, 1954–56), 2:18.
2. Spencer W. Kimball, "Small Acts of Service," *Ensign*, December 1974, 5.
3. Ezra Taft Benson, "Fundamentals of Enduring Family Relationships," *Ensign*,
   November 1982, 60.

6

Ministering in Marriage

Kent R. Brooks

In the Church and in the home, we are called upon to both administer and minister. While both words imply forms of service, the service rendered through administering tends to be quite different from the service given through ministering. To *administer* is to manage, to regulate, to organize, to supervise, to oversee, or to take charge. An efficient home requires good administration. Problems can easily arise if there are inadequate organization, leadership, planning, follow-up, and accountability. But most of what we do, or should do, in our marriages and in our homes falls into the category of ministering. To *minister* is to serve, to look after the needs of another, to provide companionship, comfort, aid, or relief. It is to "*succor* the weak, *lift* up the hands which hang down, and *strengthen* the feeble knees" (D&C 81:5; emphasis added). Good administration facilitates effective ministering.

"The Family: A Proclamation to the World" states that "in the premortal realm, spirit sons and daughters . . . accepted [Heavenly Father's] plan by which His children could obtain a physical body and gain earthly experience to progress toward perfection and ultimately realize his or her divine destiny as an heir of eternal life."[1] Let me review three points from that statement and how they relate to ministering in the context of marriage.

Obtaining a Physical Body

First, we came to earth to obtain a physical body. As premortal spirits, we had progressed as far as we could without a physical body.

Our imperfect physical tabernacles would be subject to pain, to the physiological changes of childbirth, to sickness or other physical limitations, to fatigue, physical cravings, and appetites, and to aging and death. These physical realities present many common challenges to and between husbands and wives—challenges that influence our own happiness as well as our capacity to bring happiness to others. In these circumstances, there are many opportunities to minister to each other—to succor, lift, and strengthen; to look after the needs of our partners; to provide companionship, comfort, aid, or relief.

As a teenager, I witnessed an angel mother who ministered to my diabetic father. A teacher by profession, my father eventually lost his sight. Since he was unable to read or study in preparation for his classes, my mother succored my father (*succor* literally means "to run to"[2]) by reading to him and helping him review the material he would teach each day. Her voice "did speak peace to [his] soul" (Alma 58:11). She lifted and comforted him as he struggled to learn Braille, deal with the social and emotional trauma of blindness, and adjust to a world of darkness. As the Savior is for each one of us, she was a "light which shineth in the darkness" (D&C 6:21) for my father. Later, after many years of widowhood, she remarried another wonderful man. They had many years of happiness together before he was stricken with Alzheimer's disease and, once again, she found herself being called upon to minister in extraordinary ways. In the latter stages of his disease, when his mental capacities were little more than a child's, she continued to look after his needs and provide him with loving companionship. I observed that her ministering efforts required that *she* become even more "as a child, submissive, meek, humble, patient, [and] full of love" (Mosiah 3:19). My mother has been, and is, a ministering angel.

Our mortal bodies, with their inherent weaknesses and susceptibilities, are often the source of emotional and spiritual pain or sorrow in marriage when we succumb to any of the myriad temptations of the flesh. Our physical bodies represent "*the* great prize of mortal life."[3]

As such, "all the assaults that [Satan] will make to capture us will be through the . . . lusts, the appetites, [and] the ambitions of the flesh."[4] In marriage, these assaults may come through pornography, infidelity, overeating or eating disorders, abuse, an overemphasis or underemphasis on physical fitness and beauty, violations of the Word of Wisdom, procrastination, too little or too much sleep, trying to "run faster or labor more than [we] have strength" (D&C 10:4), or through worldly ambitions that cause us to live beyond our means or neglect our family duties. "The natural man is an enemy to God [and to a happy marriage] . . . and will be, forever and ever, unless he yields to the enticings of the Holy Spirit, and putteth off the natural man and becometh a saint through the atonement of Christ the Lord" (Mosiah 3:19).

The natural man is given to pride and selfishness. Sin is essentially the animation of those two vices. President Ezra Taft Benson taught:

> Our will in competition to God's will allows desires, appetites, and passions to go unbridled. . . .
>
> Pride . . . is manifest in so many ways, such as faultfinding, . . . murmuring, living beyond our means, . . . withholding gratitude and praise that might lift another, and being unforgiving and jealous. . . .
>
> Selfishness is one of the more common faces of pride. "How everything affects me" is the center of all that matters—self-conceit, self-pity, worldly self-fulfillment, self-gratification, and self-seeking. . . .
>
> The scriptures testify that the proud are easily offended and hold grudges. (See 1 Ne. 16:1–3.) They withhold forgiveness to keep another in their debt and to justify their injured feelings.[5]

"Selfishness," Elder Neal A. Maxwell taught, "is much more than an ordinary problem because it activates all the cardinal sins! It is the detonator in the breaking of the Ten Commandments. . . . Unchecked selfishness . . . blocks the way for developing all of the divine quali-ties: love, mercy, patience, long-suffering, kindness, graciousness, goodness, and gentleness."⁶

The manifestations of pride and selfishness mentioned by President Benson and Elder Maxwell are common in marriage. The greater the pride and selfishness, the lesser the capacity (and usually the desire) to minister. Couples overcome by pride tend to adopt a repeating cycle of *self*-justification and *other*-blaming. Blind to per-sonal sin and thus rejecting any personal responsibility for the dys-functional pattern, each spouse selfishly blames the other and justifies his or her own continued acts of unrighteousness. One spouse says: "If *you* were not so critical of me all the time and were more appre-ciative, it would be natural for *me* to show affection. You certainly can't expect *me* to be intimate with one who is so unkind and rude." The other responds, "Well, *I* only criticize *you* because *you* only care about *yourself*. If *you* would show some sensitivity to *my* needs, *I* would be kind and appreciative." Focused on how everything affects them personally, spouses justify their injured feelings and withhold forgiveness. As the cycle repeats itself, they feel more and more justi-fied in being angry and hurt and less and less likely to forgive and min-ister to each other. How do couples break the cycle? How do they increase their desire and capacity to minister to each other? How do they become more like the Savior, who "came not to be ministered unto, but to minister" (Matthew 20:28)?

First, they must look *inward*. Elder Neal A. Maxwell said: "Life really becomes better only when we become better. The diversions and the illusions are such that, unless we are very careful, we will be diverted. Life unfolds only as we unfold spiritually."⁷ Each spouse must cease blaming, recognize and accept personal responsibility for sin, and then repent. Repentance and personal change require humility, the "antidote for pride."⁸ Husbands and wives show humility when they devote their time and energy to "lifting [their partners] as high or higher than [they] are, . . . by forgiving those who have offended

[them], . . . by rendering selfless service, . . . by getting to the temple more frequently, . . . by confessing and forsaking [their] sins, . . . by loving God, submitting [their] will to His, and putting Him first in [their] lives."[9]

Elder Boyd K. Packer taught:

[Husbands and wives,] can we first consider the most painful part of your problem? If you want to reclaim your [spouse], why don't you leave off trying to alter your [spouse] just for a little while and concentrate on yourself. The changes must begin with you, not with your [spouse].

You can't continue to do what you have been doing (even though you thought it was right) and expect to unproduce some behavior in your [spouse], when your conduct was one of the things that produced it.

It's you, not the [spouse], that needs immediate attention. . . .

And [husbands or wives], if you seek for a cure that ignores faith and religious doctrine, you look for a cure where it never will be found.[10]

Many, feeling the weight of unhappiness, erroneously conclude that the burden lies in an unhappy marriage, a heavy Church calling, or a stressful job. Their conclusion leads them to believe that the solution to their unhappiness lies in a change of *circumstance*—divorce, being released from their Church calling, or finding a different job. But Elder Neal A. Maxwell noted that "the heaviest load we feel is often from the weight of our unkept promises and our unresolved sins, which press down relentlessly upon us."[11] Changing *circumstances* merely shifts the burden from one part of our back to another. The full weight remains, still, on our shoulders. The Savior said, "Come unto me, all ye that labour and are heavy laden, and I will give you rest" (Matthew 11:28). Only when we change our *heart* through personal repentance can the burdensome weight of sin really be lifted from our weary shoulders. True happiness is not found in circumstances. They are ever changing. True happiness is found in Christ, "who is infinite and eternal, from everlasting to everlasting the same unchangeable God" (D&C 20:17).

Second, couples must look *forward*. Many couples get mired in the past. They lose hope that things can ever change for the better. To look *forward* is to be proactive in implementing positive, preventive measures that will keep the cycle from recurring. The Savior counseled that "whosoever will be great among you, let him be your minister; and whosoever will be chief among you, let him be your servant" (Matthew 20:26–27). "How can I help you today?" or "How can I serve you today?" are good questions to ask of each other. Continued courtship, acts of kindness, expressions of appreciation and affection, and a willingness to forgive, help, serve, and sacrifice for each other are other examples of proactive behaviors that move couples "forward and not backward" (D&C 128:22). Couples cannot look forward without faith. Faith brings hope (see Ether 12:4). Hope, which comes through the "power of the Holy Ghost" (Romans 15:13), motivates us to keep trying and fills us with "perfect love, which love endureth by diligence unto prayer" (Moroni 8:26).

Third, and most important, the couple must look *heavenward*. The proclamation on the family states that "happiness in family life is most likely to be achieved when founded upon the teachings of the Lord Jesus Christ."[12] Couples must recognize that they cannot break the cycle on their own. Each must humbly come unto Christ through personal repentance and be determined to let the Savior be the center of his or her life and of their relationship. Elder Richard G. Scott taught: "Now, the most important principle I can share: Anchor your life in Jesus Christ, your Redeemer. Make your Eternal Father and his Beloved Son the most important priority in your life—more important than life itself, more important than a beloved companion or children or anyone on earth. Make their will your central desire. Then all that you need for happiness will come to you."[13]

95

In the October 1979 general conference of the Church, Elder Howard W. Hunter recounted the story of Jesus raising from the dead the twelve-year-old daughter of Jairus, the ruler of a synagogue near the western shore of the Sea of Galilee. Elder Hunter said: "'And [Jairus] besought him greatly, saying, My little daughter lieth at the point of death. I pray thee, come and lay thy hands on her, that she may be healed; and she shall live.' . . . These are not only the words of faith of a father torn with grief but are also a reminder to us that whatever Jesus lays his hands upon lives. If Jesus lays his hands upon a marriage, it lives. If he is allowed to lay his hands on the family, it lives."[14]

In addition to these three keys, I would offer one additional thought. President Benson said: "Most people fall into sexual sin in a misguided attempt to fulfill basic human needs. We all have a need to feel loved and worthwhile. We all seek to have joy and happiness in our lives. Knowing this, Satan often lures people into immorality by playing on their basic needs."[15] I believe that same principle could be applied to other sins as well. Many sins represent misguided attempts to meet basic human needs. Often, when a person lets a passion of any kind go unbridled, it is an attempt to meet an underlying need. The passion is mistaken for the need. Therefore, no matter how much we try to satisfy the passion, the fundamental need (to feel loved, to feel worthwhile, to feel joy or happiness, to feel validated or appreciated) remains unsatisfied. Jacob counseled his people: "Do not spend money for that which is of no worth, nor your labor for that which cannot satisfy" (2 Nephi 9:51).

In marriage, we can minister to each other by working together to identify underlying needs and looking for appropriate and truly satisfying ways to meet those needs. For example, if the underlying need is to feel *loved*, each spouse could ponder the question: "How can I help my partner to feel *loved* today?" If the underlying need is to feel *validated*, each partner might consider the question: "How can I help my spouse to feel *validated* today?" and so on with other underlying needs, such as feeling worthwhile or appreciated. In the early years of

marriage, and then periodically in the ensuing years, it is wise to for-
mally ask each other those questions. We need to let our partners
teach us how to meet their underlying needs. Without their input we
often try to meet their needs *our* way, or the way *we* would like to
have those needs met if they were *ours*. Then when our efforts seem
unappreciated or unfruitful, we feel frustrated and may be tempted to
give up trying. Save for the influence of the divine, the best authority
we have on how to meet the needs of our spouse is our spouse!

As we identify and seek to fulfill the needs of our spouse, we
should bear in mind that some needs are beyond *our* capacity to satisfy. Many individuals seeking a marriage partner seem to believe that
the *right* person is the one who will meet all their needs. Much of the
frustration many couples feel in marriage is related to that unrealistic
and erroneous expectation. For example, it is unlikely that all of our
social needs can or will be met by our spouse. Part of our social needs
will be satisfied through continued association with our extended
family. Part of our social needs may be met through good friends and
neighbors, or through quorums, committees, auxiliary organizations,
clubs, or other such groups. Each of us has underlying spiritual needs
that cannot be met by the spouse. They can be satisfied only through
our personal relationship with Deity—through personal repentance,
personal prayer, personal scripture study, personal righteousness, and
by individually coming unto Christ. Ultimately, at-one-ment with God
is our deepest and most basic need. I know that the Bread of Life and
the Living Water can satisfy even the most hungry and the most thirsty
soul. Only when there is at-one-ment with God can there be true at-
one-ment in a marriage.

Gaining Earthly Experience

The next phrase from the proclamation on the family teaches that
we came to earth to gain experience. Faithful in our first, premortal
state, we were granted a second, mortal state. The two estates would,
of necessity, be different. No longer in the presence of God, we would

be required to live by faith (in Jesus Christ) and demonstrate our willingness to keep the commandments of God in circumstances wherein we had no memory of our premortal existence. Our second estate, then, was to be a time of testing and of learning that we can overcome the natural and necessary effects of the Fall only through Christ and his atonement.

In my work as a marriage counselor, I have observed that many couples struggle because they fail to understand the nature of mortality. Their doctrinal misconception carries over into marriage. Rather than understanding that marriage will be characterized by many *earthly* experiences, they expect their relationship to be an unbroken sequence of *heavenly* experiences—sort of like a Disneyland vacation with one thrilling ride after another and with only occasional long lines and slightly more heat than is comfortable. When they find that there are plenty of "spills" to go with the thrills, that the heat of some days is scorching and quite uncomfortable, that some lines seem endless and require great patience, and that some of the rides may even be temporarily "closed for repair," they feel cheated or unjustly dealt with by their spouse, by life, or even by God. Some even insist on a new riding partner or demand their money back!

President Gordon B. Hinckley said: "Too many who come to marriage have been coddled and spoiled and somehow led to feel that everything must be precisely right at all times, that life is a series of entertainments, that appetites are to be satisfied without regard to principle. How tragic the consequences of such hollow and unreasonable thinking!"[16] No, as Elder Boyd K. Packer clearly taught: "It was meant to be that life [and marriage] would be a challenge. To suffer some anxiety, some depression, some disappointment, even some failure is normal. [We must] teach our members that if they have a good, miserable day once in a while, or several in a row, to stand steady and face them. Things will straighten out. There is great purpose in our struggle in life [and marriage]."[17]

It is through our *earthly* experiences, particularly in the home, that we learn what it really means to "bear one another's burdens, that they may be light; . . . to mourn with those that mourn; . . . and [to] comfort those that stand in need of comfort" (Mosiah 18:8–9). The nature of mortality is that some *earthly* burdens *are* heavier than one can bear alone and *will* test the *willingness* of a partner to shoulder part of the load. Beyond the prescription of "take two aspirin and call me in the morning," some earthly experiences will test our *availability* to *mourn*—morning, noon, and night, if necessary—with those we love. Some disappointments, unmet needs, sins, and afflictions will test our *capacity* to deeply comfort those with deep hurt. Ironically, some of the sharpest pain of all, some of the discomfort most in need of *our* comfort, is the pain *we* inflict upon our own partners.

These *earthly* experiences certainly try our "patience and [our] faith" (Mosiah 23:21) and remind us of our absolute dependence upon the Savior and his atonement. But they are also tutoring experiences about the opportunities and responsibilities of those who are bound to God and to each other by covenant (see D&C 82:11). "However long and hard the road may be,"[18] disciples of Christ have covenanted "to stand as witnesses of God at all times and in all things, and in all places that [they] may be in, even until death" (Mosiah 18:9), and to "act in all holiness" (D&C 43:9) as they emulate the Savior and "seek that which was lost, [to] bring again that which was driven away, . . . [to] bind up that which was broken, and [to] strengthen that which was sick" (Ezekiel 34:16). Indeed, "in one sense," Elder Boyd K. Packer taught, "we ourselves may participate in an atonement. When we are willing to restore to others that which we have not taken, or heal wounds that we did not inflict, or pay a debt that we did not incur, we are emulating His part in the Atonement."[19]

Failing to understand the nature of mortality with its *earthly* experiences causes some couples to expect a *celestial* marriage after making only a short-term, *telestial* investment—perhaps the ultimate example of a "get-rich-quick scheme"! When the anticipated returns on their investment don't materialize or when the market drops, they are tempted, or even threaten, to sell out. They take counsel from their fears, their frustrations, and their partner's failings. Instead of holding on and "hold[ing] out faithful to the end" (D&C 6:13), they give in and give up. Couples must understand that a celestial marriage comes only "in process of time" (Moses 7:21). Even for remarkable Enoch, it required 365 years (see Moses 7:68 and 8:1) to transform people whose "hearts [had] waxed hard, . . . [whose] ears [were] dull of hearing, and [whose] eyes [could] not see afar off" (Moses 6:27) into a community of people who "were of one heart and one mind, and [who] dwelt in righteousness; and . . . [had] no poor among them" (Moses 7:18).

Nephi taught, "Men [or husbands and wives] are, that they *might* [not *will*] have joy" (2 Nephi 2:25; emphasis added). Joy, a gift of the Spirit (see Galatians 5:22), comes to the meek (see Isaiah 29:19), the faithful (see Matthew 25:21; D&C 59:13), the obedient (see Mosiah 2:41), and the humble and prayerful (see D&C 136:29). When one has an eternal perspective, centered in Christ, it is possible even to be "exceeding joyful in all our tribulation" (2 Corinthians 7:4). We have the faith that while "weeping may endure for a night, . . . joy cometh in the morning" (Psalm 30:5). That joy *will* come to those who learn to "[wait] patiently on the Lord" (D&C 98:2) and who through continued meekness, faithfulness, obedience, humility, and prayerfulness learn to "endure it well" (D&C 121:8). "If ye know these things, happy are ye if ye do them" (John 13:17).

Having and maintaining an eternal perspective is a prerequisite to joy. That relationship was impressed upon me several years ago when I had the opportunity to visit Liberty Jail, where the Prophet Joseph Smith and others of the Brethren languished for many months in miserable conditions. The fourteen foot by fourteen foot quarters were cramped. The ceiling was so low that the Brethren could not stand up straight without hitting their heads. The floor was cold and hard. The walls, four feet thick, comprised an inner and outer layer with loose rocks placed in between. Illuminated by only one window measuring one foot by two feet, the dungeon was dark and damp. Yet in that prison, the Prophet Joseph Smith received some of the greatest revelation ever recorded, excerpts of which are found in sections 121 and 122 of the Doctrine and Covenants. Before visiting the jail, I took the opportunity to carefully study and ponder those revelations. I reviewed the full account of the experience as recorded in the histories of the Church. I was impressed by Elder B. H. Roberts's insight that the Prophet Joseph Smith had transformed Liberty Jail into a place "more temple than prison." [20]

While most of us, gratefully, will never know literal incarceration, we all in one way or another can relate to feelings of being trapped or in some way confined by our *earthly* experiences. Some feel confined by disease, by an addictive habit, or by pride, selfishness, or other characteristics of the natural man. Some feel trapped by a never-ending list of "things to do" in a day or by the excessive demands of others. Many feel bound by their finances, an unhappy marriage, a wayward child, or a stressful job. Many know feelings of imprisonment from fear, rejection, loneliness, disappointment, abuse, or betrayal. Whatever the form or fashion of these *earthly* experiences, and however long or deeply they may afflict us or our marriages, our perspective determines whether or not these experiences become paralyzing prisons or tutoring temples. Elder Neal A. Maxwell noted that "this life's temporal lens distorts. The things of the moment are grossly magnified, and the things of eternity are blurred or diminished." [21] Without the liberating perspective of eternity, our eyes "cannot see afar off" (Moses 6:27). And "where there is no vision, the people [or marriages] perish" (Proverbs 29:18).

For *Brandon and Janelle, a couple with whom I worked some years ago, the things of the moment had been magnified and the things of eternity had diminished and become blurred. Their eyes could not see afar off. Brandon and Janelle met during their junior

* The names of people used in the examples have been changed.

year in high school. Janelle was, at that time, an active member of another faith. Through her association with Brandon and his family, she became interested in The Church of Jesus Christ of Latter-day Saints. After graduating from high school, Janelle joined the Church. A year later, Brandon accepted a mission call. Janelle was thrilled. Her greatest desire was to marry a returned missionary in the temple and raise a righteous family. Brandon and Janelle wrote to each other over the next two years. Though she dated others during that time, Janelle felt that none could compare to Brandon. Brandon's family thought very highly of Janelle. Neither family was surprised when Brandon and Janelle announced their engagement three months after his return from the mission field. They were married in the temple. Janelle felt that her greatest dreams were coming true.

Soon after their marriage, Brandon stopped going to Church. He refused to attend the temple or to pray with Janelle. He seemed apathetic about everything, including his desires to work and further his education. Janelle's dream world was shattered. It seemed that the more she tried to help and draw close to Brandon, the more he resisted and the further he pulled away from her. Brandon seemed to be getting more and more depressed. Though she did not know what else to do, Janelle was determined to never give up. But after nearly a year of marriage with no apparent progress, Janelle began to lose hope that Brandon would ever change. Many family members and friends counseled her to divorce, reasoning that she had been patient long enough and had exhausted every reasonable effort to help an unwilling, unresponsive husband. Feelings of personal hurt and disappointment made it increasingly difficult for Janelle to see past the moment and to have any hope for the future. Obviously Brandon's focus on eternity had diminished, but Janelle's view had also been blurred by the unforeseen, unexpected circumstances of her marriage.

As I visited with Janelle, I said, "You have told me something of *your* hurt, *your* pain, *your* sorrow and disappointment. What can you tell me of *Brandon's?*" She looked a little surprised. I suggested that

Brandon's behavior was probably influenced by some deep hurt of his own or by a basic underlying need that was not being met. She replied, "I guess I had never thought of it that way." We reviewed an experience from the life of Peter. Along with other disciples, Peter was in a ship, in the midst of the sea, when a terrible (and possibly unexpected) wind arose. The vessel was tossed about by the turbulent waves. Looking out across the sea, sometime between three and six in the morning, the disciples saw what appeared to be a spirit walking upon the water. The unexpected sight caused them to fear. The personage was Christ. He quickly calmed their fears, saying, "Be of good cheer; it is I" (Matthew 14:27). Peter replied, saying, "Lord, if it be thou, bid me come unto thee on the water. And [Jesus] said, Come" (Matthew 14:28–29).

In spite of the darkness, the wind, and the waves, regardless of the "binding" law of gravity, Peter began to walk to the Savior on the water! Impossible? Absolutely—without faith. Absolutely—without Christ or without an eternal, Christ-centered perspective. As long as Peter had both, he was able to do the "impossible." I asked Janelle, "What seems impossible to *you* right now?" She responded, and we discussed her feelings and her perspective. Then I asked, "What do you think seems impossible to *Brandon?* Why is he *sinking?*" She pondered my questions deeply. Sensing that she was really trying to see things from Brandon's point of view, I silently prayed that the Spirit would help her to do that. Tears began to stream down her cheeks. We sat, for some time, in sacred silence. When she was able, she responded to my questions. The "eyes of [her] understanding were opened" (D&C 138:11), and she was blessed with inspired insights that reflected her compassion and tenderness for Brandon.

In "process of time," both Janelle and Brandon came to know the at-one-ment possible through Christ, and each experienced personal healing. Each came to better understand and minister to the other's underlying needs. Each became a witness of a loving Savior "moving in his majesty and power" (D&C 88:47), "working miracles in them"

(Alma 23:6), and reassuring them that "all things *are* possible to [them] that believeth" (Mark 9:23; emphasis added). Their eternal perspective returned.

To any who have faith, who strive to maintain an eternal, Christ-centered perspective, and who are true to their covenants, Elder Neal A. Maxwell promised, "Let the winds and the storms beat and pound upon . . . faithful Saints; they [and their marriages] will overcome the world—not vice versa. Let others falter; these will not! Let others pout and doubt; these will not!"[22] "With God," wrote Luke, "nothing *can* be impossible" (JST Luke 1:37)—even the changing of hearts and the renewal of confidence that might prompt one spouse to affectionately say of the other: "In my eyes, I almost think he or she walks on water!" A recent study has shown that 86 percent of those who reported being unhappy in their marriages, but who did not divorce, five years later described their marriage as either "very happy" or "quite happy."[23]

None of us is exempt from "waves" of disappointment or "winds" of discouragement as we navigate the stormy seas of mortality. But these *earthly* experiences can help us to become more tender and compassionate toward others when they face trials of their own. Following his experiences in Liberty Jail, the Prophet Joseph Smith said, "It seems to me that my heart will always be more tender after this than ever it was before. . . . I think I never could have felt as I now do if I had not suffered."[24]

Do you see, then, one of the great relationship truths of mortality? Our capacity to love a spouse deeply and our ability to experience great joy in marriage are commensurate with the degree to which we are willing to suffer and hurt, to labor and toil, and to persevere through moments of unhappiness, stress, disappointment, and tests of our patience and love for our partners. You cannot have one without the other. They are flip sides of the same coin. Lehi taught that, while in the Garden of Eden, Adam and Eve could have "no joy, for they knew no misery; [they could do] no good, for they knew no sin"

(2 Nephi 2:23). After the Fall, having come to "know according to the flesh" (Alma 7:12) the necessity, the significance, and the blessing of "opposition in all things" (2 Nephi 2:11), mortal Eve expressed her eternal perspective when she declared, "Were it not for our transgression we never should have had seed, and never should have known good and evil, and the joy of our redemption, and the eternal life which God giveth unto all the obedient" (Moses 5:11).

Successful couples, then, are not those who *bypass* challenging earthly experiences, but rather those who, facing them with faith, gain the hope that these things too *shall pass* and will be "but a small moment" (D&C 121:7). With faith and hope, successful couples can minister to each other with charity, the pure love of Christ. As did the Savior for the people of Alma, husbands and wives can demonstrate that they will and "do visit [their spouses] *in* their afflictions" (Mosiah 24:14; emphasis added). Those kindly visitations calm seas. They dispel fears. They restore hope and perspective. The voices of these ministering angels soothe the troubled heart and resonate with the same comforting words spoken by the Savior to his chief apostle on that dark, stormy night, "Be of good cheer; it is I." That "voice of gladness" (D&C 128:19) surely helps a struggling spouse to feel "encircled about eternally in the arms of [a partner's] love" (2 Nephi 1:15), and to declare also "I feel my *Savior's* love."[25]

In the early days of open-heart surgery, which in the words of Elder Russell M. Nelson were like "like sailing an uncharted sea," not many lives were saved. In 1957 a married couple brought one of their children to Dr. Nelson in hopes that he could heal the child of congenital heart disease. The couple had lost their first child to the same ailment before heart surgery was an option. Their second child died following an unsuccessful open-heart operation performed by Dr. Nelson. Now the couple had returned to entrust their third child into his hands. The surgery was performed, but the child died later that night.

Dr. Nelson said: "My grief was beyond expression. When I went home, I told [my wife about it] and said, 'I'm through. I'll never do another heart operation as long as I live!' I wept most of the night. . . . I determined that my inadequacies would never be inflicted on another human family. When morning came, [my wife] finally said, 'Isn't it better to keep trying than to quit now and require others to go through the same grief of learning what you already know?' I listened to her counsel. I returned to the laboratory to work a little harder, learn a little more, and strive further."[26] Sister Nelson's timely ministering helped her husband continue on and become a world-renowned heart surgeon who would later minister himself in saving the lives of Elder Spencer W. Kimball, Elder James E. Faust, and many, many others through his surgical skills.

Progressing toward Perfection

In our Heavenly Father's plan, our earthly experiences were designed to help us progress toward perfection and "ultimately realize [our] divine destiny as an heir of eternal life"—the third truth we are examining from the proclamation on the family. Unfortunately, for many couples, those experiences cause personal and relationship digression or regression from where we should be on life's path. Instead of stepping stones, they become stumbling blocks to progress. What makes the difference? Why are some couples able to grow and become perfected by their earthly experiences while others are destroyed by them? I would suggest that one reason for the divergence is the disparity of perceptions regarding the nature of change and how change is to be facilitated in marriage. What *is* the best way to help a spouse grow or progress toward perfection? Judging by the actions of most couples I have worked with as a therapist, the majority seem to believe that the best way to encourage change is by nagging, criticizing, withholding gratitude and praise, or by pointing out what is wrong or in need of change. Yet, as Elder Joe J. Christensen noted, "Few people have ever changed for the better as a result of constant criticism or nagging."[27]

What is the nature of change? Let me suggest four elements of change.

First, change is gradual. We cannot "microwave" growth—in ourselves or in others. It is more like a "slow-roast over a low heat." Even the Savior "continued from grace to grace, until he received a fulness" (D&C 93:13). Even he "increased in wisdom and stature, and in favour with God and man" (Luke 2:52). Yet some spouses impose unrealistic and soul-deflating expectations on their partners. They expect, even demand, immediate change. When it does not come, they assume their companions are not trying or do not care. If we remember that growth is *gradual,* we will minister with a patient pace that will not demand that a spouse unrealistically "run faster or labor more than [he or she has] strength" (D&C 10:4). We will better understand the *when* and *where* of ministering.

President N. Eldon Tanner said: "Women, you are of great strength and support to the men in your lives, and they sometimes need your help most *when* they are least deserving. A man can have no greater incentive, no greater hope, no greater strength than to know his mother, his sweetheart, or his wife has confidence in him and loves him. And men should strive every day to live worthy of that love and confidence." [28]

President Harold B. Lee counseled: "Several years ago when Sister David O. McKay, the wife of our President, was in the hospital, I called to see her just after the President had been there, and she said in her sweet way, 'You know, I think he misses me.' And I replied, 'I am sure he does.' Then she said with a smile, 'I have always tried to be *where* I thought he needed me the most.' There you are, you sisters, try to be *where* you feel your husbands need you the most." [29] Of course, both of those statements would have equal application to men.

Second, change is painful. It requires the *surrendering* of our will. It follows a broken heart and a contrite spirit. Elder Neal A. Maxwell taught that "the enlarging of the soul requires not only some remodeling, but some excavating. Hypocrisy, guile, and other imbedded traits do not go gladly or easily. . . . The harrowing of the soul can be like the harrowing of the soil to increase the yield with things being turned upside down."[30] When we perceive that growing pains are turning our partners upside down, we can minister by returning their upside back up! That is, our desire and our efforts should be to "strengthen [our spouses] in *all* [our] conversations, in *all* [our] prayers, in *all* [our] exhortations, and in *all* [our] doings" (D&C 108:7; emphasis added). Change, by its very nature, is painful enough. We certainly do not want to inflict greater pain by being critical of a partner or by communicating that unless they change, they are not worthy of our love, our acceptance, our gratitude, our attention, or our validation.

Third, because change is painful, the nature of fallen man is to resist or avoid it. We much prefer to stay in our comfort zones—even, ironically, when we have become comfortable with trying to find "happiness in sin" (Mormon 2:13; 2 see also Corinthians 7:10). Hence, it is to be expected that our efforts to encourage change in our partners will most likely be met by their resistance. We should not be surprised by their "comfort zone–defense" as they zealously seek the path of least personal resistance by resisting our attempts to facilitate growth. Further, it is common for a partner's behavior to get worse before it gets better. In those moments it is essential that we apply our own form of resistance to the temptation to concede correct principles and to be sure that *our* behavior does not also get worse before it gets better. "Sometimes," Elder Neal A. Maxwell noted, "that which we are doing is correct enough but simply needs to be persisted in—patiently—not for a minute or a moment but sometimes for years."[31]

Fourth, real change, permanent change, comes through Christ. If a spouse perceives that it is his "job" to *make* his partner change, it won't matter whether the approach taken is "microwave" or "slow-roast"—either way, both of you will be cooked! At best, we *subtract* from our efforts to minister and *add* to our efforts to administer. Generally, that kind of arithmetic is not likely to produce the best bottom line in a marriage. And, at worst, we become guilty of practicing a doctrine similar to that taught by Korihor some two thousand years ago. With ideas just as false and just as destructive, we approach the changing of our spouses with the belief that our partner will fare "according to [my] management of the creature" and will prosper "according to [my] genius" and will conquer his or her *weaknesses* "according to [my] *strength*" and that whatsoever I say or do to make my spouse change is "no crime" (Alma 30:17; emphasis added)—since the end justifies the means—no matter how *mean!*

President Benson said that "men and women who turn their lives over to God will find out that he can make a lot more out of their lives than they can."[32] Similarly, spouses who are willing to turn their partners over to Christ will find that he can make a lot more out of their partners' lives than they can.

Now, I am not suggesting that the best thing to do is to do nothing! Bringing someone to Christ is not a passive process. It is active and proactive. But the belief that it is our "job" or our "role" to bring about change in our spouses is not only one of the most common evidences that we are trying to *administer* rather than *minister* in marriage, but is also evidence that we are "looking beyond the mark" (Jacob 4:14). Christ is the mark. Permanent change comes through him. We can assist in that process by bringing our partners to Christ through *ministering*. Let me suggest five ways that can be done.

First, minister to a spouse by shifting *your* paradigm. A paradigm is a model or pattern used to view and interpret the world. Many couples with whom I have counseled have found it helpful to shift their paradigm from "My spouse needs to *change*" to "My spouse needs to be *healed*." That simple paradigm shift seems to make a difference in how we view and interpret our spouse's behavior or attitudes and, in turn, elicits different behaviors and attitudes from us. We see ourselves as ministers of healing. We are reminded of the need to have faith and to be humble, since the spiritual gift of healing is given only to those who "have faith to heal" (D&C 46:20).

With faith in Christ, we humbly seek heavenly direction on how we can best minister to our spouse, vowing, "Let there be peace on earth [and in my marriage], and let it begin with me."[33] It takes humility and faith to rise above our own pain and to minister relief to another as did "the Sun of righteousness," who arose "with healing in his wings" (Malachi 4:2) and did heal "all manner of sickness" (Matthew 4:23). It takes humility and faith to continue to express soothing words of love and appreciation to those who may, at times, seem unlovable and hard to appreciate. Yet it is when our spouses are the least lovable that we must love them the most. That kind of "intensive care" brings healing.

Second, minister to a spouse by burying *your* weapons of war. After one group of Lamanites had been enlightened by the truths taught by Ammon, they desired to make a covenant with God that they would never again take up their weapons of war against their brethren. True to their promise, "they did bury them up deep in the earth. And this they did, . . . vouching and covenanting with God, that rather than shed the blood of their brethren they would give up their own lives; and rather than take away from a brother they would give unto him" (Alma 24:17–18).

In marriage, those weapons of war can take many forms. Weapons of war are great inhibitors to healing and change because they keep the wounds continuously open. One of the most powerful ways to minister to a spouse is to be willing to "bury the hatchet" once and for all—in the ground—not in our partner's back. No one likes a back-stabber! If we continue to reopen the same wound, healing cannot occur. And generally, it seems, growth follows healing.

The Savior taught: "And unto him who smiteth thee on the cheek, offer also the other; or in other words, *it is better to offer the other [cheek], than to revile again.* And him who taketh away thy cloak, forbid not to take thy coat also. For *it is better that thou suffer thine enemy to take these things, than to contend with him*" (JST Luke 6:29–30; emphasis added; compare 3 Nephi 12:39–40). In marriage, it is better to bury our weapons of war than to wield them. And, it is better to turn our own cheeks than to cause tears to fall on the cheeks of our spouses. President Thomas S. Monson warned the brethren of the Church, "Tears inevitably follow transgression. Men, take care not to make women weep, for God counts their tears."[34] Since tears and "all things are numbered unto [God]" (Moses 1:35), we should wisely post "no trespassing" signs on our cache of weapons and throw away the shovel.

Third, minister to a spouse by forgiving and forgetting his or her offenses. Elder Marion D. Hanks said that "the ultimate form of love . . . is forgiveness."[35] Elder Neal A. Maxwell pointed out that "one important dimension of loving-kindness is forgiveness. Our generosity, forgetfulness, and forgiveness can often be the equivalent of an 'emancipation proclamation' for someone who has erred."[36] In my counseling, I have many times heard a spouse say, "What incentive is there for me to repent and become better if my partner is unwilling to forgive and forget?" One of the greatest blessings that can come to those who "always remember [the Lord]" (D&C 20:77) is the ability to forgive and forget offenses. To bury our weapons of war yet continue to rebroadcast a "wide-screen" version of old battles and old wounds, complete with "instant replay," "slow-motion," and our own exaggerated form of "special effects," undermines the process of healing and the prospects for growth—for both spouses.

In his epistle to the Galatians, Paul wrote, "But now, after that ye have known God, or rather are known of God, how turn ye again to the *weak and beggarly elements,* whereunto ye desire again to be in *bondage?*" (Galatians 4:9; emphasis added). President Hinckley asked Church members, "Is there anything more weak or beggarly than the disposition to wear out one's life in an unending round of bitter thoughts and scheming gestures toward those who may have affronted us?"[37] "Time devoted by one injured to ensure the offender is punished [or suffers] is time wasted in the healing process,"[38] added Elder Richard G. Scott.

The Lord issued the solemn warning that "he that forgiveth not his brother his trespasses standeth condemned before the Lord; for there remaineth in him the greater sin" (D&C 64:9). I believe, in marriage or anywhere else, there would be more repentance if there were more forgiveness. We must resist the temptation to hold our spouses hostage by refusing to forgive them. When we hold back forgiveness and reconciliation, we are the ones who are really held back! When He who was without sin omnisciently determines that we must forgive others, and yet we who are guilty of sin (or guilty as sin!) are unwilling to do so, we set ourselves up as the better, more qualified judges of motive and heart and interfere with the sacred process of at-one-ment. No wonder the Lord regards our action as the greater sin!

Fourth, minister to a partner with a voice of gladness. "Now, what do we hear in the gospel [or "good news"] which we have received? A voice of *gladness!* A voice of *mercy* . . . ; glad tidings of great *joy*" (D&C 128:19; emphasis added). Is that what *your* spouse hears in the gospel you have received? What does your voice sound like to your spouse? A voice of sadness, criticism, judgment, and condemnation might cause a spouse to lament, "Reproach hath broken my heart; and I am full of heaviness: and I looked for some to take pity, but there was none; and for comforters, but I found none" (Psalm 69:20). President James E. Faust said: "Some want to justify their criticism by claiming, 'But it is the truth.' My answer is, 'How can you be so sure?' . . . The Apostle Paul reminded us that the misuse of the truth changes it into a lie. (See Rom. 1:18–25.)" [39] Joseph Smith counseled the Saints: "A wise head keeps a still tongue. . . . It is far better, many times . . . to forget all [you] know, than to tell all [you] know. And better still to forget than to tell some great things which [you] do not know." [40]

Shortly after the Relief Society was organized, the Prophet Joseph Smith counseled the sisters regarding the way to minister to their husbands. He said: "When a man is borne down with trouble, when he is perplexed with care and difficulty, if he can meet a smile instead of an argument or a murmur—if he can meet with mildness, it will calm down his soul and soothe his feelings; when the mind is going to despair, it needs a solace of affection and kindness. . . . When you go home, never give a cross or unkind word to your husbands, but let kindness, charity and love crown your works henceforward."[41]

The joyous declaration "How beautiful upon the mountains are the feet of him that bringeth good tidings, that publisheth peace; that bringeth good tidings of good" (Isaiah 52:7) could also be said of those who minister with a voice of gladness. "God loveth a cheerful giver" (2 Corinthians 9:7), for "a merry heart doeth good like a medicine" (Proverbs 17:22). A voice of gladness is like "a spoonful of sugar [that] helps the medicine go down!"[42] Even a Primary child understands that "no one likes a frowning face/Change it for a smile. Make the world [and your home] a better place/By smiling all the while."[43] When trying to facilitate healing and growth in a spouse, our voices and our words should communicate optimism, hope, confidence, and encouragement. Seeds of change grow best in fertile soil. If our reactions to our spouse's failings, weaknesses, or sins have been repeatedly negative and condemning, the "soil" will be stripped of all its nutrients, and we will find ourselves trying to plant "between a rock and a hard place."

Our voices can either cause "fear and trembling" (Philippians 2:12) or dispel fear and bring peace and hope. When John the Baptist appeared to Joseph Smith and Oliver Cowdery to restore the Aaronic Priesthood, it was the first time that Oliver had been in the presence of a heavenly messenger. He was afraid. Oliver Cowdery recorded: "The angel of God came down clothed with glory, and delivered the . . . keys of the gospel of repentance. . . . *His voice,* though mild, pierced to the center, and *his words,* 'I am thy fellow-servant,' *dispelled every fear."*[44]

If "all the world's a stage"[45]—and if marriage is then a stage—then we don't want to add to our spouse's "stage fright" by continually shouting corrections from the wings or by responding to our partner's performance with "boos and hisses." There are enough "critics" in the audience! It is reassuring to know that we have at least one "fan" who will find something to applaud, whose voice of gladness will resonate with a kind "bravo!" or an encouraging "encore!" or even with a "standing ovation"! How we respond today to our partner's feelings, attitudes, opinions, and failings will largely determine the number of return engagements. We don't want the theater to close after "opening night"! Whenever invited onto a partner's stage, remember to "put off thy shoes from off thy feet, for the place whereon thou standest is holy ground" (Exodus 3:5).

Fifth, minister to a partner with a tender touch—even the touch of the Master's hand. Jesus ministered to others by lifting them with his hand. While in Galilee, Jesus encountered a leper, who petitioned, "Lord, if thou wilt, thou canst make me clean. And Jesus put forth his hand, and touched him, saying, I will; be thou clean. And immediately his leprosy was cleansed" (Matthew 8:2–3). On another occasion the Master was at the house of Peter in Capernaum. Peter's mother-in-law was sick with a fever. Jesus came "and took her by the hand, and lifted her up; and immediately the fever left her" (Mark 1:31). In marriage, that same lifting hand can be extended to our spouses as we "lead, guide, and walk beside them. And help them find the way."[46] Ministers of healing learn not to give their spouses "the back of their hand," but rather "with pure hearts and clean hands" (2 Nephi 25:16) they become "an instrument in [the Lord's] hands" (Mosiah 23:10) to bring their partners to Christ. In that way, a husband and wife "become one in [God's] hand" (Ezekiel 37:17).

Joseph Smith said: "Nothing is so much calculated to lead people to forsake sin as to *take them by the hand,* and *watch over them with tenderness.* When persons manifest the least *kindness and love* to me, O what power it has over my mind, while the opposite course has a tendency to harrow up all the harsh feelings and depress the human mind."[47] A tender touch is evident as we lead with love, guide without guile, walk in the ways of the Lord, and help with faith and hope.

Brigham Young wisely counseled the Saints, "If you are ever called upon to chasten a person, never chasten beyond the balm you have within you to bind up."[48] We must always show "forth afterwards an increase of love" (D&C 121:43) and conscientiously apply the healing "balm of Gilead."

Conclusion

Our divine destiny is to be an "heir of eternal life." We cannot achieve that destiny alone, for "neither is the man without the woman, neither the woman without the man, in the Lord" (1 Corinthians 11:11). "The complementing differences [between men and women] are the very key to the plan of happiness."[49] They are our blessing, not our curse. They help to complete or make us whole. So much of the special and unique ministering that should take place in marriage is a reflection of those individual differences. The greatest blessings and powers of ministering in marriage come when those personalized gifts are used, in partnership, to serve each other, to look after the needs of one another, and to provide companionship, comfort, aid, and relief. Those complementing differences, determined by "divine design,"[50] enable us to "succor the weak, lift up the hands which hang down, and strengthen the feeble knees" (D&C 81:5).

Notes

1. "The Family: A Proclamation to the World," *Ensign,* November 1995, 102.
2. Jeffrey R. Holland, "Come unto Me," *Ensign,* April 1998, 22.
3. Jeffrey R. Holland, *Of Souls, Symbols, and Sacraments* (Salt Lake City: Deseret Book, 2001), 11; emphasis in original.
4. Melvin J. Ballard, "Struggle for the Soul," *New Era,* March 1984, 35.
5. Ezra Taft Benson, "Beware of Pride," *Ensign,* May 1989, 4–6.
6. Neal A. Maxwell, "Put Off the Natural Man, and Come Off Conqueror," *Ensign,* November 1990, 14–15.
7. Neal A. Maxwell, *We Will Prove Them Herewith* (Salt Lake City: Deseret Book, 1982), 73.
8. Benson, "Beware of Pride," 6.
9. Ibid., 7.

10. Boyd K. Packer, "Families and Fences," *Improvement Era*, December 1970, 106–7.
11. Neal A. Maxwell, "Murmur Not," *Ensign*, November 1989, 85.
12. "The Family: A Proclamation to the World," *Ensign*, November 1995, 102.
13. Richard G. Scott, "The Power of Correct Principles," *Ensign*, May 1993, 34.
14. Howard W. Hunter, "Reading the Scriptures," *Ensign*, November 1979, 65.
15. Ezra Taft Benson, "The Law of Chastity," in *Morality* (Salt Lake City: Bookcraft, 1992), 86.
16. Gordon B. Hinckley, "What God Hath Joined Together," *Ensign*, May 1991, 73.
17. Boyd K. Packer, "Solving Emotional Problems in the Lord's Own Way," *Ensign*, May 1978, 93.
18. Winston Churchill, first speech as prime minister, House of Commons, 13 May 1940, in *Churchill, the Life Triumphant*, comp. American Heritage Magazine and United Press International (New York: American Heritage Publishing Co., 1965), 90.
19. Boyd K. Packer, "The Brilliant Morning of Forgiveness," *Ensign*, November 1995, 20.
20. B. H. Roberts, *A Comprehensive History of The Church of Jesus Christ of Latter-day Saints, Century One*, 6 vols. (Salt Lake City: The Church of Jesus Christ of Latter-day Saints, 1930), 1:526.
21. Neal A. Maxwell, *If Thou Endure It Well* (Salt Lake City: Bookcraft, 1996), 26.
22. Neal A. Maxwell, "Shine As Lights in the World," *Ensign*, May 1983, 11.
23. Linda Waite and Maggie Gallagher, *The Case for Marriage* (New York: Broadway Books, 2000), 148.
24. Joseph Smith, in *The Personal Writings of Joseph Smith*, ed. Dean C. Jessee (Salt Lake City: Deseret Book, 1984), 386–87.
25. *Children's Songbook* (Salt Lake City: The Church of Jesus Christ of Latter-day Saints, 1989), 74–75; emphasis added.
26. Lane Johnson, "Russell M. Nelson: A Study in Obedience," *Ensign*, August 1982, 21.
27. Joe J. Christensen, "Marriage and the Great Plan of Happiness," *Ensign*, May 1995, 64–65.
28. N. Eldon Tanner, "No Greater Honor: The Woman's Role," *Ensign*, January 1974, 8; emphasis added.
29. Harold B. Lee, *The Teachings of Harold B. Lee*, ed. Clyde J. Williams (Salt Lake City: Bookcraft, 1996), 253; emphasis added.
30. Neal A. Maxwell, "Endure It Well," *Ensign*, May 1990, 34–35.
31. Neal A. Maxwell, "Patience," *Ensign*, October 1980, 28.
32. Ezra Taft Benson, "Jesus Christ—Gifts and Expectations," *New Era*, May 1975, 20.

33. From Jill Jackson and Sy Miller, "Let There Be Peace on Earth" © Jan-Lee Music 1955, 1983. Used by permission.

34. Thomas S. Monson, "That We May Touch Heaven," *Ensign*, November 1990, 47.

35. Marion D. Hanks, "Forgiveness: The Ultimate Form of Love," *Ensign*, January 1974, 20.

36. Neal A. Maxwell, *That Ye May Believe* (Salt Lake City: Bookcraft, 1992), 22.

37. Gordon B. Hinckley, "Of You It Is Required to Forgive," *Ensign*, June 1991, 4.

38. Richard G. Scott, "To Be Healed," *Ensign*, May 1994, 9.

39. James E. Faust, "The Abundant Life," *Ensign*, November 1985, 9.

40. Joseph Smith, *History of The Church of Jesus Christ of Latter-day Saints*, ed. B. H. Roberts, 7 vols., 2d ed. rev. (Salt Lake City: The Church of Jesus Christ of Latter-day Saints, 1932–51), 7:413.

41. Ibid., 4:606–7.

42. Richard M. Sherman and Robert B. Sherman, "A Spoonful of Sugar," from *Mary Poppins*, soundtrack (Disney 1964).

43. *Children's Songbook*, 267.

44. Oliver Cowdery to W. W. Phelps, in *Messenger and Advocate* 1, no. 1 (October 1834): 15; emphasis added.

45. William Shakespeare, *As You Like It*, 2.7.1118.

46. Paraphrased from "I Am a Child of God," *Children's Songbook*, 2–3.

47. Joseph Smith, *Teachings of the Prophet Joseph Smith*, sel. Joseph Fielding Smith (Salt Lake City: Deseret Book, 1976), 240; emphasis added.

48. Brigham Young, *Discourses of Brigham Young*, comp. John A. Widtsoe (Salt Lake City: Deseret Book, 1977), 278.

49. Boyd K. Packer, "For Time and All Eternity," *Ensign*, November 1993, 21.

50. Neal A. Maxwell, "The Women of God," *Ensign*, May 1978, 10.

7

Being Realistic in Marriage Relationships

Terrance Olson

Perhaps as Latter-day Saints we suffer from an abundance of advice—good and bad. Perhaps we attend only to the counsel we feel is "realistic." But how do we decide what is realistic? This chapter proposes that we play a major role in what we are willing to receive regarding how to foster high-quality marriage relationships and regarding what solutions we are willing to consider when relationships become problematic. We will see that *willingness,* and not ability, is the key to being realistic about how to create and maintain quality relationships.

When we are unwilling to imagine or recall such experiences as marital harmony, shared sorrow, unity and oneness, mutual sacrifice, bearing one another's burdens, and so on, we are saying that these ways of being are either unrealistic or temporary. In that view we are giving ourselves an excuse to be unwilling to try. At the least, when we take seriously these possibilities of being harmonious, united, one, and so forth, we are demonstrating a willingness to see them as realistic, and as available to us in the present moment. When we take gospel principles so seriously that harmony and unity are restored to us as realistic, we should notice a difference in how we experience everyday life, as well as a difference in how we walk toward the future. Specifically, this reality means that, no matter what our circumstances, the present moment is our best and most realistic starting point to partake of the Restoration and make its truths fundamental to our marriage relationships. Our ideals, to be of worth to us, should be absolutely realistic to meet the demands of everyday life.

Yet we live in a world where the simple truths of gospel living—principles such as "love thy neighbor as thyself" or "forgive seventy times seven"—seem far removed from reality. While it is certainly realistic to acknowledge that we cannot decide what other people are going to do, in matters social-emotional and spiritual we can always decide what *we* are going to do. This is true whether we are subjected to honesty or to injustice, whether our children are obedient or disobedient, whether we feel close to or distant from family members.

This chapter assumes the following:

1. Gospel ideals are realistic.
2. Humans are moral agents.
3. Mortal life is a blessing.
4. Marital harmony is something mutually constructed by willing marriage partners.
5. It is realistic to think that living the principles of the gospel (honoring our ideals) has an impact on the quality of married life.

Perhaps this chapter is written most to those who find some of these assumptions to be unrealistic or even outrageous. My hope is that my words will help you see how these assumptions *are* realistic and especially applicable to the ongoing unexpected and even unwanted events of daily living.

The Restored Gospel and the Quality of Everyday Life

A good friend of mine, Cheryl, was searching for a parking place in a grocery store parking lot that is perennially full. Her goal wasn't to get a place close to the front of the store. She simply wanted to find an empty space anywhere, just anywhere, on the lot. Finally, after ten minutes of searching, she was heading south along a lane of cars when she saw, one lane over, an empty space. Her problem was that, in order to reach it, she had to go two-thirds of the way to the end of the row she was in, and then two-thirds of the way back up the row with the empty space. Just after she turned into the row with the coveted empty space, a car entered the other end of the row. That car,

119

if searching for a space, had only half the distance to cover that my friend did. Cheryl pressed on the accelerator and closed the gap quickly—but not quickly enough. This newcomer, this Johnny-or-Janie-come-lately, managed to slide into the space just before my friend. She slammed on the brakes and was full of furious thoughts. How *dare* this person usurp what was rightfully hers! Here Cheryl had been waiting in line, biding her time, paying the price of vigilance for victory, when an illegitimate pretender to the parking space scooped it up—almost certainly without regret, guilt, or any other of the feelings such people ought to suffer from if they had any sensitivity or conscience at all. Cheryl decided to let this lucky but insensitive stealer of spaces know exactly what she had so rudely done. Cheryl got out of the car, slammed the door on her still-idling automobile, angled awkwardly in the middle of the lane, and turned to confront her thoughtless tormenter. "Cheryl, how *are* you? I haven't seen you forever!" The voice of Cheryl's enemy was that of her favorite aunt. Cheryl immediately gave her a big hug and said, "I know, I feel terrible I haven't come over lately."

Now, how is an event such as this possible? How is it possible to be furious in one moment and hugging in the next? What is it about humans which makes such a transformation possible? If we can answer this question, we can answer an important question about how the gospel can and ought to make a difference in the way we conduct ourselves in everyday life. And if the gospel can help explain and solve simple circumstances such as parking-lot frustrations, then it likely can address even more dramatic, intense, or distressing circumstances that are a part of marriage.

Perhaps the value of the gospel in our lives is most dramatically illustrated in matters of life and death. The coming forth of the Restoration did, itself, involve life and death. From Doctrine and Covenants 135 we are reminded: "When Joseph went to Carthage to deliver himself up to the pretended requirements of the law, two or three days previous to his assassination, he said: 'I am going like a lamb to the slaughter; but I am calm as a summer's morning; I have a conscience void of offense towards God, and towards all men. I shall die innocent, and it shall yet be said of me—he was murdered in cold blood'" (v. 4).

It is significant that a feature of Joseph's knowing journey to his last imprisonment was his own declaration that he had "a conscience void of offense towards God, and towards all men." To be *void of offense* is to not be resentful of, angry with, or blaming someone. In other words, Joseph is not blaming God for his situation. He is not shaking his fists at the heavens. And it is significant that Joseph held nothing against God for his circumstances, for his sorrows, or even for events about to transpire. It is as if he remembered that we all shouted for joy to be able to come to earth and that all things work together for the good of those who love the Lord. Perhaps the idea of taking the gospel seriously in everyday life suggests to us a *way of being,* even when those we love or who should love us seem to have abandoned us or moved against us. Joseph was realistic without being in despair.

This *way of being* does not mean we have no feelings or emotions about injustice, murder, false witness, or a host of other wrongs against ourselves or our neighbors. It does mean that the quality of emotions we experience is different when we are faithful and humble as compared to when we live without faith and with the kind of arrogance that makes us independent of God.

Hyrum Smith, who died with his brother Joseph in that Carthage jail in Illinois, read a paragraph of scripture from Ether, chapter 12, just before they left for the final imprisonment. It is a significant thought that relates to not being offended by what befalls us during our lives on the earth. Moroni is speaking and has just acknowledged the Lord's mission of love, of charity. Then Moroni says:

> I prayed unto the Lord that he would give unto the
> Gentiles grace, that they might have charity. And it came to
> pass that the Lord said unto me: If they have not charity it

121

mattereth not unto thee, thou hast been faithful; wherefore thy garments shall be made clean. And because thou hast seen thy weakness, thou shalt be made strong, even unto the sitting down in the place which I have prepared in the mansions of my Father. And now I . . . bid farewell unto the Gentiles; yea, and also unto my brethren whom I love, until we shall meet before the judgment-seat of Christ, where all men shall know that my garments are not spotted with your blood (Ether 12:36–38, as quoted by John Taylor in D&C 135:5).

Hyrum seems to sense he is also bidding farewell to the brethren he loves, perhaps confident about how he will fare before the judgment-seat of Christ.

So at the least, while we may always pray for those who raise their hands against us to be "smitten with charity," we must remember that the Lord taught Moroni that the first issue is not whether the Gentiles have charity, but *do we?* The Lord's testimony to Moroni, which Hyrum found comforting, was "thou hast been faithful; . . . thou hast seen thy weakness." Such simple starting points as faith and admitting weakness are more important to the Lord than whether our enemies have charity. In a gospel view of everyday life, *who we are* is the first concern. Who they are will be understood by us only according to who we are.

The thoughts of Joseph and Hyrum, then, on the eve of their martyrdom, express some simple and stunning thoughts regarding how we are to be while on this earth. For if they believed these thoughts even in the face of death, surely we too are to take them seriously as we approach the simple tasks of daily living. Solutions to our difficulties seem to be grounded in receiving gospel principles in a way that sees them as realistic in informing our experience.

The Reality of Our Ideals

Lehi, in teaching his son Jacob, asserts that "men are, that they might have joy" (2 Nephi 2:25). That is a bold doctrine to declare in a world where so much injustice, misery, and pain can be documented. Joy, however, is a function of obedience, not cultural circumstance. That is, when my backyard is washed away in a flash flood, my response will depend on the quality of life I am living. If I am living in such a way that I am willing to receive those realities of mortal life that "afflict" me, I will properly feel sorrow at the loss and seek realistic ways of rebuilding my backyard and preventing a reoccurrence of the problem. In those efforts, I will succeed or fail, but I will, if I am being realistic about it, give my best. I will receive the condolences of others, their willingness to help me with my problem, and the compassion they offer. This response finds gospel principles such as compassion, forgiveness, charity, and humility to be realistic. Living by them helps us connect to others, even in the midst of trials and injustice.

Alternatively, if I am unwilling to "receive" the reality of the washed-away backyard, I will be bitter and resentful about my circumstance, the decisions I made about where to live, the faults of the contractor or the city for allowing me to place my home in harm's way, and so on. If I do embark on a course of restoring and rebuilding the backyard, it will be under a constant cloud of hostile feelings that I have to do it at all. Even if others are at fault in some way for the disaster, instead of seeking justice I am more likely to seek revenge, inasmuch as what is most on my mind is to punish those who contributed to my suffering. Those who offer help will find me often in a rage, if not vengeful, and brooding with resentment with every shovelful of dirt or foot of retaining wall necessary to forestall any future flooding problems. In this condition, by the way, I would find the idea of being merely sorrowful and hardworking to be pretty unrealistic. As far as gospel principles of forgiveness or compassion are concerned, they would seem to be abstract platitudes that have no place in the face of water and mud rampaging down a hill.

How do I know these two scenarios are plausible? More importantly, how do I know that the source of these two contrasting responses to a flood are due to the "quality" of life I am living?

To answer the first question, I appeal to our own experiences. I assume that we all can think of people in our acquaintance who, when faced with temporal setbacks, responded with grace, compassion, humility, forgiveness, determination, and faith. Surely we have also known people whose response to setbacks has been to rant, rave, resent, accuse, complain, and essentially meet the events with utter despair. The quality of the first response leaves no room for resentment or despair. The quality of the second response leaves no room for compassion, humility, forgiveness, or faith. Those qualities are unavailable to the resentful, because their own resentment cannot coexist with compassion. The difference is illustrated by a woman's comment to me in a parent education class: "The principles I believe in most strongly abandon me just at the moment I need them most." Perhaps, as we shall see, it is not the principles that abandon us, but it is we who abandon the principles.

In answer to the second question as to where the quality of our responses "come from," I am claiming the difference is in living true to, or in being false regarding, the gospel ideals that are meant to be central to our *way of being* in the face of mortal "realities." If we take the relevant gospel principles seriously (if we continue to live true to them), then we find them not only to be realistic, but to be a feature of living that excludes resentment or despair. Similarly, if I have abandoned those principles, I no longer see the solutions they make possible as realistic.

I once found the idea of forgiving my stepfather to be unrealistic. After all, he had become resentful over how involved I was in school activities when they interfered with the needs at his neighborhood grocery store. He had, in various ways, found my growing interest in Church matters to be evidence of my excluding him from my life. Only later, as I reconsidered the practical reality of forgiveness, did I find the doctrine realistic. I also discovered, incidentally, that once I began to live true to the doctrine of forgiveness, there was much less to forgive him for than I originally felt. In fact, my concerns turned first to the necessity of my own repentance. In personal repentance the magnitude of others' sins often shrinks. But my point is that once I began living true to gospel principles, they were absolutely realistic and turned out to be exactly what I needed to "solve" my problem with my stepdad. But as long as I resisted being forgiving, I easily found forgiveness unrealistic and therefore nigh to impossible. So again, it may be that our ideals are realistic only when we are willing to live them.

Consider a similar circumstance. The wife of a long-distance truck driver is worried about dinner being late. She and her husband always celebrate his return from his three or four days on the road with a quiet dinner. Although he is a little later than she expected, she is grateful she has not yet heard the brakes of the big rig in front of the house, because she wants the whole thing to be ready, and it's not. Alas, there is the noise she had been both dreading and hoping for. She begins to imagine his coming in the back door, hanging up his jacket and then, before washing up, leaning around the hall entrance and smiling a greeting. She worries he will see the unset table and discover the unready meal. She is worried that his face will fall, that he will think his homecoming is no longer a big deal or will not include the spirit of welcome she typically offers. In other words, she is imagining him being offended—perhaps even resentful—at her unpreparedness. She worries he will hold it against her. Her imaginings seem absolutely realistic to her.

Her husband, however, presents her with an alternative reality. When he actually does lean around the corner and sees that dinner preparations are incomplete, he smiles, catches her eye, and says, "Hi, honey. Looks like I got here just in time to help. Be right there." His *way of being* in that moment makes her imaginations look unrealistic (if not foolish)—and the harmony in their marriage appears effortless. For this couple, who are as imperfect as any of us, the counsel from Mosiah 18:21 is—well, realistic: "And he commanded them that there should be no contention one with another, but that they should look forward with one eye, having one faith and one baptism, having their hearts knit together in unity and in love one towards another."

In that moment of reunion, their *way of being* with each other—and with the gospel—made unity not only realistic, but seemingly the most natural reality they could experience. Make no mistake. Had either the husband or the wife in this example "taken offense" at the circumstance, gospel ideals regarding unity or lack of contention would have been inaccessible to them, and thus unrealistic.

These examples suggest that when we take our ideals to be realistic, we accept the following as realistic descriptions of mortal living:

1. Commandments are given to be blessings, not burdens.
2. The Lord asks nothing but that which is possible for us to receive and live by.
3. To the obedient, all things given us work together for our good (see D&C 90:24).
4. It is possible to choose liberty and eternal life over captivity and death (see 2 Nephi 2:27).

When We Do What Is Right, We Are Being Realistic

To be human is to be a moral agent who sees moral meaning and lives in accordance with the light and truth we have received—or who refuses so to live. We have the choice to receive or reject. Our obedience is fundamental to seeing realistically. When we do what is right, we invite others to live similarly, but we have no guarantee of what their response will be. We are realistic when we admit we must let the consequence follow. We can give our best, try our hardest, and seek to make things happen. Ultimately, however, certain consequences cannot be dictated by us. This is, in part, because others are agents also, capable of choosing either that which will promote or that which will undermine their own well-being and the welfare of family members.

But when we do what is right, we do our part to create and maintain relationships that are mutually a blessing and that foster peace, love, unity, and confidence. When the long-distance truck driver did not take offense at the late meal, he was doing his part to live harmoniously. Since our choice to do right does not guarantee others will do right, our harmony is always at risk. But by our obedience and example we issue a powerful invitation to our loved ones to so live. If the truck driver's wife lived in an uncompassionate way that night he was late, she may well have ruined the dinner by complaining and resenting that he was late. But such was not in her spirit, not in her soul.

However, we do face others, including our loved ones, who have their moments of being negative or even hostile. We can then live in ways that either feed the problem and make things worse, or, in our responses, we can continue to walk in the light and encourage the negative, destructive ways of living to cease.

Laura, a mother of four, found her high school daughter becoming increasingly impudent and disrespectful. Laura began to dread Cindy's return from school every day, because the peace of the household exploded into questions, complaints, accusations, resentments, and sullen silences. Laura noticed that when the grandfather clock chimed at 3:00 P.M., she stiffened—in spirit and body—because she knew she had only fifteen minutes before Cindy, with her defensive demeanor, would burst through the door. For a few weeks, Laura found herself rehearsing how to greet Cindy in a civil manner. She sought ideas from self-help books; she read newspaper columns; she rehearsed opening lines of dialogue in front of the mirror. It never worked. Cindy always seemed to know how to torpedo the best line. The most rehearsed kindness fell flat. Cindy would say things that cut right to the thoughts or feelings Laura was trying to hide or control. If Laura said, "Cindy, tell me the best part of your day today," Cindy would say, "Been reading another how-to-get-along-with-your-teenage-daughter book, Mother?" If Laura said, "Hi, Hon, welcome home," Cindy would say, "Gee, Mom, you ought to try singing that one to the Primary children." Laura would fight back either tears or rage, and she would always bite her tongue.

Then one day Laura, between 3:00 P.M. and 3:15 P.M., was rehearsing, in front of the mirror, the latest civil greeting to *Cindy the Barbarian*. Laura looked into her own eyes and heart and began to chuckle in an "I can't believe I'm doing this" way. She had this thought come to her: "What attitude must I really have toward my daughter if I have to actually *practice* being nice to her? Is being kind really a burden?" Laura suspended the attitudes and labels she had constructed to protect herself from Cindy and saw how she had become part of the problem. In a way, Cindy was hitting the nail on the head with her sarcastic comments. Laura had indeed gotten that line about the best part of the day from a book. Welcoming Cindy home was not a spontaneous greeting but a contrived, memorized, and rehearsed protective device.

This realization did not mean Cindy was not part of the problem, but it did mean that Laura also had become part of the problem. Laura was so preoccupied with this realization that she was caught by surprise when Cindy strolled into the kitchen, saw Laura's faraway look, and said, "Hey, Mom, kidnapped by aliens again?"

Laura laughed and sputtered out, "Well, no, but the good news is that I no longer want to be."

Here was a response Cindy couldn't have predicted and Laura couldn't have rehearsed. Things were different already. Cindy did her part further by asking, in all genuineness, "What do you mean, Mom, you 'no longer want to be'?"

What followed was a discussion of Laura's frustrations at not getting things done around the house, of wanting to enroll in those last two classes to complete her college degree, of her fear of competing in some English class with students half her age. To Laura's surprise, Cindy made no sarcastic remarks, no cocky comebacks. Cindy listened. She encouraged. She asked her mom questions about how art history had ever gotten in her blood in the first place. The conversation didn't end, but it wandered. Their talk was like traveling a path in an unexplored meadow—something new around every corner. The direction of the conversation shifted after a brief silence, which was broken by Laura saying, "How about you—ever felt you wanted to be kidnapped by aliens?" Cindy actually had something to say about that—a lot to say.

This conversation was not the end of Laura-Cindy problems, but it was the beginning of their solutions. It began in an unexpected place—not in skills or rehearsals or strategies, but in giving up labels and the insistence that the other person had become *the* problem. It began in seeing another person in a right way—a realistic way, as it turns out. Doing what is right means seeing others compassionately, even when they are being uncompassionate.

Later, in further private reflections, Laura saw that, as soon as she decided Cindy was the problem, she had ceased doing what was right. She had used Cindy's hostility and resentment and her times of destructive action to justify abandoning gospel principles (such as love or long-suffering), because in the face of Cindy's hardness, Laura had become hard. In those weeks she had lived that way, gospel principles had become unrealistic to her. She thought she was a victim of the real world. Once she returned to personal humility, she experienced a *way of being* in that real world that was not foreign to her, but that she had not experienced recently.

It is also realistic to understand that just because we become obedient or do what is right, others will not necessarily follow suit. We can hope for that, pray for it, long for it to happen, but we must relentlessly do what is right even if all the consequences we righteously strive for do not unfold. Václav Havel, before Czechoslovakia was freed from the Iron Curtain, wrote from the prison in which the communists had placed him: "When a person tries to act in accordance with his conscience, when he tries to speak the truth, when he tries to behave like a citizen, even in conditions where citizenship is degraded, it won't necessarily lead anywhere, but it might. There's one thing, however, that will never lead anywhere, and that is speculating that such behavior will lead somewhere."[1]

In other words, we must never abandon the right as we see it just because some might not respond or agree. Havel was speaking broadly, and his individual case involved a conflict between a government and an individual. Laura and Cindy were merely mother and daughter. But what can be said of citizenship can be fundamental to success in families. Parents are most realistic when they live true to the principles they believe. The most important times to take the gospel seriously in the family are those very moments we are tempted to see them as unrealistic.

When We Take Offense, the Gospel Becomes Unrealistic

We could say that Laura's problems with Cindy began when she "took offense" at the hardness, disrespect, or offensiveness of her daughter. In our culture, the phrase "you have offended me" is common. It describes the source of feelings of someone who feels wronged, betrayed, or mistreated, and whose life has been made hard, if not miserable, by the conduct of others. The feelings of the offended are such that they would say they cannot help how they feel and that their feelings are someone else's fault.

In families, being offended is illustrated by being hurt or being denied attention or being given too little of the family resources. A brother thinks another brother is Dad's favorite. A daughter resents her sister borrowing her clothes without permission. A husband thinks he is unappreciated. A wife feels as if she is the family's pack animal. All such feelings are signs of "having been offended" by the actions and attitudes of others.

The sources of our offended feelings can be petty, yet when we are offended, our feelings are real and cannot be denied. Our culture accepts the idea that it is possible and even typical for other people to "offend" us and therefore to produce feelings, attitudes, and actions we may not like and may not necessarily be proud of. Yet when we experience them, it feels as if we can't help having them at all. We believe such feelings have been produced by others. If this view is legitimate, then in a fundamental sense we are saying such feelings are not our fault. Another symptom of this is to believe we are victims, emotionally, of how other people treat us. Such is my claim about what our culture at large believes.

How could Joseph Smith, then, testify that he was void of offense? That offensive things had been done to him and to the Saints from the beginning is well-documented. The imprisonment to which he was submitting was unjust. So Joseph couldn't have meant that he was not subject to offensive, unjust acts. It is more likely that he is describing the spirit of *his response* to virtually all the wicked acts mounted against him. To be void of offense can refer to not being offended at the offensive conduct of those who considered Joseph an enemy. To be void of offense invokes the idea that *we have the ability not to take offense* at offensive behavior—and *we have the ability to refuse to give offense* in response to the offensive acts of others. That is, we need not adopt the contentious, hateful spirit of those who are contentious and hateful. If we do so, we become like those who are offensive. And then we are no longer void of offense ourselves. When our attitudes are resentful and offensive, we become like the people who have been offensive toward us. Certainly Joseph Smith was not guilty of committing offenses against others—and he was also not guilty of taking offense at the choices and actions of others.

Even in more mundane contexts where we are offended, we usually become, in spirit and attitude, like the people we are accusing. The person offended at her clothes being borrowed without permission is doing more than saying "It is not right you would use my property this way." The offended person is emotionally caught up in the other person's wrongdoing and uses the injustice to justify hate, resentment, impatience, frustration, moral superiority, and a host of other possible accusatory feelings. It is this kind of retaliatory emotional response which Joseph testified he was free of. Hence, he was calm as a summer's morning, because he was not, in spirit or attitude, regarding his tormenters as they regarded him. This did not mean Joseph was naive to injustice, wickedness, or the likelihood he was in mortal danger. On the contrary, he understood better than the jailers did what the stakes were. The issue was the work of the Lord, the reality of the contest between good and evil, between the Lord's plan and Satan's resistance. He was not offended because he did not take offense. As Terry Warner has helped point out, the difference between being offended and taking offense is the difference between being a victim and being a moral agent.[2]

By Taking Offense, We Become Victims of Our Emotions

Using the offended emotion of anger as his prime example, Elder Lynn G. Robbins of the Seventy addressed this issue. In referring to the family as Satan's primary target, Elder Robbins notes how Satan seeks to damage and destroy families within the walls of their own homes by stirring up anger among family members. The scriptures command that contention and anger be done away with (see 3 Nephi 11:29–30). In referring to Satan's tactics, Elder Robbins said: "A cunning part of his strategy is to dissociate anger from agency, making us believe that we are victims of an emotion that we cannot control. We hear, 'I lost my temper.' Losing one's temper is an interesting choice of words that has become a widely used idiom. To 'lose something' implies 'not meaning to,' 'accidental,' 'involuntary,' 'not responsible.' "[3]

He notes that anger and similar emotions are matters of agency, not matters of helplessness. His thoughts are not only consistent with scripture but also with the idea that we may not be the emotional victims of others' offensive conduct, even though our culture finds such an idea unrealistic.

So the Restoration may very well give us a different view of the phrase "you have offended me." Perhaps with the gospel in our everyday life, we would transform the phrase from "you have offended me," to "I have taken offense." This moves the focus from being a helpless emotional victim of the lack of charity in others to how we as agents can respond to those who mistreat us. Another clue to this possibility is in the counsel of the Lord to Moroni, which Hyrum quoted: "If they have not charity it mattereth not unto thee, thou hast been faithful; wherefore, thy garments shall be made clean. And because thou hast seen thy weakness thou shalt be made strong, even unto the sitting down in the place which I have prepared in the mansions of my Father" (Ether 12:37). This response implies that in the gospel the starting point to dealing with injustice or lack of appreciation or favoritism or all kinds of offensive conduct lies not in the offender, but in those who would be offended.

Thus it may be that when we say, "You have offended me," we do not find the idea of "I have taken offense" to be realistic. This is because, when I act as if you have offended me, I am saying also that you have caused feelings in me which I can't help. I begin to experience life as your victim. My evidence—which is your behavior or attitude toward me—is simple, and my case against you seems logical and strong. When I, seeing myself as a victim, simply rehearse in my soul or verbally declare your wrongs against me, I am perfectly justified in experiencing certain feelings against you.

This is a pervasive world view *in our culture*. I suspect many family arguments, grudges, and feelings of alienation are based on taking this view seriously. People retaliate emotionally or physically for those wrongs against them which they experience as more than they can bear and which they feel will have to be controlled or agonizingly expunged. Teenagers feel justified in feelings of embarrassment against their parents or in feelings of frustration against limits and expectations placed upon them. Parents feel they can't help being resentful for the lack of gratitude in their children or for the refusal of the children to attend to their schoolwork or their chores or their piano practice or their Church assignments. Each person who is offended by the conduct of others simultaneously experiences emotions that seem so logical and inescapable that we have come to call such feelings "human nature."

And, in a certain sense, that view does describe much of how some people experience life. That is, we can all recall incidents where we have been resentful, hostile, and angry—and where we simultaneously feel justified, precisely because of how we have been treated. Such feelings are especially disheartening when they involve people we care about. So some of our own experiences can sustain the idea that offended feelings are "human nature." Surely we are all offended at one time or another, even if just in heavy traffic or just by our two-year-old throwing her food dish on the floor. However, if we also accept the doctrine that we are moral agents, there is something inconsistent and unsettling about accepting the idea that we are *not* agents when it comes to our attitudes and feelings toward others.

As noted, it is common to see ourselves as victims of emotions and thus faced merely with having to control the destructive ones. The phrase "I lost my temper" is common in our culture. It invokes the idea that we are victims of some tendency that gets the better of us. President David O. McKay confronted that notion:

> I wonder how long it will take us to realize that in matters of temper nothing can bring us damage but ourselves—we are responsible for what helps us and for what injures us—that the harm that each one sustains he carries about with him, and never is he a real sufferer but by his own fault. I think you get that thought, and yet the tendency of each one is to blame somebody else, the wife blaming the husband, the husband blaming the wife, children finding fault with the parents when the fault lies with themselves. If in the dignity of manhood such a man would cease to magnify his troubles; would face things as they really are; recognize blessings that immediately surround him; cease to entertain disparaging wishes for another; how much more of a man he would be, to say nothing about being a better husband and a more worthy father! A man who cannot control his temper is not very likely to control his passion, and no matter what his pretensions in religion, he moves in daily life very close to the animal plane.[4]

If we are responsible, we cannot be victims of temper. If we are victims, we cannot be responsible. The gospel idea of moral agency would have to be revised if we are unwilling to receive President McKay's assessment of this.

In summary, then, when we are offended we are really *taking offense*. When we are hurt by others or when we feel justified in our arrogant treatment of our children or when we are contentious against our mates for their real or imagined wrongdoings, we are behaving as agents, even though we feel as if we are victims. And we are not void of offense ourselves. This whole idea suggests that our emotions—those related to circumstances, situations, relationships—are, in any given moment, of a certain quality, a quality we can choose.

Think of the parking lot incident. In one moment Cheryl was taking offense at an anonymous parking-space stealer. In the next she was embracing her favorite aunt. That her emotions could change so quickly is testimony to her being an agent rather than a victim in regard to the quality of her feelings. That her feelings did change suggests that in one moment she was taking offense and in the next moment she was void of offense. Some will say, "Well, yes, but it is because of her love of her aunt that she changed." Precisely! That fact makes the case for agency and being void of offense. If Cheryl were to see the anonymous driver with charity, her response to the parking lot hunt would be of a different quality. She would still, by the way, need to find a parking place, and there would still be a problem to be solved. The question is whether the solution will be with or without feelings of offense.

The suggestion here is not that we become emotionless zombies droning through a life of unpleasant events putting on a happy face. On the contrary, when we are not taking offense, our emotions are deep; we just aren't out of control. Our feelings are real; they just don't reflect our becoming offended. Our emotions, when we are not taking offense, are of a completely different quality than when we are offended. Some emotions—such as sorrow, grief, joy, charity, compassion, love, forgiveness, humility, and meekness—are what we experience when we walk by faith. Other emotions—such as resentment, hostility, revenge, rage, and bitterness—are expressions of our faithless moments. Laura's change of heart toward her disrespectful daughter was a move from being offended to no longer taking offense. The quality of our emotions turns on whether we, as agents, take offense or are void of offense; whether we, as agents, walk by faith, acknowledging our weakness, or abandon our faith and humility and find fault with others.

It is popular, especially in marriage, to see the situation or the circumstance or the spouse as the "cause" of our feelings. But it is who *we* are in those circumstances that tells the truth about the meaning of our feelings. When we take offense, our feelings themselves become offensive, perhaps even to ourselves. When we are void of offense, our feelings become invitations to others to give up their offensiveness. Of course, we have no guarantee others will change. Whatever Joseph and Hyrum learned about being void of offense and being personally faithful, they learned the world can be oblivious to, if not actively against, such gospel truths.

Being Realistic Is Possible and Helps Create Marital Harmony

We have the ability, in every moment, to live true to the light we have. Marital harmony is primarily a matter of morality—of living true to the light—rather than a matter of skill or knowledge. Of course, skill and knowledge matter, but they are secondary to whether we are true to our moral sense. Because harmony is a moral issue, we cannot extinguish, ignore, or sidestep our moral feelings just because of our past experiences or current stress and strife. If we see our moral sense as subject to either current pressures or past events, we can excuse ourselves from our role in promoting harmony just by saying, "I know I did wrong, but I just couldn't help it." If you can't help it, you cannot be held accountable for your actions. If you are a moral agent, then there must be some manner in which you could have helped it.

In matters of accountability and agency, the present moment is not hostage to the past.

Moreover, we don't learn from our experiences unless we are walking in the light during those experiences (see D&C 90:24). Otherwise, life seems to be a burden, and the best we feel we can do is cope. The hope, the reality, the longed-for humility, and the promises of the gospel seem to be devoured by reality. We cut ourselves off from the chance to learn from our experiences when we go against the light *during* those experiences. Even our way of explaining our helplessness—the meanings we assign to our circumstances—reveals more about our moral condition than about the reality of the situation. We have suggested that only when we are obedient to truth are we truly realistic about our relationships. Only then do we see that we always have a role in fostering harmony, compassion, forgiveness, and peace—or their counterfeits. Only then are we being real in the real world.

Our beliefs about what is right in married life include how we believe we should treat others, as declared by the Lord himself: "Whatsoever ye would that men should do to you, do ye even so to them: for this is the law and the prophets" (Matthew 7:12). Is this realistic? It is realistic to those willing to be obedient. If we take the Lord seriously, moral commitment is not burdensome, but beneficial, and we are willing, in our trying moments especially, to receive his call realistically: "Come unto me, all ye that labour and are heavy laden, and I will give you rest. Take my yoke upon you, and learn of me; for I am meek and lowly in heart: and ye shall find rest unto your souls. For my yoke is easy, and my burden is light" (Matthew 11:28–30). When we are realistic we don't escape yokes and burdens; we just find them bearable.

Being realistic also suggests we have an ability to sense what other people need and to take upon us the Savior's yoke precisely because "hereby perceive we the love of God, because he laid down his life for us: and we ought to lay down our lives for the brethren. But whoso hath this world's good, and seeth his brother have need, and shutteth up his bowels of compassion from him, how dwelleth the love of God in him?" (1 John 3:16–17).

We experience the reality of such commandments when we simply love our spouse as ourselves and refuse to be contentious in the marriage (see Mosiah 23:15). Loving another as ourselves is seeking to act in their best interests. When we live in meekness and humility, it is realistic so to act. Their best interests are now our best interests. When I act in the best interests of my marriage partner, I invite harmony. Being committed to another's best interests is the moral alternative to serving self-interests. It is possible to betray, or go against, our personal sense of how to treat others. James describes it as knowing to do good and not doing it (see James 4:17). When we betray our beliefs, we usually don't act in anyone's best interests. The description of unrighteous dominion in Doctrine and Covenants 121 is an apt rendition of how, when we do not seek first the kingdom of God (and therefore the best interests of others), we lose a realistic understanding of the Lord's counsel. Instead, we feel driven to such activities as covering our sins, gratifying our pride, pursuing vain ambition, or, perhaps in its worst manifestations, exercising control, dominion, or compulsion upon others (see vv. 36–38).

The ultimate disruption of harmony is found in our mistreatment of others. Lack of harmony is fundamentally a moral problem—a sign of unwillingness. As suggested earlier, it is possible for us to experience different qualities of feeling in a marriage. We wonder, when things go wrong, "what happened" to the way we used to feel, without realizing *we* are "happening" the difference. It is our refusal to stay true to what we know regarding how to give our heart to another. When we withhold our hearts, our feelings change. (It is not that when our feelings change, we then withhold our hearts, although it looks that way to us when we are blind to what is realistic.)

So harmony is possible in a marriage when two people give up being self-centered in favor of *doing right* by each other. Harmony is possible when we look to ourselves as to how to improve, how to give our best. This is impossible when we insist that the other must change first.

Marital harmony is realistic and available when two people find the sacrifice of a broken heart and a contrite spirit to be realistic (see 3 Nephi 9:20). When we abandon our hard-heartedness, we experience a world that is unavailable to us while we are hard.

Marital harmony, then, becomes a symptom of the moral quality of the life we are living. Harmony is invited by our willingness, as moral agents, to be true to our moral sense of how to treat others. We discover that repentance and forgiveness are the foundations of quality living. Then (and only then) are we realistic about money and indebtedness, about how to help the children develop, about compassionate mutuality in intimate marital relationships, about how to serve family members in times of illness, about how to address matters of injustice or intergenerational squabbles.

Being Realistic in the Real World

The question never is: Will others respond to my being void of offense? It always is: How can I live so as to not be guilty of offenses? Then we are inviting others so to live. This chapter has proposed that ideals are livable and that when we live by our ideals, we have a way of meeting the joys and sorrows of everyday family life. We have not said that the righteous will avoid challenges, injustice, disease, rebellious children, unresponsive governments, a bully in a fourth-grade classroom, or flat tires in the middle of the desert. The rain of mortal trouble falls on the just and the unjust (see Matthew 5:45)—on the righteous and the wicked—so no Latter-day Saint can expect to be free of the realities of mortal living. We knew before we came here that the bitter and the sweet were to be a part of this mortal life (see D&C 29:39; Alma 60:13).

Sometimes we are seduced into thinking that our obedience will spare us from the rains and storms of life. The relationship of ideals to real life is this: We can, by holding on to the iron rod of faith and our ideals, always have the Lord with us to face our trials and troubles. We can, by our willingness to do and to be true, have a starting point by which we face the less-than-ideal situations this mortal life presents us. The Lord is bound when we do what he says (see D&C 82:10), and one expression of that promise is that we will never be confronted in this mortal life by more than we can bear (see 1 Corinthians 10:13; D&C 90:24).

It is possible, of course, to feel as if we cannot bear the loss of a child or the injustice of an employer or a myriad of other bitter realities. But our choice is not to escape such circumstances altogether, but to confront them with or without our ideals. When we accept our ideals and allow ourselves "to do and to be" true to them, we have hope. When we reject our ideals or let go of the iron rod, we are lost, and our feelings truly can include being overwhelmed or in despair. As mortals, we do let go of the iron rod. But the solution to that problem is not to be found in any superficial excuses or in trying to reduce our guilt because we are human. It is to be found only in restoring our grasp on the iron rod—holding to our ideals. When we are lost or in despair, bitterness, or resentment, it is not because of the troubles we face, but because we have let go of our ideals in the face of our troubles. We have let go of the very way out of our despair.

So here is our predicament. We will not, on this earth, escape the mortal conditions that include more than enough of attitudes and actions, in ourselves and others, that are less than ideal. However, as moral agents, we have the ability to hold to our ideals, to learn line upon line, and to learn through experience, through the things which we suffer (see D&C 105:6). Our decision is this: will we meet our suffering with or without the gospel, with or without holding to the iron rod, with or without our ideals? This is what makes our ideals *realistic*. It is not that our ideals are somehow not connected to real life. Our ideals are the very way we connect to life in a real way. When we hold to the iron rod, our trials are bearable. We experience sorrow rather than despair; we rejoice in others' blessings, rather than become envious. This truth is no more sobering than when we seek to invite and entice our children to do good, and they reject our efforts. Our choice, however, is not to say that our ideals "don't work," that holding on to the iron rod is not worth it. Rather, it is only by turning to God, by living our ideals, that we can bear the heartbreak or loss that seems to be on the horizon. Consider, then, how we can participate, as moral agents, as family members who love each other, in meeting the realities of life.

Real Examples from the Real World

A boy attends BYU-Idaho and joins the Church. A year passes, and he accepts a mission call. He hasn't seen his parents since they became offended at his joining the Church. But he lives void of offense toward them. They agree to drive to an airport where he has a layover on the way to the mission field. His mother is softening; his father is seemingly distant. He lives void of offense toward them. He writes them faithfully. His mother is baptized before he finishes his mission. After his mission, he returns to baptize his father. He never had any guarantee that his parents' hearts would soften. But he always, as an agent, had the power to live void of offense toward them. It is one of the reasons he was such a good missionary.

A college student drives to exhaustion to be home for Thanksgiving. For several years she does so, offended by the fact that once home, she must help the family in their bakery business—which is especially busy at holiday times. Then, one Christmas, penniless, she determines that her gift to her family that season must be her heart. She actually resolves not to take offense at the early morning work with her mother at the ovens and the constant home deliveries of cinnamon rolls and cakes. Although she is involved in the same demands that to her had been drudgery for so many holidays, this season the work became a time of conversation and reflection with her mother—a time, she decided, that made this her most memorable Christmas.

A demanding father who has reared his two children by violating every aspect of Doctrine and Covenants 121—he is virtually without meekness, patience, longsuffering, or love unfeigned—finds himself resenting the rudeness of his children and accuses them of ingratitude. They retreat from him ever further. At first he sees their alienation as proof they are unworthy of being in his household. Then one night, after prayer, he is consumed with love for them and goes to each individually. He asks forgiveness for the way he has treated them. With one child, he begins anew. The other child rejects the plea and is hard-hearted against the father. Even though one child does not respond, the father resolves to never give up and to live void of offense, seeking to recover his children by taking correct principles seriously. He has no guarantee of the outcome, but faces the joy and sorrow of giving his best. He moves from bitterness to sorrow regarding the child who continues to reject him.

So What?—A Summary

So how are we to be realistic? What does it mean to take a gospel view of life into our marriage and family relations? The starting point requires us to *take our agency seriously* and therefore live so that the quality of our lives—as reflected in our thoughts, attitudes, emotions, actions—is worthy of our faith. We learn from our experiences according to *who we are,* not according to what the situation is. To live void of offense is to choose to be faithful and to understand we need not make ourselves into emotional victims of real or imagined tormentors. It is to acknowledge that our agency is more fundamental to our emotional well-being than those who may treat us uncharitably. I have suggested that when we treat the uncharitable without charity, we obviously become like them. We then almost live to take offense, and we become offended in our feelings. When we live with resentment, impatience, and even hostile frustration, we push people away from us and give them ammunition with which to accuse and resent us.

We are to put contention and anger far from us, and because we are agents, such a commandment is realistic and possible. When we live with love, compassion, humility, and, in the words of Joseph

Smith, are "void of offense," our faith and humility become invitations to others to so live. They may not. We never give up.

Ultimately, the proposal I have considered is that since it was possible for Joseph Smith to be void of offense in a life-and-death situation, it is possible for us to be void of offense, especially regarding lesser injustices. Perhaps the insights drawn by Joseph and Hyrum from Moroni's words in Ether 12 include giving up worrying about whether the Gentiles will ever have charity. Rather, the more immediate concern for all of us must be, at the least, our personal faithfulness and our willingness to acknowledge our weaknesses. Those two acts—of faith and meekness—are the acts of agents, not victims, and are evidently completely possible no matter what our circumstances may be. We can be concerned about the Gentiles' lack of charity out of concern for them and their ultimate fate, but not as an excuse to resent or hate them. And the issue certainly is not to look at our tormentors through some self-righteous lens where we are thankful we are not like them. If we were to be in the business of acknowledging our own weaknesses, we would be too busy being humble and faithful to partake of such arrogance. Then we would see our spouse as a person to serve and bless, as a person whose best interests we can watch out for—and we would find the idea of being free of contention, but experiencing much mutual joy and sorrow, to be absolutely realistic.

Notes

1. Václav Havel, *Disturbing the Peace: A Conversation with Karel Hvíždala* (New York: Alfred A. Knopf, 1990), xvi.
2. See C. Terry Warner, *Bonds That Make Us Free: Healing Our Relationships, Coming to Ourselves* (Salt Lake City: Shadow Mountain, 2001).
3. Lynn G. Robbins, "Agency and Anger," *Ensign*, May 1998, 80.
4. David O. McKay, in Conference Report, April 1958, 5.

8

Marriage Crossroads:
Why Divorce Is Often Not the Best Option

Brent A. Barlow

In past decades we have seen more and more people choose divorce as a solution to marital unhappiness.[1] Initially, it was thought that divorce was perhaps the best solution to difficult problems between marriage partners. However, experience, research, and hindsight show that divorce often has a negative impact on both adults and children—sometimes for generations. What was once accepted as a way out of an unhappy marriage now can be viewed with a little more objectivity. Serious emotional repercussions often result from this decision, causing many people to rethink the divorce option. An increasing number of national publications have pointed out that divorce can bring great hardship and serious side effects to adults and children.

As Latter-day Saints, we are strongly in favor of marriage. We expect people to stay married. We expect them to create and to remain in a stable and vibrant marriage that they build together. The Lord created the earth so that his children from the premortal life could come and participate in the great adventure of mortality—marriage and parenthood. The marital relationship between a man and woman is "ordained of God" (D&C 49:15). We build temples to perform ceremonies that can qualify a couple for an "eternal marriage." Sadly, one of the things I run across quite often is young couples who, while considering marriage themselves, find their parents contemplating divorce! These prospective brides and grooms want their parents to reassess their decision to break marriage covenants. It is a serious decision.

Therapist and author Michele Weiner Davis noted: "The decision to divorce or remain together to work things out is one of the most important decisions you will ever make. It is crucial for those considering divorce to anticipate what lies ahead in order to make informed decisions. Too often the fallout from divorce is far more devastating than many people realize when contemplating the move."[2]

The purpose of this chapter is to assist married couples to make informed decisions about staying together in the light of ideas and current research on the topic. While I am thinking primarily here of couples with troubled marriages, I feel the information will be beneficial to all Church members. I say at the outset that I believe it to be in the best interests of married couples (and their children) to stay married, where possible, and work to improve their marriage relationship. I have outlined those reasons below.

Large Numbers of Married Couples at the Crossroads

There are many married couples in the United Sates who approach the crossroads of whether to stay in a marriage or split up. At the present time approximately 40 to 50 percent of couples in *first marriages* choose the divorce path.[3] While the divorce rate for Latter-day Saint couples is lower than the national average—especially for those sealed in the temple—it is still a major concern to Church leaders. The Church proclamation on marriage and families is an outgrowth of that concern.[4]

The divorce rate for couples in *second marriages* in the United States is between 50 and 60 percent. Other couples reach the crossroads and then decide, for various reasons, to stay married. One report, from a United States Gallup poll, found that 40 percent of married individuals had considered leaving their partners at one time, and 20 percent said they were dissatisfied with their marriage about half the time.[5] Stated another way, nearly half the couples in the United States divorce, while another 20 percent seriously consider it at one time during their marriage.

Even newlyweds face serious problems during the first year of marriage. A study of several hundred newlywed couples found that 63 percent had serious problems related to their finances, 51 percent had serious doubts about their marriage lasting, 49 percent had significant marital problems, 45 percent were not satisfied with their sexual relationship, 41 percent found marriage harder than they had expected, and 35 percent stated their partner was often critical of them.[6]

Divorce for recently married couples is most likely to occur in the second or third year of marriage. Half of all first marriages that end in divorce end within the first seven years.[7]

After years of marriage, there is a large group of married couples in the United States who face the crossroads. There is a 16 percent increase in the divorce rate among those who have been married longer than thirty years.[8] This may be due to "the float of isolation"—a gradual emotional separation—that begins early in many marriages and often expands as the marriage continues.[9]

Some Divorces Are Warranted

While as Latter-day Saints we are promarriage, we are also sensitive to those who had to choose to terminate their marriage. There certainly *are* legitimate reasons for divorce. An estimated 30 percent of the divorces in the United States involve marital relationships with a high degree of conflict.[10] Usually we find that violence, physical and mental abuse, or even murder of spouse or children exist in highly conflicted relationships. Most would agree that in such extreme cases, divorce is in the best interest of those involved. While scripture speaks strongly against divorce and appears to support divorce only in rare circumstances (see Matthew 19:3–9; 1 Corinthians 7:10–16), modern prophets have indicated that there are justifiable reasons for breaking a marriage contract. Elder James E. Faust shared these thoughts on what constitutes a just cause for divorce:

> What, then, might be "just cause" for breaking the covenants of marriage? Over a lifetime of dealing with human

problems, I have struggled to understand what might be considered "just cause" for breaking of covenants. I confess I do not claim the wisdom nor authority to definitely state what is "just cause." Only the parties to the marriage can determine this. They must bear the responsibility for the train of consequences which inevitably follow if these covenants are not honored. In my opinion, "just cause" should be nothing less serious than a prolonged and apparently irredeemable relationship which is destructive of a person's dignity as a human being.

At the same time, I have strong feelings about what is not provocation for breaking the sacred covenants of marriage. Surely it is not simply "mental distress," nor "personality differences," nor "having grown apart," nor having "fallen out of love." This is especially so where there are children. Enduring divine counsel comes from Paul: "Husbands, love your wives, even as Christ also loved the church, and gave himself for it" (Eph. 5:25).[11]

In her book *The Case Against Divorce,* Diane Medved entitled a chapter "Exceptional Situations: When You Should Divorce." Chronic addiction or substance abuse, psychosis or extreme mental illness, and physical or mental abuse are among those situations or conditions that qualify, according to her. Medved also gives additional insights as to when wisdom dictates the need to say good-bye.[12]

Couples who make the decision to divorce need the help and support of family, friends, neighbors, and religious leaders, particularly where children are involved. The adjustment to divorce is difficult for the parties involved and can last a considerable length of time. Legal assistance is usually needed, and couples and children may need counseling or therapy before, during, and after the separation. Competent counselors, therapists, and priesthood leaders can assist in the transition. More and more couples are using the services of divorce mediation organizations to help lessen the trauma of divorce both before and after it occurs.

We wish those well who decide that divorce is a necessary option. But I also offer encouragement to those couples at the crossroads to stay together, if possible, and work through differences and difficulties. The apostle Paul provided the following counsel to Church members in Corinth who were contemplating divorce: "For what knowest thou, O wife, whether thou shalt save thy husband? or how knowest thou, O man, whether thou shalt save thy wife?" (1 Corinthians 7:16).

Some Considerations

Carefully consider the following items as you think about the consequences of divorce on you and your children.

1. Most Divorces Can Be Avoided

While I note that 30 percent of divorces involve couples in highly conflicted marriages, what about the other 70 percent who are wondering if they should divorce or stay married? There are, perhaps, legitimate reasons for breaking up the marriage in about 10 percent of these relationships as well.

One study reported that the major reasons marriages fail are (in rank order): (1) infidelity, (2) no longer in love, (3) emotional problems, (4) financial problems, (5) sexual problems, (6) problems with in-laws, (7) neglect of children, (8) physical abuse, (9) alcohol, (10) job conflicts, (11) communication problems, and (12) married too young.[13]

Notice that physical abuse was ranked number eight in reasons for divorce, and "no longer in love" ranked number two. It would appear from this that many marriages end from "burnout" rather than "blowout." That means that a significant number of these couples could work through their problems, revive their love, and stay married if they made the effort to do so. Only the two spouses, however, can make the decision to stay married or divorce, since they are the ones who must ultimately abide by the consequences of the decision, as Elder Faust indicated.

It is becoming increasingly evident to those who study marriage trends in the United States that an estimated 50 to 60 percent of divorces could be avoided and should be avoided. Consider the following point:

> The divorce revolution—the steady displacement of a marriage culture by a culture of divorce and unwed parenthood—has failed. It has created terrible hardships for children, incurred insupportable social costs, and failed to deliver on its promise of greater adult happiness. The time has come to shift the focus of national attention from divorce to marriage and to rebuild a family culture based on enduring marital relationships.[14]

After acknowledging the need for some to divorce, therapist Diane Medved wrote of the negative consequences of divorce. She made the following observation and suggestion:

> It is finally time to renounce—openly and clearly—the self-serving platitudes about independence and fulfillment and look at the reality of divorce. We act too frequently as if every infirm marriage deserves to die, based simply upon the emotional report of one distressed partner. Rather than viewing a separation first with alarm, we're full of sympathy for a divorcing friend, and we offer understanding of the temporary insanity involved in severing old ties. Still influenced by the "do your own thing" era we don't act constructively. We don't take a husband (or wife) by the shoulders and shake him. We don't shout in his ear that he might be making a disastrous mistake. Even if we care immensely about him, we feel it's too intrusively "judgmental" to do more than step back and say, "Okay, if that's what you want," and close our eyes to the consequences. My research suggests that this is more cruelty than friendship.[15]

Medved also noted:

> If you hear someone for whom you have any feeling at all hinting at separation, instead of tacitly endorsing the move, instantly protest. Nearly every marriage has something worth preserving, something that can be restored. Revitalizing a relationship brings triumph and ongoing reward. . . . Avoiding divorce spares those concerned from the greatest trauma of their lives.[16]

2. The Stable Marriage Has Significant Benefits

In *Why Marriage Matters*, Glenn T. Stanton has written:

> As the researchers have gone to press with their work and produced an enormous literature, one of the most consistent findings is that men and women do markedly better in all measures of specific and general well-being when they are married, compared to any of their unmarried counterparts. Married couples are healthier—physically and mentally—and they live longer, enjoy a more fulfilled life, and take better care of themselves (and each other). This has been shown consistently over decades, but it is rarely mentioned in the popular debate on the family. One of social science's best-kept secrets is that marriage is much more than a legal agreement between two people. Marriage truly makes a difference in the lives of men and women.[17]

Three other authors, David B. Larson, James P. Swyers, and Susan S. Larson, observed the damage of divorce in their book, *The Costly Consequences of Divorce:*

> What would you say if someone told you that a particular social bond could add years to your life and ensure your children a better education and economic livelihood? Furthermore, what would you say if you also found out that breaking

this social bond was only slightly less harmful to your health than smoking a pack or more of cigarettes per day and could significantly increase your risk of depression, alcohol abuse, and committing suicide? And what would you say if you found out that this social bond that was potentially so beneficial to you and your children's health and personal well-being was marriage? Truly, the research is striking. For decades, studies have shown that the married live longer and have a lower risk of a variety of physical and psychological illness than the unmarried.[18]

In an article entitled "Marital Status and Personal Well-Being," Robert H. Coombs of the UCLA School of Medicine noted:

> The therapeutic benefits of marriage remain relatively unrecognized by most youths, the media, and some helping professionals who, preoccupied with accelerating divorce rates and variant family forms, question the value of marriage in contemporary society. Media messages have minimized marriage, implying it is an outdated institution, an "uncool" survivor of a simpler society. . . . Family educators can serve an important function by teaching the therapeutic benefits of marriage and that it is in each person's own best interest to establish and maintain a durable relationship with an emotionally supportive spouse. The lack of this resource is a mental health deficit.[19]

3. Divorce Has a Detrimental Impact on Many Children

It is clear that a large number of children of divorced parents survive the experience and become capable and stable adults. However, the opposite is also true. Many children of divorce face risks of developing detrimental behaviors, personality disorders, and disruptive lifestyles. Some of the variables in adjustment of children to parental divorce are (1) age of child at divorce, (2) amount of conflict in the marriage, (3) access to both parents after the divorce, (4) adjustment to a stepparent, if there is one, and (5) access to other nurturing adults during the childhood years. What does the research say about many children of divorced parents? David B. Larson, James P. Swyers, and Susan S. Larson have noted:

> Coming from a disrupted family does not necessarily doom a child to later chronic unhappiness or academic or personal failure. Indeed, many resilient children and young people from disrupted families not only finish high school, but go on to college and graduate school and have successful careers, marriages and families. Unfortunately, the preponderance of evidence clearly shows that when compared to their peers from intact families, children, adolescents, and young adults from disrupted families are disproportionately represented among individuals with academic, behavioral and interpersonal problems.[20]

In the executive summary of a forty-nine-page report titled "The Effects of Divorce on America," authors Patrick F. Fagan and Robert Rector of the Heritage Foundation observed the following:

> Each year, over 1 million American children suffer the divorce of their parents; moreover, half of the children born this year to parents who are married will see their parents divorce before they turn 18. Mounting evidence in social science journals demonstrates that the devastating physical, emotional, and financial effects that divorce is having on these children will last well into adulthood and affect future generations. Among these broad and damaging effects are the following: 1) Children whose parents have divorced are increasingly the victims of abuse. They exhibit more health, behavioral, and emotional problems, are involved more frequently in crime and drug abuse, and have higher rates of suicide. 2) Children of divorced parents perform more poorly

in reading, spelling, and math. They are also more likely to repeat a grade and to have a higher drop-out rates and lower rates of college graduation. 3) Families with children that were not poor before the divorce see their income drop as much as 50 percent. Almost 50 percent of the parents with children that are going through a divorce move into poverty after the divorce. 4) Religious worship, which has been linked to better health, longer marriages, and better family life, drops after the parents divorce. 5) The divorce of parents, even if it is amicable, tears apart the fundamental unit of American society. Today, according to the Federal Reserve Board's 1995 Survey of Consumer Finance, only 42 percent of children aged 14–18 live in a "first marriage" family—an intact two-parent family. It should be no surprise to find that divorce is having such effects on society.[21]

Authors Lisa Laumann-Billings and Robert E. Emery make a similar point:

> Current research indicates that the majority of children of divorced parents do not manifest behavioral problems that can be outwardly noticed or measured. But the absence of an observable behavior disorder does not mean an absence of emotional distress. A significant number of children of divorce apparently do experience a variety of emotional problems that often go undetected until late adolescence or early and even later adulthood. One of the most prevalent sources of distress reported by researchers was the child's distant relationship or infrequent contact with their biological fathers. Many children blamed their fathers for the divorce, and some were still angry with their fathers later in their adult lives. One-third of the children studied questioned their father's love for them.[22]

Judith Wallerstein and colleagues also explored two major myths about divorce in their book, *The Unexpected Legacy of Divorce, A Twenty-Five Year Landmark Study:*

> Two faulty beliefs provide the foundation for our current attitudes towards divorce. The first holds that if the parents are happier the children will be happier, too. . . . Children are not considered separately from their parents; their needs, and even their thoughts are subsumed under the adult agenda. . . . Indeed, many adults who are trapped in very unhappy marriages would be surprised to learn that their children are relatively content. They don't care if mom and dad sleep in different beds as long as the family is together. . . .
>
> A second myth is based on the premise that divorce is a temporary crisis that exerts its more harmful effects on parents and children at the time of the breakup. . . . The belief that the crisis is temporary underlies the notion that if acceptable legal arrangements for custody, visits, and child support are made at the time of the divorce and parents are provided with a few lectures, the child will soon be fine. It is a view we have fervently embraced and continue to hold. But it's misguided.[23]

In their book, *The Case for Marriage,* Linda J. Waite and Maggie Gallagher made this summary observation:

> Less than a third of divorces are ending angry high-conflict marriages. Here's what the best evidence suggests: most current divorces leave children worse off, educationally and financially, than they would have been if their parents stay married, and a majority of divorces leave children psychologically worse off as well. Only a minority of divorces in this country are taking place in families where children are likely to benefit in any way from their parents' separation.[24]

Those with children who file for divorce in Utah are required to attend a two-hour class on divorce education before the decree is granted. The class is not designed to make the decision for people, but it reviews how to deal with divorce so it will have the least negative impact on their children. Perhaps serious thought about the impact of divorce on children should precede filing for divorce as well.

4. Many Later Regret Divorce

Once people have divorced, how do they later feel about the choice they made? There is often some immediate relief after the divorce, but the question remains: How do husbands and wives feel about their decision months or even years later? My current estimates are that about one-third of the couples who divorce feel they made the right decision, another one-third are uncertain or have mixed feelings about their divorce, and approximately one-third of divorced couples eventually regret the decision within five years.

In addition, many divorced people in the United States feel that they could have made a greater effort to make their marriage work. In Minnesota, 66 percent of those who are currently divorced answered "yes" to the question, "Do you wish you and your ex-spouse had tried harder to work through your differences?" And in a New Jersey poll, 46 percent of divorced people reported that they wished they and their ex-spouse had tried harder to work through their differences. Research from Australia indicates that of all people who divorce, "one third regret the decision five years later. Of the individuals involved, two in five (40 percent) believe their divorce could have been avoided."[25]

A recent letter to the editor in a Utah newspaper reflected the sentiments of one man among the estimated one-third who regretted his divorce. Under the title "Divorce Isn't Worth the Cost," he wrote:

> I would wish to comment on the letter that ran Jan. 2 concerning the weakening of men and children through divorce. Anne Smart-Pearce was the author. To my great sorrow, I must admit I am a divorced husband and father. Anne speaks of the terrible price that is being paid and then asks, "If a mother had an equal fear of losing her children, would she so

readily seek a divorce? Or would she do all in her power to avert such a tragic outcome?"

Might I add this, husbands and wives, if there is even one-half of an ounce of friendliness left in your marriage, take each other by the hand, look at each other's eyes and then remember of the love that brought you together in the first place! Let each other know, somehow, that you are needed, loved and wanted! If you fail, you will reap the whirlwind, especially you, fathers. You will lose all that is important, near and dear to you. And that is your sweet wife, your wonderful children and your home.

Oh, that I had been more wise and not let my pride be my downfall. I can tell you with knowledge that a seemingly endless tragedy does await! The mornings do come when you awake, call her name and then realize that you are alone in a house that is ever silent and does not answer back.[26]

5. Marriage Is Usually Worth the Work

If a substantial number of couples regret their decision to divorce, the question arises: Should couples try to restore what they once enjoyed in marriage? The answer to this question is a simple "yes" in a large number of cases. Many have learned to do so. Again from Michele Weiner Davis in her book, *Divorce Busting:*

> It appears that more and more couples are beginning to take a skeptical view of divorce. . . . Some say the growing threat of AIDS is keeping couples together. However, my explanation is different. I believe that people are beginning to realize how devastating divorce is—emotionally, financially, and spiritually—for everyone involved. With enough time under our belts to have observed the results of rampant divorce, we are beginning to recognize the price we have paid for the freedom of disposable marriages.[27]

Nearly all, if not all, marriages go through peaks and valleys, times of highs and lows. Most of married life, however, is spent cycling between these two extremes. During difficult times, between 40 and 50 percent of currently married spouses seek divorce and follow through with it. And, as previously noted, about 20 percent of those who remain married consider leaving a marriage partner but do not.

Although many married couples contemplate divorce and may even see a lawyer or file for divorce, they change their minds about it. In Utah, for example, in the year 2000, 12,574 couples filed for divorce, but only 10,138 divorces were actually granted.[28] Thus, for a variety of reasons, one in five couples who file for divorce decide not to go ahead with the process. Their decision may be well-founded. The vast majority of unhappily married couples in the United States apparently do improve their relationship when they stay married.

6. Unhappy Marriages Can Often Be Saved

In their recent book, Waite and Gallagher ask and then answer this question:

> How many unhappy couples turn their marriages around? The truth is shocking: 86 percent of unhappily married people who stick it out find that, five years later, their marriages are happier, according to an analysis of the National Survey of Families And Households. Most say they've become very happy indeed. In fact, nearly three-fifths of those who said their marriage was unhappy in the late 80's and who stay married, rated this same marriage as either "very happy" or "quite happy" when reinterviewed in the early 1990's.

> The very worst marriages showed the most dramatic turn-arounds: 77 percent of the stably married people who rated their marriage as very unhappy (a one on a scale of one to seven) in the late eighties said that the same marriage was either "very happy" or "quite happy" five years later. Permanent marital unhappiness is surprisingly rare among couples who

stick it out. Five years later, just 15 percent of those who initially said they were very unhappy married (and who stayed married) ranked their marriage as not unhappy at all.[29]

In the last paragraph, these two authors conclude:

Decades of social-science research have confirmed the deepest intuitions of the human heart: as frightening, exhilarating, and improbable as this wild vow of constancy may seem, there is no substitute. When love seeks permanence, a safe home for children, who long for both parents, when men and women look for someone they can count on, there are no substitutes. The word for what we want is marriage.[30]

7. Divorce Has Significant Financial Costs

The financial costs of divorce for married couples are usually substantial. These costs include legal or lawyers' fees, which average $7,000 per couple ($3,500 per person) in the United States.[31] Some divorces cost more, others less. An uncontested divorce involving no children in Utah costs between $500 and $1,000. If there is litigation, or custody battles, costs can go as high as $10,000 to $30,000 for legal fees. If there is a sizeable amount of property and prolonged litigation, costs could go as high as $100,000. The hourly wage for many lawyers is $200 to $300. The use of accredited divorce mediation services can help reduce the financial costs of divorce.

There are also additional costs for housing, moving expenses, transportation, potential loss of income during divorce proceedings and transition, additional occupational training (particularly for the custodial spouse of children, if such are involved), child care, and partial loss of retirement benefits. Sometimes there are additional costs to state government, extended family members, and charities if initial income is minimal. There may also be considerable financial consequences during retirement for husband, wife, or both.

According to another report: "Families with children that were not poor before the divorce see their income drop as much as 50 percent. Almost 50 percent of the parents with children that are going through a divorce move into poverty after the divorce."[32] Perhaps the greatest costs of divorce, however, are emotional rather than financial.

8. Divorce Has Long-Term Consequences

Many who divorce are satisfied with their decision to end the marriage. But as I said, it is becoming increasingly evident that as many as one-third later regret their decision. This is particularly so when they experience long-term consequences. Sometimes the immediate benefits cloud the negative effects of long-term consequences. Many problems in marriage are temporary, even though those problems may continue for years. But most divorces are forever.

9. It Is Worth It to Take Time to Make a Decision

Your decision to divorce is one of the most important choices you will ever make. If you do decide not to divorce immediately and want to work on improving your marriage, plan on taking several months to do so. Remember that 86 percent of unhappily married couples bounce back within five years. Your marriage, however, may not take as long to turn around. Also, be aware that peers who are divorced or unhappily married may give you bad advice during this time. With new skills and new effort, it is possible to regain love that is lost.

10. Couples Should Use Discretion in Seeking Marriage Counseling

If you seek marriage counseling, be careful in choosing a therapist. Make sure the therapist understands your desire to work to make your marriage succeed. Also, make sure the therapist has been trained in helping couples stay together, where possible. Let the therapist know of your intentions. Professional and competent counselors will honor this request. Discuss the fees in advance, which range from $60 to $100 or more for a fifty-minute session. Many health maintenance organizations (HMOs) currently do not pay for marriage counseling. In addition, if you seek personal counseling, HMOs will often determine who you will see and the number of sessions you are allowed. Choose wisely from among the therapists allowed on your insurance program, if you have one. Remember: they are working for you and your marriage! Before you choose a counselor, review "How Therapy Can Be Hazardous to Your Marital Health," by William J. Doherty. Read his comments about "therapy-induced marital suicide." (The article is available at www.smartmarriages.com.)

11. Couples Should Stay Close to Bishops or Stake Presidents

Keep the bishop advised of your decisions and progress. A bishop can be a great source of hope and encouragement, helping you add the spiritual dimension to your marriage during difficult times. Be active in the Church while you are making your decisions. Married couples who attend religious services on a weekly basis have a one-third lower divorce rate than those who do not.[33]

12. Couples Can Learn from Other Married Couples Who Have Made Decisions

As noted, many couples have come close to divorce and then decided to work on their marriages and stay together. Some of these couples are available to conduct seminars and workshops. One national and nondenominational group conducting such seminars is Retrouvaille (a French word meaning "rediscovery" and pronounced "retro-vi"). When both husband and wife attend Retrouvaille meetings and work at their marriage, the success rate of staying together is 85 percent.[34]

13. Couples Can Consider Reading Books That May Help

There are many books in the marketplace that put divorce in perspective—and that offer helpful alternatives. Here are a few that you may find helpful. (If these books are not available in your local library or bookstore, they can usually be obtained within a week on web sites such as www.amazon.com or www.bn.com.)

- Diane Medved, *The Case against Divorce* (New York: Donald I. Fine, 1989).
- Michele Weiner Davis, *The Divorce Remedy: The Proven 7-Step Program for Saving Your Marriage* (New York: Simon and Schuster, 2001).
- Michele Weiner Davis, *Divorce Busting: A Step-By-Step Approach to Making Your Marriage Loving Again* (New York: Simon and Schuster, 1992).
- Judith S. Wallerstein, Julia M. Lewis, and Sandra Blakeslee, *The Unexpected Legacy of Divorce* (New York: Hyperion, 2000).
- Linda J. Waite and Maggie Gallagher, *The Case for Marriage: Why Married People Are Happier, Healthier, and Better Off Financially* (New York: Doubleday, 2000).
- Howard Markman, Scott Stanley, and Susan Blumburg, *Fighting for Your Marriage* (New York: Jossey-Bass Publishers, 2001).
- Glenn T. Stanton, *Why Marriage Matters* (Colorado Springs, Colorado: Piñon Press, 1997).
- James Dobson, *Love Must Be Tough: New Hope for Families in Crisis* (Nashville: Word Publishing, 1996). (This book discusses such issues as husbands or wives who are in the process of losing a spouse to another person, excessive hours at work, or various kinds of addiction, including drugs and pornography. Written from a Christian perspective, this book has been helpful to many.)

14. Couples Can Consider the Following Web Sites

a) *www.utahmarriage.org*. This web site was created especially for Utah residents. The site contains a variety of helpful information and resources for married couples and individuals. Or you can call the toll-free number (800–472–4716) for additional help and information. People in Salt Lake, Summit, Tooele, and Utah Counties can simply dial 211.

b) *www.divorcebusting.com*. This web site has many tips for helping couples to strengthen marriage. Michele Weiner Davis has also created a ten-hour audiocassette program and workbook titled "Keeping Love Alive" that is advertised on this web site—$59.95 plus $5.95 shipping and handling—and is highly recommended. This web site also gives instructions on how to become "Keeping Love Alive" group leaders in your community.

c) *www.smartmarriages.com* was created and is maintained by Diane Sollee. This web site lists a number of current articles on marriage and marriage education programs available throughout the United States. Numerous organizations promoting marriage are also listed. A few questions are posted to test your knowledge about contemporary marriage. Information on the annual Smart Marriage Conference is provided, and you can also subscribe to the free e-mail newsletter listed on the web site.

d) *www.marriagemovement.org*. This twenty-nine page document describes the current "marriage movement" in the United States. You are invited to read it and be a signer if you care to endorse the document. (I was honored to be one of the thirty individuals who attended the organization's first meeting in New York City on January 25, 2000, and was also one of the original one hundred signers of the document.)

e) *www.family.org*. This web site has many helpful materials on marriage from Focus on the Family, a Christian organization founded by Dr. James Dobson.

f) *www.divorcereform.org*. This web site details fascinating trends in divorce reform legislation in the United States and has some interesting statistics on contemporary divorce.

15. Remember the 9-11 Alert!

Almost everyone in the United States will remember September 11, 2001, when two planes crashed into the World Trade Center in New York City, another plane crashed into the Pentagon building in Washington, D.C., and a fourth crashed in Pennsylvania. We all witnessed over and over the tragic details of these events and their aftermath. These vivid images will likely remain with us for many years to come. What some may not know, however, is that immediately following these tragic events, many married couples withdrew applications for divorce that had been filed before September 11, 2001. In Houston, Texas, for example, "Dismissals in divorce cases have sky-rocketed in the Harris County Family Law courts since the terrorist attack of September 11th. Family-law cases, the vast majority of which are divorces, have been dismissed in nearly three times the volume in the days after the tragedy as in the days before it."[35] Similar trends apparently occurred elsewhere.

What does this trend after September 11, 2001, suggest? Why were so many military personnel married in the following weeks, before they were deployed for duty abroad? Why is it that in times of crisis we place higher value on marriage and family relationships? Michael Von Blon, a family law attorney in Texas, stated that in times of tragedy, "people stop and think about the most basic things in life—companionship, love and family."[36] Why do we need a national tragedy to remind us, once again, of the importance of marriage and family relationships? Apparently, such events help us realize the value of ancient wisdom:

> Two are better than one; because they have a good reward for their labour.
>
> For if they fall, the one will lift up his fellow; but woe to him that is alone when he falleth; for he hath not another to help him up.
>
> Again, if two lie together, then they have heat: but how can one be warm alone?

And if one prevail against him, two shall withstand him; and a threefold cord is not quickly broken (Ecclesiastes 4:9–12).

In this chapter, I have tried to present a balanced view, noting there are situations when divorce *is* warranted. Some individuals, where abuse, addiction, and other such problems exist, are better off not married to each other. On the other hand, I have given many reasons why I believe it is beneficial for most husbands and wives to stay together, if they can, and work through the differences in their marriages. It is important that married couples take time to make an informed decision about this most serious issue of divorce, for we know that "marriage between a man and a woman is ordained of God and that the family is central to the Creator's plan for the eternal destiny of His children."[37] More than two thousand years ago, Roman statesman and orator Marcus Tullius Cicero (106–43 B.C.) stated, "The first bond of society is marriage." I believe it still is.

Notes

1. Adapted from an article "Marriage Crossroads: Why Divorce Is Often Not the Best Option: Rationale, Resources, and References" by the author in *Marriage & Families*, January 2002, 21–28. The publication is a production of the School of Family Life at Brigham Young University.
2. Michele Weiner Davis, *Divorce Busting: A Step-by Step Approach to Making Your Marriage Loving Again* (New York: Simon & Schuster, 1992), 25.
3. Divorce statistics can be misleading. For example, if you measure all the couples married in the year 2003 against those couples who divorced the same year, the figures will be inflated because the pool from which divorced come is much larger than the newlyweds of one year. However, that is the way statistics are generated.
4. See "The Family: A Proclamation to the World," *Ensign*, November 1995, 102.
5. See David H. Olson and John Defrain, *Marriage and the Family, Diversity and Strengths* (Mountain View, Calif.: Mayfield Publishing Company, 1994), 6.
6. See Ibid.
7. Ibid., 517.
8. See David Arp and Claudia Arp, *The Second Half of Marriage* (Grand Rapids, Mich.: Zondervan Publishing House, 1998), 31.

9. Dennis Rainey, *Staying Close: Stopping the Natural Drive Toward Isolation in Marriage* (Dallas, Tex.: Word Publishing, 1992), 7.

10. See Paul R. Amato and Alan Booth, *A Generation at Risk: Growing Up in an Era of Family Upheaval* (Cambridge, Mass.: Harvard University Press, 1997), 220.

11. James E. Faust, "Father, Come Home," *Ensign,* May 1993, 36–37.

12. See Diane Medved, *The Case Against Divorce: Discover the Lures, the Lies, and the Emotional Traps of Divorce—Plus the Seven Vital Reasons to Stay Together* (New York: Donald I. Fine, Inc., 1989), 103–30.

13. See Olson and Defrain, *Marriage and the Family, Diversity and Strengths,* 522.

14. "Marriage in America: A Report to the Nation," Council on Families in America, 1995, 4–5. Institute for American Values, 1841 Broadway, Suite 211, New York, New York 10023.

15. Medved, *The Case Against Divorce,* 8.

16. Ibid., 11.

17. Glenn T. Stanton, *Why Marriage Matters* (Colorado Springs, Colo.: Piñon Press, 1997), 73.

18. David B. Larson, James P. Swyers, and Susan S. Larson, *The Costly Consequences of Divorce: Assessing the Clinical, Economic, and Public Health Impact of Marital Disruption in the United States* (Rockville, Md.: National Institute for Healthcare Research, 1995), 1.

19. Robert H. Coombs, "Marital Status and Personal Well-Being: A Literature Review," *Family Relations* 40 (January 1991): 100–101.

20. Larson, Swyers, and Larson, *The Costly Consequences of Divorce,* 136.

21. Patrick F. Fagan and Robert Rector, "The Effects of Divorce on America," 5 June 2000, retrieved from www.heritage.org/research/family/bg1373.cfm on 22 January 2004.

22. Lisa Laumann-Billings and Robert E. Emery, "Distress Among Young Adults from Divorced Families," *Journal of Family Psychology* 14, no. 4 (December 2000): 671–87.

23. Judith Wallerstein, Julia M. Lewis, and Sandra Blakeslee, *The Unexpected Legacy of Divorce, A Twenty-Five Year Landmark Study* (New York: Hyperion, 2000), xxiii–xxiv.

24. Linda J. Waite and Maggie Gallagher, *The Case for Marriage: Why Married People Are Happier, Healthier, and Better Off Financially* (New York: Doubleday, 2000), 147–48.

25. William J. Doherty, "The Covenant Marriage Option Bill: Overview and Response to Questions," 1999, retrieved from http://fsos.che.umn.edu/doherty/covenant.html on 22 January 2004.

26. Guy M. Bradley, "Divorce Isn't Worth the Cost," *Deseret News,* 11 January 2001, A-10.

27. Davis, *Divorce Busting,* 27.

28. See Court Record and Information System (CORIS database), Information Services Department, State of Utah, 2000.

29. Waite and Gallagher, *The Case for Marriage,* 148–49.

30. Ibid., 203.

31. See Steve Nock, "Calculating the Financial Cost of Divorce," presentation at the Smart Marriages Conference, Washington, D.C., 1999. See also David G. Schramm, "What Could Divorce Be Costing Your State?" 25 June 2003, retrieved from www.utahmarriage.org.

32. Fagan and Rector, "The Effects of Divorce on America."

33. See Larson, Swyers, and Larson, *The Costly Consequences of Divorce,* 246.

34. The web site is www.retrouvaille.org. For information on Retrouvaille in Utah, call (801) 773–4587.

35. Mary Flood, "Divorce Case Dismissals Soar Since Sept. 11," *Houston Chronicle,* 25 September 2001.

36. Michael Von Blon, in ibid.

37. "The Family: A Proclamation to the World," *Ensign,* November 1995, 102.

9
Resolving Marital Differences
Kenneth W. Matheson

Dealing with differences in life, and especially in marriage relationships, is part of Heavenly Father's plan for his children in their second estate. Lehi explained the principle: "For it must needs be, that there is an opposition in all things. If not so, . . . righteousness could not be brought to pass, neither wickedness, neither holiness nor misery, neither good nor bad" (2 Nephi 2:11). Every married couple experiences marital differences because they think independently, because they come from different backgrounds—and because they are male and female! Enough said. However, differences don't mean that one spouse has to be right and the other wrong, nor does it mean that one opinion is better than the other, nor does it mean that all differences need to be resolved. Only those differences that have a negative effect on the marriage or cause conflict between partners need be resolved. It is those differences that I will address in this chapter.

In order to achieve success in marriage, there must be a willingness on the part of each marriage partner to give and take, to compromise personal views and opinions occasionally for the good of the marriage, especially in those areas where differences are destructive to the relationship. When a couple is totally committed to each other and to their marriage, compromising views and opinions are less traumatic. I have found through counseling couples that even those with major differences can love and respect each other and work toward the goal of "having their hearts knit together in unity and in love one towards another" (Mosiah 18:21).

Myths about Marriage

Before focusing on specific principles and solutions to resolve marital differences, there are two myths about marriage I want to explore.

Myth #1: Couples believe that "most other couples and families never have conflict in their homes." In reality, as Elder Neal A. Maxwell explained, "there are no perfect families [or marriages], either in the world or in the Church, but there are many good [ones]."[1] We all lose our composure on occasion. We all get our dander up in the course of living together. I once heard an individual say, "We have been married for forty years, and we have never had a disagreement in all that time." If that is truly the case, then I think we are talking about "selective memory," or else one of the partners just patiently puts up with the differences. For example, Aunt Jenny may have never expressed her difference of opinion to Uncle George about his habit of repeatedly dropping muddy clothes on the kitchen floor. To her it just wasn't worth the fuss to constantly mention it to him. She just picked them up, and she never let it become an issue in her marriage. However, not everyone can just ignore things as easily as Aunt Jenny. As Elder Joe J. Christensen taught, "Any intelligent couple will have differences of opinion. Our challenge is to be sure that we know how to resolve them."[2]

Though it is impossible for two people to see every issue the same way, their differences need not turn into anger or arguments.

Myth #2: "If we are obedient to the commandments of God, there will be no differences in our marriage." If you have been married for any length of time or been observant of other marriages, you know the fallacy of this myth. More often than not, we ask ourselves, "How can two apparently well-adjusted, celestial candidates marry each other only to have the marriage turn into a telestial relationship?" The answer is that marriage brings into the life of a couple complexities new and different than those encountered in living alone. Living with someone day in and day out in close proximity, sharing intimate exchanges, being dependent on each other, and learning to appreciate the uniqueness of each other all create an entirely different situation from being single, where the primary focus is on self and meeting one's own needs. Marriage brings a requirement that we think in terms of someone else. It is "we," not "I," starting even before the ceremony begins. The principles of building healthy interpersonal relationships in marriage are more difficult than dealing with just yourself, because marital relationships require that we be concerned for the feelings, desires, wants, needs, and attitudes of someone else.

No matter how well a couple thinks they know each other before they marry or how compatible they think they are beforehand, they cannot possibly foresee the multitude of experiences that reveal major differences in areas such as money management, housekeeping, yard care, sexual interest, food preparation and taste, apartment decoration, where to live, work schedules, and a multitude of other issues. Someone has said that "every marriage is happy; it's the living together afterwards that causes problems."

Differences Naturally Come with Marriage

Sometimes after the marriage a couple finds so many differences between them that they may feel, as a newlywed couple, that they made a mistake and married the wrong person. Even though we encourage people to choose a partner with similar values to their own, it does not follow that a successful marriage stems solely from how much we are originally alike. Rather, a successful marriage is the result of a couple's ability to resolve conflict and to tolerate a number of differences that show up *after* marriage. Let me put it this way: a lasting marriage comes from a couple's ability to resolve inevitable differences in marriage in healthy and productive ways.

My wife learned this lesson while visiting a lady who had been married for more than fifty years. She could just sense that the woman was extremely happy in her marriage. My wife had seen the individual and her husband do many things together, and it was obvious that they had a terrific marriage. My wife commented to her, "It must be nice to have reached the point in your marriage where you two are so compatible." The lady smiled and replied, "It all depends on how much you are willing to overlook." Any couple's marriage, even after many years together, never quite reaches total perfection.

As this lady suggested, not all individual expectations are met by our spouses. One marital partner may have an expectation that no human being on earth could meet. And when a specific expectation is not met by the spouse, the potential exists for disharmony to develop. Sometimes we just need to realize that marriage in mortality will not meet all of our expectations—and that is okay. Marriage can still be a vibrant and stable thing, an "exultant ecstasy," as President Spencer W. Kimball reminded us.[3] (Of course, it is obvious that we must meet some of each other's major expectations if happiness is to be achieved.)

Experienced married couples report that as long as the essential expectations are met—loyalty, caring, kindness, understanding, fidelity, honesty, affection—then nonessential expectations and preferences that are not met so well by a spouse are much more tolerable.

A fulfilling marital relationship will not happen without a continued, consistent effort on the part of both spouses. Another adage is that "creating and achieving a successful marriage depends as much on being the 'right' partner as it does on marrying the 'right' partner." Periodic personal introspection ought to be a part of every married couple's repertoire. Suppose, for example, a married person asked himself or herself:

"What is it like to be married to me?"

"If I were married to me, would I be happy?"

"Am I easy to love?"

"How well do I meet the needs of my spouse?"

"Am I the kind of spouse my companion wants and needs me to be?"

"Is my spouse happy he or she made the choice to marry me?"

"What things do I do that really frustrate my spouse that I can and ought to change?"

Resolving Marital Differences

The effort to resolve marital differences, though sometimes painful, can be a healthy part of life. In successfully resolving issues together, a couple comes to appreciate the individual talents and strengths of one another and the unique contributions that masculine and feminine traits and thought processes bring to the table. Spouses also increase in their faith in each other to resolve differences respectfully, and their appreciation of the Christlike attributes needed for an effective and loving marriage partnership—patience, kindness, love, cooperation, compromise, and faithful observance in living gospel principles.

When serious differences go unresolved, it is because of our stubbornness, our unwillingness to bend, our hard heart, and our selfishness. Then conflict, contention, unhappiness, and the divorce option come up. Contention and fighting between married companions is unacceptable in the gospel perspective. Jesus counseled the Nephites: "There shall be no disputations among you. . . . He that hath the spirit of contention is not of me, but is of the devil, who is the father of contention, and he stirred up the hearts of men to contend with anger, one with another. Behold, . . . this is my doctrine, that such things should be done away" (3 Nephi 11:28–30).

If we hope to be Jesus' disciples, he was saying, we must avoid argument and contention. And why should we yield to those temptations? We have never had this marriage role before. We were never married, nor were we ever parents in the premortal sphere. Mortality is our first time, ever, to learn the ins and outs of being a spouse and parent. That doctrinal truth alone should make us more charitable when either of us errs or makes mistakes. Come to think of it, we really don't know enough as mortals to be angry and caustic with each other, because we are all so fallible. Though differences in marriage are natural and a part of our spiritual, emotional, and social growth as a couple, if differences cause hard feelings, are left unresolved, or become serious disagreements that lead to interpersonal conflict and then on to anger and rage, then we have put ourselves into spiritual hot water. We have offended not only each other but also our Heavenly Father and his Son. To be a disciple of the Lord Jesus Christ requires that we be peacemakers, not warmongers. The penalty for escalating unresolved differences into pain and hurt is a loss of the Spirit of the Lord.

I once worked with a couple who ended up in a heated argument over just about every topic that came up between them. After I brought this destructive pattern to their attention, they told me that their fighting was the result of an unresolved difference that occurred three years earlier, which they adamantly refused to talk about or address together! Excuse me! Something had been festering for three years and had not been resolved between them? I felt sorry for them. There is great spiritual damage in harboring negative feelings against a brother or sister, much less your spouse. Such silly behavior has a detrimental effect on any marriage relationship.

I want to again emphasize that differences in a relationship do not mean that the marriage is doomed to fail. It is how differences are handled by both spouses that really matters in the long run. Managing differences in charitable ways strengthens marriage. One wife told me that her husband's habit of constantly cracking his knuckles annoyed her immensely. She mentioned this to him many times over the years, but he simply continued the obnoxious behavior. She realized then that she had two choices—she could either continue to focus on his negative knuckle-cracking behavior, or she could ignore it and focus on his admirable and positive qualities. She chose the latter, and as a result, she stopped all sarcastic and critical comments. Interestingly enough, when she stopped focusing on his knuckle cracking, he stopped doing it in front of her! What lesson does that teach us?

Principles That Help Us Resolve Differences

I want to share some basic principles that I have found to be effective in resolving differences in almost any marital situation. Though not exhaustive, the following principles can help couples cope and deal with each other and the inevitable differences in marriage. You'll note that I have already touched on some of them.

1. Resolve Differences in an Environment of Mutual Love and Consideration

Before any of us is inclined to change behavior patterns, we must have enough love and respect for each other that we desire to please one another. The positive values of love, respect, understanding, courtesy, consideration, kindness, trust, commitment, caring, and a host of other Christlike attributes must be well established in our marriage relationship. There is an old adage that says "Behavioral problems are simply relationship problems." Though secular counselors suggest a number of what to me are gimmicks to help couples resolve serious differences, I am of the opinion that the root causes of marital conflict are *pride* and *selfishness*. These twin plagues of marital unhappiness make it difficult for spouses to apologize, take responsibility, and want to change themselves to better the relationship. Those who are selfish and proud have a hard time admitting that they could be at fault.

I have found the following to be a useful exercise for a couple to utilize. On a sheet of paper, place three column headings; then, under each heading, list the issues and ideas that apply. On the following page are the headings with a few examples.

This exercise can help you focus on relevant problems in your marriage. Getting a problem down on paper, agreeing with each other that it needs attention, brainstorming together about a workable solution, and then deciding how to implement the agreed-upon solution can be very therapeutic. It engenders a spirit of cooperation and re-kindles confidence in both of you that you are capable of solving your

Problem in Our Marriage	Workable Solutions	Consequences
Use of remote control	Take turns— sense of humor	Both happy
Use of leisure time	Compromise or alternate choices	Both satisfied
Sexual frequency	Share feelings	Both more satisfied
Debt management	Discuss income/expenses	Both participate in decisions

own problems. However, even this simple exercise assumes a spirit of cooperation and respect for each other and each one's ideas. President Gordon B. Hinckley made this point: "I am satisfied that a happy marriage is not so much a matter of romance as it is an anxious concern for the comfort and well-being of one's companion."[4] When we have an "anxious concern" for the welfare of each other, then we are able to resolve any differences that need our attention. The late Elder Loren C. Dunn remarked:

> "There is a need for us, perhaps more than ever before . . . to be able to disagree without becoming disagreeable; to lower our voices and build on common ground. . . .
>
> People will always have opposing views, and I suppose there will always be conflict and even misunderstanding; but the principle of *mutual respect* mixed with charity and forgiveness can lay the foundation for the resolving of differences and the solving of problems."[5]

2. Realize That Marital Differences Are Normal

Undoubtedly we acquired definite male and female attributes in the premortal sphere, attributes that are specific to our gender. Surely we brought them with us to this second estate. That does not mean that a man cannot possess traits commonly attributed to women, such as caring, nurturing, nourishing, and so forth. Nor does it mean that a woman can't have traits normally thought of as masculine—driven, task-oriented, logical, less feeling oriented, and so on. But it is obvious that, in general, men and women are quite different.

We also are socialized by family and friends who develop certain attributes of character and personality in us. When differences surface in marriage, we are prone to explain them by our family background and characteristics or our gender socialization. But there is no reason why male and female differences should not be complementary. Brigham Young said, in essence, that differences are not a sign of failure or unrighteous living, but a manifestation of the novelty that exists in personal needs and values.[6]

Thus, when differences exist in a relationship, it does not mean that the relationship has failed or that one is unrighteousness. Instead, differences have to do with our being human; we have certain idiosyncrasies that make up our character. If one spouse likes hard-boiled eggs, for example, and the other likes soft-boiled eggs, the difference has nothing to do with righteousness but simply represents unique preferences that seem to be inherent in our character.

3. Enhance Personal Growth and Cohesion in a Marital Relationship by Resolving Differences

Why is it that as soon as we hear the word *differences,* negative thoughts spring to mind? Most of us are inclined to believe that differences are negative, and therefore one spouse must change—and we are pretty sure it is not us.

I worked with a couple where the husband told me that he was doing everything correctly, and if any changes were to be made in the marital relationship his wife was going to have to be the one to make them! I honestly think that he viewed himself as guiltless. How silly of him! As mortals, we simply are not perfect. This man could not admit to any errors, and it was obvious that he expected his wife to make the needed changes. Every marriage has its own unique challenges, and by working as a partnership on those challenges we grow and progress. Differences are essential to character building. Elder Boyd K. Packer suggested that it is through overcoming our challenges that we can reach our potential: "Marriage is not without trials of many kinds. These tests forge virtue and strength. The tempering that comes in marriage and family life produces men and women who will someday be exalted."[7]

Now, couples need not go out of their way to accentuate or create differences; those will just naturally come in the course of living together. Differences are plentiful even in healthy relationships. It is important that a couple solve their own issues and not take their problems home to their parents. After all, parents usually take their child's side of an issue and validate their feelings of frustration. Couples need to work on their problems together.

President Spencer W. Kimball stated: "No combination of [external] power can destroy that marriage except the power within either or both of the spouses themselves. . . . Other people and agencies may influence. . . . But the marriage depends first and always on the two spouses, who can always make their marriage successful and happy if they are determined, unselfish, and righteous."[8]

When differences exist, a couple can decide to (1) resolve them if they are important or (2) ignore them if they are not—as did the lady whose husband liked to crack his knuckles. Either of these approaches can help us to be more compatible and loving partners.

4. Resolve Differences with the Help of the Spirit of the Lord

As Latter-day Saints, we understand that spirituality is very important in helping us be more charitable in our treatment of each other. We strive to be more spiritual in our lives, that is, to be more Christlike in the way we live and relate to others. Spiritual people are kind and considerate individuals. They have soft hearts. They love others and desire to serve those they live with and work with. Every

176

married couple ought to consider this matter: "What can we do to increase our spirituality?" Generally most of us would respond by saying that the keys would be delving more into the scriptures, attending the temple more frequently, holding effective family home evenings, and praying more meaningfully and consistently together. And these things would certainly help. President Ezra Taft Benson gave some additional ideas to increase spirituality:

> Rely on the Lord [exercise our faith in Jesus Christ], the teachings of the prophets [Conference Reports or *Ensign* every six months], and the scriptures [especially the Book of Mormon, Doctrine and Covenants, and Pearl of Great Price] for guidance and help, particularly when there may be disagreements and problems.
>
> Spiritual growth *comes by solving problems together,* . . . *not by running from them.* . . .
>
> The more we serve one another, the greater is our spiritual and emotional growth.[9]

What couple would not be helped by exercising their spiritual muscles? The prophet said that we must not run from our problems, but face them and resolve them—that is how we increase our spiritual capacity and personal growth. The point is that by resolving our differences in Christlike, charitable ways, we grow in confidence that we can handle any challenge mortality throws in our direction.

5. Acknowledge the Effort Your Partner Makes to Meet Your Needs and Marital Expectations

Sometimes we withhold expressions of love and appreciation for our companions. Every person has a need to be loved, appreciated, valued, and accepted—even us. If we need it, so do our spouse and children. There is much that we can do to lighten the load each carries. Marriage demands that we learn from each other how to meet individual needs. I recall the wife of a couple I visited with who said to her husband, "I would really like you to be more affectionate with me: hold my hand, put your arm around my waist, send me little love notes, be more expressive in letting me know that you love me." The husband, who had not done these things in the past, struggled with his wife's requests. However, he loved his wife and he wanted to make an effort to meet her needs.

On one occasion, he reached over to grab her hand, but it was rather abrupt. Her initial reaction was surprise and shock, and she almost said to him: "Are you trying to crush my hand? Can't you do any better than that? That's not what I need." However, she restrained herself, thought about it, and a few minutes later said to him: "Dear, thanks for holding my hand today, it meant a lot to me." How was that response different than her first reaction? Because of her restraint, her husband was encouraged by her comment. (She realized that she could refine his hand-holding technique later.) Had she given in to her first impulse and voiced her initial feelings she could have discouraged her husband, who might not have made the effort again.

I have learned that it is important for individuals to positively reward the efforts of their partner to meet their needs, even though the performance may not be perfect. Even though it may not be exactly what was wanted, as in this case with this wife, she gave him credit for his effort.

6. Understand That Divorce Is Rarely an Acceptable Response to Marital Differences

It is not uncommon for individuals to conclude that they have "done all they can" to change their companion's behavior, and yet it hasn't worked. They conclude that the relationship was "not meant to be." They begin to think that if they get out of the marriage and find a "more compatible spouse" they will be happier. I've observed over many years of working with couples, however, that when they divorce they are likely to find problems in the new marriage that are very much like those they left in the former one. Personality and character are difficult to change, and trading partners seldom makes things better.

Satan loves to see Latter-day Saint marriages dissolved. He thrives on broken marriages and broken covenants. Elder Boyd K. Packer observed: "The ultimate purpose of the adversary . . . is to disrupt, disturb, and to destroy the home and the family." [10] And from current divorce statistics it appears that Satan is doing very well in his goal. I have seen few friendly divorces. Divorce destroys character in addition to families. I consider it to be a great tragedy when children are left without much influence from one of their biological parents. President Spencer W. Kimball condemned divorce in this statement:

"Divorce . . . is one of the principal tools of Satan to destroy faith, through breaking up happy homes and bringing frustration of life and distortion of thought. . . .

"The divorce itself does not constitute the entire evil, but the very acceptance of divorce as a cure is also a serious sin of this generation.

"Every divorce is the result of selfishness on the part of one or the other or both parties." [11]

President Gordon B. Hinckley echoed President Kimball: "There is a remedy for all of this [marital disharmony]. It is not found in divorce. It is found in the gospel of the Son of God. . . . The remedy for most marriage stress is not in divorce. It is in repentance. It is not in separation. It is in simple integrity that leads a man [or woman] to square up his shoulders and meet his obligations. It is found in the Golden Rule." [12]

Now, I must say that I am grateful that divorce is an option for some. I have watched people stay in a marriage when repeated adultery and abuse appeared to be justifiable grounds for separation. I have also seen people bail out of a marriage over trivial causes. But wo to that person who is responsible for breaking marriage covenants. In this same address, President Gordon B. Hinckley continued: "There may be now and again a legitimate cause for divorce. I am not one to say that it is never justified. But I say without hesitation that this plague among us, which seems to be growing everywhere, is not of God, but rather is the work of the adversary of righteousness and peace and truth." [13]

The question naturally arises as to when divorce might be justified. When is it acceptable in the eyes of the Lord to remove yourself from an abusive situation? Elder James E. Faust gave his opinion:

> What, then, might be "just cause" for breaking the covenants of marriage? Over a lifetime of dealing with human problems, I have struggled to understand what might be considered "just cause" for breaking of covenants. I confess I do not claim the wisdom nor authority to definitely state what is "just cause." Only the parties to the marriage can determine this. They must bear the responsibility for the train of consequences which inevitably follow if these covenants are not honored. In my opinion, "just cause" should be nothing less serious than a prolonged and apparently irredeemable relationship which is destructive of a person's dignity as a human being.
>
> At the same time, I have strong feelings about what is not provocation for breaking the sacred covenants of marriage. Surely it is not simply "mental distress" nor "personality differences" nor "having grown apart" nor having "fallen out of love." This is especially so where there are children. [14]

When a marriage is destroying the personal dignity and integrity of a spouse after repeated attempts to reconcile, perhaps then there is sufficient justification to break the marriage vow. Though priesthood leaders cannot counsel an individual to divorce, it is important that they be kept abreast of what is happening so they can lend support.

7. When Resolving Differences, View the Problem As Being Separate from Your Spouse

In resolving differences, we must be gentle and kind with each other. We love each other, but we have issues that need joint attention. It is our responsibility to be charitable with each other. Attack your problems together—details, facts, time line, outcomes—in the spirit of cooperation and love. Accusing, blaming, labeling, excusing, or attacking each other are not helpful in resolving differences. Keep in mind that you are jointly addressing a problem that needs your attention, not attacking each other or putting your partner down emotionally.

For example, a wife might want to say to her husband, "We are always broke because you don't work hard enough." Such a comment would only lead to defensiveness on the part of the husband. A better approach where financial strain exists might sound like this: "Honey, it is obvious that we are in trouble financially. As I see it, we have a choice to make: (1) We can either earn more income by my going back to work; or (2) we have to cut expenses quickly. What do you think is the best choice?"

A wife might feel like saying, "If you would stop trying to convince me that you are right all the time, we could have a better relationship." A better approach might be: "Sweetheart, I need your help. I feel that when we talk together, we generally end up having to do it your way and I feel like I'm not worth much in our marriage. It is as if my ideas are not worthwhile. I think you have some great ideas, but there are times when I think mine aren't that bad either. I have a couple of ideas that I think will help us. May I share them with you?" The wife could then give her suggestions. If the husband accepted or agreed with her ideas, she would then express her appreciation for his willingness to look at the problem together. It is important that we treat each other with respect and kindness.

A good model on this issue comes in the Lord's counsel to Oliver Cowdery in his relationship with Joseph Smith: "Admonish him [your husband or your wife] in his [or her] faults, and also receive admonition of him [or her]. Be patient; be sober; be temperate; have patience, faith, hope and charity" (D&C 6:19). This is good counsel for any couple seeking to improve their relationship.

8. Develop a Sense of Humor

Life is filled with a variety of pressures that face every couple: finances, schooling, vocation, deciding where to live, leaving parents and family behind, Church callings, and so forth. Marriage brings its own set of challenges: compatibility, in-laws, children, power and decision-making issues—issues that can overwhelm a couple. If a husband and wife focus only on negative issues and stress, tension levels escalate. Developing a sense of humor is one way to balance the normal and abnormal stresses of life. That doesn't mean that everything is a joke, can be laughed away, or justifies sarcasm. But we all need to be able to see the lighter side of life. Elder Hugh B. Brown stated: "Both husband and wife should keep a sense of humor. They should laugh with each other. . . . Each needs the assurance and reassurance of the other's love and laughter. The love that is not nurtured by repeated endearments and refreshed by a bit of humor is liable to wither and die on the vine."[15]

President Gordon B. Hinckley, who demonstrates a great sense of humor, stated: "We've got to have a little humor in our lives. You had better take seriously that which should be taken seriously but, at the same time, we can bring in a touch of humor now and again. If the time ever comes when we can't smile at ourselves, it will be a sad time."[16]

9. Control and Discipline Your Emotions

Someone has said that the size of the man can be measured by the size of the things that make him angry. Anger is the great destroyer of many families. When resolving differences, it is important for a couple to be open and honest in their communication, but that does not mean that we attack, belittle, or embarrass our sweetheart. President Ezra Taft Benson taught this principle: "Restraint and self-control must be ruling principles in the marriage relationship. Couples must learn to bridle their tongues as well as their passions. . . . The goal of marriage is unity and oneness, as well as self development." [17]

President Gordon B. Hinckley has warned male members of the Church:

> How tragic and utterly disgusting a phenomenon is wife abuse. Any man in this Church who abuses his wife, who demeans her, who insults her, who exercises unrighteous dominion over her is unworthy to hold the priesthood. Though he may have been ordained, the heavens will withdraw, the Spirit of the Lord will be grieved, and it will be amen to the authority of the priesthood of that man.
>
> Any man who engages in this practice is unworthy to hold a temple recommend. . . .
>
> My brethren, if there be any within the sound of my voice who are guilty of such behavior, I call upon you to repent. Get on your knees and ask the Lord to forgive you. Pray to Him for the power to control your tongue and your heavy hand. Ask for the forgiveness of your wife and your children. [18]

Note that President Hinckley does not excuse any negative treatment of women. He does not excuse abusive behavior, even if a person was abused as a child. He plainly counsels men to control their temper. Priesthood cannot be exercised in righteousness unless men are righteous, and righteousness means that we treat the daughters of God with kindness and respect.

Certainly there are women who can be trying and exasperating to their husbands. But the same is true of husbands—some are trying and exasperating. Both husband and wife should refrain from critical or destructive comments.

10. Resolve Differences through Positive Communication

We have an old adage that says, "It is impossible for a husband and wife not to communicate." Even if there are no verbal comments, communication is taking place. In working with couples over the years, I have observed that *feelings not talked about openly are acted out nevertheless.* Typically, I think that women are able to express their feelings more naturally and easily than men. That does not mean that no husband can express his ideas and feelings well—that's an exaggerated stereotype. But some husbands can learn from their wives to be more expressive, while wives can learn other meaningful things from their husbands. In fact, marriage is a profound commitment where we are to learn much from each other. Husbands can be effective listeners as well as communicators, mainly because communication is more of an attitude than a skill.

Positive communication is much more effective than negative criticism. Openness in a relationship is important, but the venting of negative feelings without regard to its effect on a spouse is detrimental. We accomplish more when we are positive and helpful to each other.

It is probably true that men grow up better trained in problem-solving techniques than women; men want to fix things, both mechanically and emotionally—now. In contrast, women usually want to just turn things over in their minds, to discuss matters thoroughly rather than worrying about an immediate solution to a specific problem. They want their husbands to understand them, their feelings, and their concerns. Sometimes when a wife is attempting to express her feelings or concerns to her husband, he interrupts her in an attempt to instruct her on how to solve the problem, much to her frustration. Both parties must be sensitive and nondefensive and learn from each other how best to communicate ideas and feelings. A wife may need to help her husband by saying: "Jim, I would appreciate it if you would hear me out first rather than solve the problem for me right now. Just help me think it through." Most husbands need that kind of information from their wives because it is a new concept at first.

And wives should not expect their husbands to know their every need without ever expressing those needs to them. Men are not good mind readers. A wife sometimes believes that if her husband really loved her, he would know what she was thinking and feeling, and what her needs are, without her having to mention them. It's always easier to respond to a verbal request than to try to mind read and guess what a spouse wants.

Husbands often counterattack when they are attacked. Men tend to be logical and, when accused, they feel the attack unjust because at the time their behavior seemed logical to them. As a result of a personal attack, husbands may believe they are justified in retaliating by labeling or putting down their wife by saying, "Who do you think you are anyway?" or "You always say that about me and I'm tired of hearing that over and over again." Remember, the days of an eye for an eye and a tooth for a tooth are over. Disciples are counseled to turn the other cheek.

I often hear a husband respond to his wife that a particular problem is "yours, not mine." Please know that any problem in marriage affects both of you. Problems are best solved together. The focus should be not on who's right, but what's right.

Positive communication is very important in resolving differences in marriage, but timing is also important. There are awkward times when trying to resolve a difference "right now" might not be wise. Know that it is acceptable to postpone important discussions for more appropriate times. There is an old adage that says you should not go to bed upset and angry—don't go to bed until you have worked through the problem. If this advice works for you, wonderful. As Erma Bombeck said, "Stay up and fight it out." My rule of thumb is that you should not let twenty-four hours elapse between any conflict and your attempt to resolve it. Some people do better at resolving differences after a good night's sleep. Elder Joe J. Christensen stated:

"Even letting the sun go down on your wrath can help bring you back to the problem in the morning more rested, calm, and with a better chance for resolution."[19]

11. Emphasize the Positive Aspects of Your Relationship

We all do better with compliments. Very few marriage partners ever change for the better because of nagging or critical partners. President Kimball called the constant nagging of a marriage partner "ceaseless pinpricking."[20] My advice to couples I work with is to "emphasize the positive without ignoring the negative." President Gordon B. Hinckley taught this principle:

"I am satisfied that if we would look to the virtues in one another and not the vices, there would be much more of happiness in the homes of our people. There would be far less of divorce, much less of infidelity, much less of anger and rancor and quarreling. There would be more of forgiveness, more of love, more of peace, more of happiness. This is as the Lord would have it."[21]

In *Why Marriages Succeed or Fail*, John Gottman, a family scientist from the University of Washington, indicates that after twenty years of research he saw that couples who remained married had a common element. In their relationships, they emphasized the positive with each other more than the negative. In fact, his research indicated that the ideal ratio between positive and negative interactions was five to one in favor of positive. In other words, for every negative interaction that occurs in a relationship, there need to be at least five positive interactions to balance out the effect of the negative.[22]

How can spouses be more positive and supportive of each other? Consider the following items based on Gottman's research:

- Show genuine interest in your spouse's life and worries by asking about how the day went, and then listening to the response.
- Be affectionate not just to receive favors, but anticipate and be attentive to your spouse's needs.

- Show you care about your spouse's thoughts and feelings by asking questions.
- Be appreciative of the services your spouse renders to you and your children.
- Show genuine interest in what concerns your spouse.
- Be honest in expressing your feelings, remembering to emphasize the positive.
- Be accepting of individual weaknesses and appreciative of specific strengths.
- Be humorous in private as well as public settings.
- Share your joy of marriage and life with each other often.

When one partner makes an attempt to change for the better, it usually motivates the other to do the same.

12. Remove Selfishness and Pride from Your Marital Relationship

Selfishness and pride, as I indicated earlier, destroy marriages and family relations. Self-centeredness makes it difficult for a person to give of self to bless a spouse and children. Differences are tough enough to resolve when one person thinks they come from the "true family" or that their ideas are never wrong. In his classic talk on this matter, President Benson stated:

[Pride] is the power by which Satan wishes to reign over us. . . .

Another face of pride is contention. Arguments, fights, unrighteous dominion, generation gaps, divorces, spouse abuse, riots, and disturbances all fall into this category. . . .

Contention in our families drives the Spirit of the Lord away. . . .

The proud are not easily taught. . . . They won't change their minds to accept truths, because to do so implies they have been wrong.

Pride adversely affects all our relationships—our relationship with God and His servants, between husband and wife, parent and child, . . . and all mankind.

The antidote for pride is humility, meekness, submissiveness. [23]

In other words, a person needs to look within himself or herself first and make sure his or her heart is right with God before attempting to change a spouse. It's the old mote-beam issue that Jesus addressed. Pride on the part of one or both marital partners is a major contributor to unresolved differences, primarily because individuals who are selfish or proud will not repent or make any changes that could improve the relationship. Prideful, selfish individuals can't believe that they could be the source of the problem.

The antidote for pride is humility. Since we are married to imperfect spouses, they will, just like us, continually make mistakes. Isn't it true that we tend to judge others by their actions, while we see only our good intentions?

When we are willing to say, "I apologize; I'm sorry; please forgive me," even if we are not totally at fault, we can open a doorway to the healing process. We should take responsibility for what we can. Humility, repentance, and a willingness to apologize are indicators of genuine discipleship and charity and are an essential ingredient to achieving a truly Christlike relationship. Elder Marvin J. Ashton provided a definition of charity that I have always enjoyed; if followed, it will help to resolve many marital differences. He said:

Perhaps the greatest charity comes when we are kind to each other, when we don't judge or categorize someone else, when we simply give each other the benefit of the doubt or remain quiet. Charity is accepting someone's differences, weaknesses, and shortcomings; having patience with someone who has let us down; or resisting the impulse to become offended when someone doesn't handle something the way we might have hoped. Charity is refusing to take advantage of another's weakness and being willing to forgive someone who has hurt us. Charity is expecting the best of each other.[24]

I counseled with a couple who were always blaming each other for problems in their marriage. At the beginning of the third session, I asked them, "How have things gone between you two during the past week?" The wife paused for a moment and said, "Wonderful." I asked her to explain what she meant by "Wonderful." She then reviewed an incident that happened the day after our last meeting in which her husband, after an argument, said to her, "Honey, I'm sorry for upsetting you. That was not my intent." After the husband said those words to her, the wife started to cry because in her memory that was the first time in their married life she could recall him ever apologizing. The impact of his remorse caused her to humble herself and ask his forgiveness. From that point on, positive changes took place in their relationship. I have learned over the years that if I can ever get a couple to apologize to each other, the other problems seem to melt away.

13. Involve the Savior More in Your Marital Relationship

Occasionally when I meet with a couple having major problems, I ask them if they are praying together, reading scriptures regularly together, holding family home evening, and so on. Invariably the answers are "No." How sad, I think to myself. The Savior has all power. He created this earth and many more like it. He can heal relationships, soften hearts, and make weak things strong if we will only let him in. His prophets plead with us to do those things that bring his Spirit into our lives and homes. The Savior's teachings and examples, when applied to our marriage relationships, make it possible for couples to realize that the Savior is interested in their marital success. The examples and teachings of the Savior also bring the ultimate source of power to resolve differences and heal wounded hearts.

No one wants you to succeed in marriage more than Jesus Christ.

He gave his life for both of you that you might (1) be forgiven of your sins and (2) be resurrected and continue as male and female companions forever. Without Christ's atonement and resurrection, death would bring an end to your marriage and your creative powers. Because of him, however, you have the opportunity to continue in the celestial kingdom what you begin in mortality. The gospel gives vision and purpose to life. It outlines the importance of marriage and family in the eternal scheme of things, and it motivates us to be our best selves. Each member of the Godhead wants you to gain immortality and eternal life. That is their goal, just as it is our goal. That goal can be achieved only by acquiring the Christlike traits that Jesus displayed in his ministry and teachings. We also have his authorized servants on hand—prophets and apostles—to provide modern counsel for living in modern times.

Remember, God can heal sick and troubled relationships, just as he can heal sick bodies. He wants us to develop Christlike qualities and become more like him. Developing those characteristics and applying them in overcoming marital differences will help us achieve that goal.

Notes

1. Neal A. Maxwell, "Take Especial Care of Your Family," *Ensign*, May 1994, 89.
2. Joe J. Christensen, "Marriage and the Great Plan of Happiness," *Ensign*, May 1995, 65.
3. Spencer W. Kimball, *Marriage* (Salt Lake City: Deseret Book, 1978), 37.
4. Gordon B. Hinckley, "What God Hath Joined Together," *Ensign*, May 1991, 73.
5. Loren C. Dunn, "Before I Build a Wall," *Ensign*, May 1991, 82–83; emphasis added.
6. Brigham Young, in *Journal of Discourses*, 26 vols. (London: Latter-day Saints' Book Depot, 1854–86), 9:121–25.
7. Boyd K. Packer, "Marriage," *Ensign*, May 1981, 15.
8. Kimball, *Marriage*, 38, 40.
9. Ezra Taft Benson, "Salvation—A Family Affair," *Ensign*, July 1992, 2–4; emphasis added.
10. Boyd K. Packer, "The Father and the Family," *Ensign*, May 1994, 19.

11. Kimball, *Marriage,* 30, 33, 42.
12. Hinckley, "What God Hath Joined Together," 73–74.
13. Ibid., 74.
14. James E. Faust, "Father, Come Home," *Ensign,* May 1993, 36–37.
15. Hugh B. Brown, *You and Your Marriage* (Salt Lake City: Bookcraft, 1960), 99–100.
16. Gordon B. Hinckley, in *Church News,* 9 September 1995, 5.
17. Benson, "Salvation—A Family Affair," 2, 4.
18. Gordon B. Hinckley, "Personal Worthiness to Exercise the Priesthood," *Ensign,* May 2002, 54.
19. Christensen, "Marriage and the Great Plan of Happiness," 65.
20. Kimball, *Marriage,* 42.
21. Gordon B. Hinckley, "Living Worthy of the Girl You Will Someday Marry," *Ensign,* May 1998, 51.
22. See John Gottman, *Why Marriages Succeed or Fail* (New York: Simon & Schuster, 1994).
23. Ezra Taft Benson, "Beware of Pride," *Ensign,* May 1989, 4, 6.
24. Marvin J. Ashton, "The Tongue Can Be a Sharp Sword," *Ensign,* May 1992, 19.

10

Happily Ever After:
Handling Anger in Marriage

John Livingstone

The first "altercation" occurred on our honeymoon. We were returning to my uncle's rustic mountain cabin after dark. Night had fallen, and as we walked the serpentine path from the parking area to the cabin, I had what I thought was a clever idea. The previous day, we had seen a little snake on this same path. Now I was carrying a large bowl in one hand and holding my new bride's hand in the other. What if I reach around my back with the bowl, I thought to myself, and touch her arm with the bowl? In the dark, she would not see what I did, and she would think a snake got her and she would jump out of her skin!

Well, she stayed in her skin, but she immediately screamed and burst into tears. But instead of getting mad at me, she got "sad" at me. That is when I began to learn about how people deal with anger. Let me explain.

I grew up in a family of boys. When something went wrong between us boys, someone got mad and someone got punched. Sometimes there was blood, sometimes not, but someone always prevailed. As the eldest son, I was used to prevailing (at least until my brother grew larger than me—then the fighting stopped, for some reason). Now that I was married to this beautiful Linda creature, I was about to learn better ways of dealing with anger than the way boys handle it. As I said, she didn't get mad, she got sad. And that turned out to be important later when, as a psychologist, I found myself meeting with couples who would sometimes shriek at each other, not only at home, but right in front of me in my office.

I remember another occasion too. It was sometime in our first two months of marriage. I think my wife conceived on our wedding night, because within a few days she felt sick, her back hurt, and she was not her bright, happy self. She was dragging, and I hoped I was not the cause. (Of course, it was because of me, but not the way I was thinking!) It happened like this: we were at my mother's house in my old bedroom. We were making the bed together. I was between the wall and the bed in an upright, but slightly cramped, position trying to help get the fitted sheet around the mattress. As we smoothed the bottom sheet, I put a hand to my aching spine and said, "My back is killing me." At that, she flopped down on the sheets and began to cry. I was stunned. Now I grew up with a four-foot-ten-inch-high single-parent mom who was a brick. I think I saw her cry maybe three times in all my childhood years, so this tearful reaction from my bride was new and very disconcerting to me. I didn't know why she was sad, but I was pretty sure it must have been something I said or did. After a slight hesitation, I thought maybe I could just softly lay the top sheet over her and continue making the bed. I felt that would be preferable to just leaving the room and letting her cry. (After all, young husbands have some sensitivity.) As I finished positioning the bedspread over the sheet and my wife, I lay down beside her and thought it best to just wait for her to respond. After several minutes, she said, "Aren't you going to say you're sorry?"

"I am really sorry," I said, mustering as much as sincerity as I could.

Another long pause on my part: "What did I do?"

"You made fun of my sore back," she replied.

It dawned on me that putting my hands on my back and saying what I did to her had come across as a mocking gesture regarding her complaints. "Uh, my back really was sore," I replied. "With my legs to the wall like that, bending over to fit the sheet was awkward, and it really did hurt." Suddenly her eyebrows rose to a peak, and she held

193

my face in her hands. "I'm sorry," she said, "I'm so sorry. I thought you were making fun of my back."

Well, again, I learned the difference between sad and mad. I was slowly learning that girls were sure different than boys. At least *this* girl was. But it was good for me. If she was angry, she wasn't showing it the same way I did. Like my brothers and I did, I mean. There were no physical blows. And that got me thinking.

Why is it that some people get angry while others don't? What is it about anger that some choose it as the first reaction while others don't make that choice? Haven't anger and contention been common human problems from the very beginning? As Cain made spiritual and temporal comparisons between himself and his brother Abel, he found himself wanting and became jealous and angry. The consequences were disastrous.

> And in process of time it came to pass, that Cain brought of the fruit of the ground an offering unto the Lord.
>
> And Abel, he also brought of the firstlings of his flock and of the fat thereof. And the Lord had respect unto Abel and to his offering:
>
> But unto Cain and to his offering he had not respect. And Cain was very *wroth*, and his countenance fell.
>
> And the Lord said unto Cain, Why art thou *wroth*? and why is thy countenance fallen?
>
> If thou doest well, shalt thou not be accepted? and if thou doest not well, sin lieth at the door. And unto thee shall *be* his desire, and thou shalt rule over him.
>
> And Cain talked with Abel his brother: and it came to pass, when they were in the field, that Cain rose up against Abel his brother, and slew him (Genesis 4:3–8; emphasis added).

Thus the hearts of Adam and Eve were broken as the first recorded murder on earth came to their family.

Temper and anger cause a great deal of pain among members of the human family. As a child, I have memories of my parents arguing. I often tried to physically step between them and distract them. Burned into my memory is a particular argument that took place upstairs in my aunt's home where my family had lived for a year. As I recall, I was five years old at the time. I don't remember the topic of their argument, but I do remember that I yelled out, "Then the workers wouldn't be able to work!" While I can't connect my outburst to the argument between them, for some reason I remember the words I used and my plaintive attempt to upstage their violent conversations. I think that those early experiences with my parents' verbal assaults resulted in a lifetime of intense desire to end contentious anger, especially in the home. When someone around me, even as an adult, chooses to be angry and raises his voice, or somehow loses control—that's how I see it, he loses control—and says or does something emotionally violent, I cringe.

Proverbs reminds us, "A wrathful man stirreth up strife: but *he that is slow to anger* appeaseth strife" (Proverbs 15:18; emphasis added). Rage causes havoc in our lives and in the lives of others. The Lord expects more of his disciples than a display of temper or anger. He commands his followers to eliminate anger, or at least control it: "But I say unto you, That whosoever is angry with his brother without a cause shall be in danger of the judgment: and whosoever shall say to his brother, Raca, shall be in danger of the council: but whosoever shall say, Thou fool, shall be in danger of hell fire" (Matthew 5:22).[1] The apostle Paul's comment in the King James Version was changed by Joseph Smith: "Can ye be angry, and not sin?" (JST Ephesians 4:26). Anger is a sin! Elder Bruce R. McConkie commented, "According to the gospel standard, unrighteous anger is evil whether provocation precedes it or not."[2]

Anger is often at the heart of domestic disputes that range from a minor tiff to full-blown verbal and physical assaults. We can be hurt deeply *by* anger, and we can hurt *with* anger. It seems that anger can be used as a verbal blunt instrument, as a mechanism to manipulate another's behavior, or as a weapon of mass destruction! Anger is an outward sign of inward turmoil. If we resolved the inner concern, outward anger would be greatly reduced or eliminated. Why would anyone use rage against a member of their own household? How can we resolve the inner issues that cause so much outward hostility?

As a young husband, I learned that my sweetheart wanted to talk. I mean *really* talk. Superficial conversation was not good enough for her. She wanted my undivided, whole, and rapt attention, and she wanted it often, or so it seemed to this barely-returned-missionary husband. I was amazed that she wanted my opinion on so many things, things I didn't even know I had any opinion about at the time! But because I loved her, and I wanted her to love me, I listened to her. And I talked. I answered. I asked. I learned from her the importance of feelings.

Now let me see if I can explain what I mean (which is really what she meant) about feelings. I want to discuss the difference between feelings and emotions. We don't normally differentiate between the two. But for the purposes of understanding and discussing anger and its resolution, I'm going to clearly separate them.

Feelings

Feelings come to us humans automatically. We experience them routinely. We can't really control them or their onset. They are a part of everyday life and come to us as the result of things and events that happen to us. Let me illustrate the point:

Shock, for example, is a feeling that comes to us automatically from a surprise event. Imagine your spouse throwing a glass of water at you. If it is totally unexpected, or if it is ice water, you are surprised and shocked. Now, you don't choose to feel shocked. It just happens. That's the way feelings are. They are unpredictable. And it is human nature to be shocked when we experience a traumatic event (a friend dies unexpectedly, we slip on the ice, we run into another car, and so forth). The point is that feelings come unexpectedly.

Embarrassment is another feeling that just comes on us. If a couple shares a romantic moment at the husband's work, for example, and during a rather passionate kiss a co-worker suddenly opens the door, feelings of embarrassment flood over both of them—even if they are married. They were not planning on this feeling. It just happened as the event occurred.

Hurt is another feeling. When someone you respect says something negative about you publicly or privately, you experience a feeling of hurt. (The more important the person is to you, the more hurt you feel). On the other hand, if some stranger unexpectedly yells at you, it may shock you, but you're not likely to experience hurt because the person is not your acquaintance. But when the statement or action is from your own child or parent, or especially a mate—ouch!

Frustration also fits in this category. And feelings of hurt, frustration, embarrassment, and shock are common across all cultures.

Worry is also a feeling. If a spouse does not arrive home at the time we expect, we worry. If their arrival is delayed, our level of worry may increase. Where could she be, we ask ourselves? Why is she not here? We can generate a host of fearful outcomes in our mind. Has there been an accident? Did the car's battery go dead? What if she has been injured?

We all have them. Feelings are the stuff of which life is made. We experience a wide range of them, and they come to us naturally on a daily basis. Feelings are wonderful. They let us know we are alive. They are reactions to life's experiences. And our feelings matter. We are also interested in what others feel. In addition to knowing what happened to other people, we want to know what they were feeling. Perhaps that is a reason why media talk shows are successful. Viewers identify with others' feelings. We don't care so much about "processed" feelings. We want to know what the original feelings were like. We relate to them, because of our own experiences. We compare our experiences and feelings with theirs to see if we are "normal."

Emotions

Emotions differ from feelings. Emotion may be viewed as "processed" or interpreted feelings. In this sense, feelings are the mother to emotion. Emotions come out of us, whereas feelings can be retained. Emotion is what we generate within ourselves when we feel something. (The "e" in "emotion" comes from the Latin and Greek term *ex,* meaning "out" or "from" and when combined with *motion* literally means to "move out or from").[3] Emotions, therefore, "come out of us." We can talk *about* our feelings, but with emotions, we actually "emote" them. Emotions can be displayed verbally or nonverbally. And, unlike feelings that come to us unpredictably, we decide what emotion, if any, we will display publicly. A few examples will illustrate the point:

Suppose your sweetheart comes through the door after being out later than you anticipated. Seeing him safely walk through the door may resolve your initial feelings of worry, but you may choose to emote something entirely different from worry. The more you think about it, the more you're upset he didn't call. He has a cell phone. You weren't worried for nothing. How inconsiderate when you were so worried! The anger in your voice replaces the original feelings of worry, as you choose now to emote anger. The worry has disappeared, but you replace it with anger. Emotion can cover up initial feelings like a smokescreen. Negative emoting can occur so forcefully that our original feelings are eclipsed entirely by what we choose to emote. Perhaps this is what Paul, Nephi, and Mormon meant when they used the term "past feeling" in the scriptures (Ephesians 4:19; 1 Nephi 17:45). "Behold, thou knowest the wickedness of this people; thou knowest that they are without principle, and *past feeling;* and their wickedness doth exceed that of the Lamanites" (Moroni 9:20; emphasis added).

People can become so emotionally angry that their normal feelings are lost.

I remember an interchange with my wife when our oldest daughter was about nine years old. I gave our daughter some instructions, and later I thought I heard my wife contradict what I told her. It hurt me. I felt it immediately. As I thought about it, my pride called for a reaction, an emotional reaction. So, I raised my voice and "hurt back," so to speak. (That's how emotion works. If we are not Christ-like in character, we may emote to get even.) My wife cried and headed out the door for a walk. I was left wondering. Some psychologist I was! Why couldn't I use all that training, which I used to help others, in my own situation?

When she returned (thankfully, she did) we went into the bedroom, reclined on the bed, and talked for a long time. (I seem to talk better while I am looking at the ceiling in the master bedroom.) My anger died down (read: I *decided* not to be angry anymore), and we were able to discuss what happened and how we both felt. I felt stupid (a feeling I have become accustomed to) and sincerely apologized to her. That discussion paved the way for a lengthy talk about what we had both experienced.

It is important to understand that it is you and I who decide to become angry. We decide what emotion to emote. It doesn't "just happen" like feelings do. We interpret a specific situation, and then we decide what emotion we are going to display (or we may choose none).

Consider this example: imagine going out to your car in the parking lot and finding the driver's side door smashed. Imagine the *feeling* that would automatically generate inside you. You look around and see a rusty, old, 1980 Camaro "burning rubber" at the far end of the parking lot. The driver appears to be a teenage boy with a girlfriend next to him in the front seat. He is laughing and tire-screeching "doughnuts" for fun! It's suddenly clear to you what happened. This kid was doing stunts with the car, trying to impress his girlfriend, and ran into your car and then had the gall to leave the scene without a note.

His car stalls, and you start marching toward him. He looks up and sees you coming, and you perceive a frightened, desperate look in his eyes. He keeps trying to start the engine, but it won't start. As you walk faster towards him, you are sure you see his eyes widening.

As you near the stalled car, however, you realize someone is calling loudly to you. "Excuse me, sir—is that your car?" You turn toward the individual, a well-dressed man who seems strangely familiar. "I have to apologize to you," he says, "I carelessly backed my car into yours." You then notice the man is your stake president.

You look back at the teenager trying to start his car. It was not him who smashed your car, after all. It was the stake president. What happens now to the "emotions" that you were going to level at the young driver? What do you do? How do you handle it now that you see the mix-up? Do you say the same thing to the stake president that you were about to say to the young man in the Camaro? No doubt your attitude and voice would change immediately. You would not say the same things or use the same tone of voice with the stake president that you were about to use on the teenager.

The point here is that we *can* change which emotion we display, and we can do it rather quickly. We can decide to be angry, or we can decide *not* to be angry. We have the capacity to make the choice.

Overcoming the choice of anger is difficult for most of us because it requires a humility that most of us struggle to develop. I remember a visiting Church leader who had the congregation repeat aloud nine words: "I am sorry. I was wrong. I love you." As I repeated it out loud with others in the congregation, I realized that an apology can reduce negative emotions. Being defensive, on the other hand, usually causes negative emotions to rise. Controlling the "rise" is critical to managing anger.

Jealousy is an example of an emotion that we choose. If I arrive home and find my wife hugging a tall, dark, and handsome stranger

200

in our driveway, I will have immediate feelings. When I discover that this is her long-lost cousin from Milwaukee, I likely will not mention my initial feeling to her. If this is our new neighbor, I may choose to emote jealousy. But *I* decide to be jealous. I may not talk to her about my initial feeling, but I choose to emote jealousy. If I obscure my original feeling and choose to display jealousy as a means to hurt her, then I create the very problem I want to avoid. On the other hand, an exchange with her about my initial feelings may soften her heart and help her understand how surprised I was to see her hugging another man and how uncomfortable I was at seeing her in his embrace.

Hate and *rage* are emotional decisions we make. We must consciously decide to hate something (stoplights) or someone (a robber). I cannot make you hate me; I can't make you angry; I can't make you jealous. I may shock, embarrass, hurt, frustrate, or worry you, but I cannot make or force you to be angry, jealous, or hateful. You must choose that outcome on your own. You don't decide what you *feel*, but you do decide what to *emote*. Feelings come spontaneously, while we choose emotions from a variety of responses open to us based on our interpretation of the initial feeling. The Lord taught his disciples:

"Love your enemies, bless them that curse you, do good to them that hate you, and pray for them which despitefully use you, and persecute you; that ye may be the children of your Father which is in heaven: for he maketh his sun to rise on the evil and on the good, and sendeth rain on the just and on the unjust" (Matthew 5:44–45).

We can *decide* to love someone, bless them, be positive with them, rather than be angry.

Case Study

As a last resort, Greg and Melissa (names changed) came to talk with me about their troubled marriage. (Most counselors see people at the "end of their rope," who "have had the last straw," or who are "at their wit's end.") Greg's temper seemed to be the root of the couple's struggles. His moodiness and lightning-quick temper alienated Melissa and the children. They were obviously miserable, and so was he. But he assumed that he had little control over his angry outbursts. They just seemed so natural. "That's just me," he rationalized. But the more we talked about how feelings came to him, the more he came to realize that he was in charge of the emotions he could display. He could decide on his response.

We started out with a simple proposition: "Shout 'stop!' in your mind," I suggested to him, "when you feel yourself emoting anger. Make a different choice. Think about the feeling that first influences you to choose anger as a response." (If you can stop a habitual choice of anger midstream, you can more easily see how you are affecting yourself and others. Often we simply fuel more anger from our initial feelings.) Understanding the relationship between feelings and emotions will help us make better choices—not unlike the earlier example of the stake president and the teenaged driver.

"When was your last anger episode?" I asked him. He complained about a "back-seat driver" comment Melissa made just as they were driving to our appointment. And as he talked about the incident, he really "got into it." It was creating negative feelings again just thinking about and describing what she said.

The three of us looked at this episode in slow motion. "What feeling caused you to choose anger?" I asked him. My question caused them both to think back to the incident. I went through a list of feelings with him:

"Were you shocked by what she said?"

"No."

"Frustrated?"

"No."

"Worried?"

"No."

"Well, maybe I was hurt," he finally blurted out. "She asked me if I saw this kid on the bike. Of course I saw the boy. She must think I'm an idiot."

"So if you felt hurt or stupid because of what she said," I repeated, "what if you had talked to her about the feelings you were feeling *rather* than immediately choosing to show your anger? In fact, let's try it right here, right now. Let's say you're in the car, and Melissa has just made her comment about the child on the bike to you. What could you say that would not be a knee-jerk reaction of anger? Give it a try."

He hesitated. Role playing is sometimes hard the first time you try it. "I don't know . . . " he trailed off. "You said she thinks you're an idiot," I reminded him. "What if you just said something like, 'When you ask me a question like you did about the child on the bike, it makes me feel dumb.' Try saying that to Melissa." So he did. And he didn't sound mad when he said it.

"Good job," I encouraged.

"And how would you have reacted to his saying it that way?" I asked Melissa.

"It was okay," she responded, "and I can see what he means now."

"What difference does it make in your relationship to talk about how you feel rather than just getting angry about something?" I asked them both. It was obvious that anger had become rather automatic and habitual to them, and they really weren't thinking about what feelings prompted the negative response. Greg and Melissa were Latter-day Saints, so I reached for my scriptures and turned to Doctrine and Covenants 121:43 and commented that as Latter-day Saints we want to emote love rather than chastise another or choose anger. The Lord counseled:

"Reproving betimes with sharpness, when moved upon by the Holy Ghost; and then showing forth afterwards an increase of love toward him whom thou hast reproved, lest he esteem thee to be his enemy."

I explained to them that when we are covenant partners in marriage, the Lord expects us to show forth "an increase of love" after any negative incident or misunderstanding. This allows us to "sandwich" correction or chastening between expressions of love and caring. "The 'sandwich' would look like this," I said, holding up three fingers to punctuate my point:

1. Express genuine care for the other.

2. Talk about what feelings both are (or were) feeling.

3. Express love and caring again so that the spouse (or child) knows you are correcting or reproving with love and kindness.

I explained to them that *betimes* is an old English word that means "promptly," which suggests the Lord would have us reprove quickly so that the one being chastened or corrected or advised will make the connection between the incident and the correction. *Sharpness* may not only mean "strongly" but "with clarity," as one would focus a pair of binoculars or a camera lens. If we express positive feelings encompassed by love, then anger will either dissipate or we will not choose it as an appropriate response because we already dealt with our initial feelings.

"So, how could you have done the 'sandwich' in the car-driving incident?" I asked.

"Uh, gee, I'm not sure . . . " was Greg's response, but I could tell he was thinking about it. I commented that often as men, we don't express love feelings outside the bedroom and even then, our love may not be as obvious to our wives as we think it is. "What if you said something like, 'Thanks, honey, for being on the lookout. I saw the boy on the bike. Sometimes when you make a comment like that I feel a little dumb, as if you don't think I am paying attention or watching carefully.'

"Would that be close to something you could say without sounding insincere?" I asked Greg.

"I could say something like that," he responded.

"Go for it," I asked. And he did. He didn't say it exactly as I did, and I was glad, because it came from him; he owned it, and it was close enough that Melissa gave a coy little smile.

"Did that sound a little better to you?" I asked her.

"Oh, yes, it is so much better," she answered.

I could tell from the look and budding smile that this was helpful. "Okay, that's the point. If you will stop the anger before it gets away from you, you can assess the situation and decide on a more Christlike emotion.

"So, let's review: You are going to ask yourself this question: 'What am I feeling right now?' Then describe the feelings you have in a gentle and straightforward way. Be humble and not accusing or defensive." I then pointed out the need for Greg to show forth love after his "feeling" comment, and I asked him how he could do that.

"I'd probably touch her leg or something," he indicated.

"Do it," I suggested.

As he gently reached for her thigh, they both burst into laughter and the tension was gone.

This strategy in dealing with anger is an important aid to healing. To be able to say something positive like, "I love you, Greg, but I have to tell you that when you answered me so roughly it hurt my feelings." "But I want you to know I love you" puts the correction in its proper context. It must be a genuine expression. Correcting or chastening someone in the absence of love may simply trade hurt for hurt.

The father, mother, husband, wife, teacher, or administrator who can overcome a tendency to choose anger as the first emotion is also making progress as a human being. Most people hesitate to deal with difficult people or situations and will go "way out of their way" to avoid contention. But then the problem is never resolved; it is perpetuated—and then it can become habitual. Being able to deal with difficulties kindly and directly instead of running from them reduces fearfulness in relationships, places problems in their proper perspective, and clarifies individual feelings rather than creating anger with its usual alienation.

I invited Greg and Melissa to not only practice this strategy a few times before going to bed that night, but to share the principle with their children. That way their entire family could learn to deal with feelings and emotions in a healthy way.

Historical Perspective

For years it was thought by many psychologists that the repression of anger did more mental and physiological damage than did the expression of outward anger. For a time "encounter groups" were formed that encouraged people to release their pent-up anger as a cathartic means to resolve the damage they assumed would take place if anger was repressed. Individuals were encouraged to punch pillows or beat symbolic objects with foam baseball bats. However, physiologists and psychologists learned over a period of time that the opposite is actually true. Expressing anger directly to other people can not only destroy relationships, but it also damages the one doing the expressing! An individual's heart and arteries are not strengthened by temperamental outbursts.[4]

With a solution as simple as stopping ourselves when feelings are generated and then choosing a more kind or loving expression than what the "natural man" would choose, we can eliminate venting negative emotions. We do not need to use emotions to hide feelings. Rather than choose to be mad or angry with the people we live with, we can make better choices in the way we respond to each other. From a gospel perspective we realize that negative behavior not only offends individual family members, but it also offends the Lord's Spirit.

Humbly talking with each other about individual hurts, without negative emoting, makes us stronger as a marital team, because we come to understand the sensitivities of those we hold dear. Moroni understood this principle when the Lord told him: "And if men come unto me I will show unto them their weakness. I give unto men weakness that they may be humble; and my grace is sufficient for all men that humble themselves before me; for if they humble themselves before me, and have faith in me, then will I make weak things become strong unto them" (Ether 12:27).

If you or someone you love has a serious problem with anger, consider the difference between feelings and emotions, and help them to understand this principle. Understanding this simple difference can bring about healthy changes in the way spouses relate to each other and how parents and children interact.

Eliminating Anger

I talked earlier about eliminating anger. That, of course, is the ideal solution. Anger is not an acceptable response for those who are mature disciples of the Lord Jesus Christ. Recall that he chastised the most righteous Nephites because of the contention and anger they were emoting among themselves. He explained:

"He that hath the spirit of contention is not of me, but is of the devil, who is the father of contention, and he stirreth up the hearts of men [and women] to contend with anger, one with another. Behold, this is not my doctrine, to stir up the hearts of men with anger, one against another; but this is my doctrine, that such things should be done away" (3 Nephi 11:29–30).

Sometimes we grow up in homes where temper and anger are frequently displayed, and we tend to model our parents' relationship. However, as we come to understand the purposes of marriage and family life in the eternal scheme of things, we realize that to make angry judgments about or to those we say we love is unacceptable.

As spouses, we are learning from each other how to relate to each other in healthy ways. Marriage is a new adventure for us. We've never done this before in all eternity. And we want our marriage to last past this mortal life. Also, we are parenting the very children of Heavenly Father, and he is concerned about how we are treating his children. He entrusts them to us so that we may learn together how to develop healthy relationships.

The Lord's remedy for anger does not stop at merely avoiding anger. We are invited to return good for evil (see Matthew 5:44–45). Resisting the urge to emote in negative ways entitles us to greater freedom from anger. As we come to understand gospel doctrine more perfectly, and as we gain greater love for our family members, we avoid angry responses in the first place. That is what Greg and Melissa did. Of course, we occasionally slip and err, but we repent and apologize and strive to do better next time. We do not want to return anger for anger. The Lord counseled us to turn the other cheek (see Matthew 5:39). Elder Dallin H. Oaks emphasized this point in quoting another writer:

> In a stimulating analysis of the application of this commandment in the circumstances of our day, Leonard E. Read, the long-time editor of *The Freeman,* concluded that it meant "not to argue with anyone. . . . In a word, away with confrontation!" He gave this illustration: "Now and then we experience shysterism: a broken promise, overcharge, underquality, an attempt to 'get the best' of one. Resist not this evil; that is, pay no heed; not a scolding word; simply walk away and fail to return. While resistance will harden the malefactor in his sins as he rises to his own defense, nonresistance leaves him alone with his soul, his shop, and his jobbery, a plight even a malefactor will ponder and understand."[5]

Summary

We cannot control the events and circumstances that naturally create feelings in our hearts. Negative feelings may come in ways that cannot always be anticipated. But emotion is a different matter. We can choose which emotions to display. We can choose to respond as men and women of God, or we can return evil for evil, as does the natural man.

My counsel is to eliminate or control anger. You can do it. And you can reach out and help others in your family to do it. Just shout

"Stop!" to yourself in your mind. Take control of your emotions rather than suffering, or causing others to suffer, because of your inability to master the feeling-emotion connection. Ponder and work on making positive choices to negative stimuli. Manifest love and kindness when you talk about your feelings. Be kind and charitable in the way you respond when your own sweetheart or child shares intimate topics with you. Work on controlling and eliminating temper—especially in your home. The next time you start to choose to be irritated, shout "Stop!" in your mind and think through what you are doing and make a better, more Christlike choice.

Eliminating or controlling your temper will improve your marriage and family life immensely. Anger and temper are the great destroyers of marriages and family life. Try it in your workplace, too. Don't just intellectualize it. Make it one of your character traits. If you gain mastery over your temper, your chances for living "happily ever after" greatly improve, and you will more closely approach the life required of a celestial candidate.

Notes

1. Both the Joseph Smith Translation and the Book of Mormon eliminate the words "without a cause" (see JST Matthew 6:24 and 3 Nephi 12:22).
2. Bruce R. McConkie, *Doctrinal New Testament Commentary*, 3 vols. (Salt Lake City: Bookcraft, 1965–73), 1:222.
3. *The American Heritage Dictionary of the English Language*, 4th ed. (Boston: Houghton Mifflin, 2000).
4. See Aron Wolfe Siegman, "Cardiovascular Consequences of Expressing and Repressing Anger," in Aron Wolfe Siegman and Timothy W. Smith, *Anger, Hostility, and the Heart* (Hillsdale, N.J.: Lawrence Erlbaum Associates, 1994), 173–97.
5. Dallin H. Oaks, *The Lord's Way* (Salt Lake City: Deseret Book, 1991), 143.

11

The Couple Connection

Charles B. Beckert

I said good-bye to the couple with whom I had been talking and looked at my appointment book. My next scheduled appointment was to be a double counseling session, one the wife had told me on the phone would provide hope for the marriage or confirm her desire for a divorce. I had encountered this type of pressure before and have never felt comfortable with it. Other than this warning, I had no idea what I would be facing during the next two hours but hoped that each partner would be willing to listen and be honest in their responses.

I opened the door that separated the counseling office from the waiting room and glanced to see if the "new" couple had arrived. There were two people in the room but I wasn't certain if they were together. These two individuals were sitting in the small waiting area as far apart as was physically possible. I did notice that one was a man and the other a woman; still, for a moment, I wondered if I had scheduled two couples for the same hour. My question was answered as I called out the names of Marty and Jodi. They both stood and looked at me but not at each other. It was obvious from the outset that we had some work to do.

I invited them into the inner office and noticed again that their preference seemed to be to sit as far apart as possible. I caught this indication before they sat down and directed them to two chairs that had been placed next to each other and turned slightly so two people could see one another and interact more comfortably. Following a few brief introductory comments, they began to unfold their story. During the initial ten or so minutes they apologized more than once for seeking counseling so late in their discomfort. Their story indicated that they had been experiencing marital problems for several years, and it was the imminent threat of divorce and the realization of what a separation or divorce might mean to their six children and to their financial situation that brought them in for help. They wanted to make certain their marriage could not be salvaged and that the decision to divorce was right for them. They had both decided they would try counseling one last time. If it didn't help, they would pursue either a separation or a divorce. The warning I had received when the appointment was made was confirmed.

From the description of their home life, it was evident this couple was as "disconnected" as a couple could be while still living under one roof. They worked opposite shifts, slept in separate bedrooms, never dated, and didn't even go to church in the same car. Once in the chapel, however, they sat together—but they informed me this was only for the sake of appearance. They had all the earmarks of being "married singles." After hearing both sides of the story I thought, "To help this couple become reconnected is going to be a real challenge." I explained to them the best I could what our plan of action might be. From the outset, we would assume they had been deeply in love when they married. Once we had agreed to this assumption, we would try to discover what had gone wrong with their relationship and caused them to do everything they could to avoid one another. Secondly, we would discuss and suggest some strategies that would help them regain a comfortable and fulfilling closeness and allow them to enjoy their marriage if each was willing to make some changes. I handed them a small card upon which was written the following statement: *"If nothing changes, nothing will change."* I wanted them both to realize that they could not continue behaving toward one another as they had been and expect anything to be different. Some things would have to change. They nodded in agreement, and I chose to ignore the "duh!" look on their faces.

Following the discussion of a basic plan, I was interested in further assessing the nature of their relationship and wanted to do so from individual perspectives. To accomplish this I handed each of them a sheet of paper containing the following words and phrases and asked them to mark the line that represented where, in their opinion, their relationship stood at the present time. The words were presented in descending order and read like this:

Successful: at the top.
Succeeding: in the process of growing.
Sailing: moving but not gaining.
Striving: putting forth effort to succeed.
Surviving: barely making it.
Struggling: not quite making it.
Sliding: slipping and going downhill.
Sinking: going under.
Submerged: under the surface and finding it difficult to breathe.
Sunk: at the bottom.

We discussed each of the options and any personal implications they might see, and then they marked their sheets. Marty was the more optimistic of the pair and checked the "Sliding" box. Jodi grimaced as she marked a darker "X" next to "Submerged." Based on their individual responses to this abbreviated exercise, it was obvious that Jodi was the more discouraged of the two. Marty appeared a little confused and had what looked to me like a worried look on his face.

My next question was designed to provide further clues as to how each felt about the marriage. There were several questions I wanted answers for. Was there still a spark between the two of them, or had the fire burned completely out? Were they discouraged to the point that change would be unlikely for either or both of them?

One question I like to pose in an initial session has to do with what brought the couple to the point of deciding to marry in the first place. I generally direct this question to the partner I feel may offer the most helpful answer. I will admit that once in a while the question backfires on me and I have some repair work to do, but generally speaking, people come in for counseling before the fire has been totally extinguished. I selected Marty to answer the question, feeling Jodi needed the boost an expected positive answer could provide. "Marty," I asked, "out of all the girls in the world whom you could have married, what was it about Jodi that caught your eye and touched your heart to the degree that you chose her?" It took a little coaching, but then Marty caught on and began talking about their early relationship, how much fun they had together, things they did together, and how they were able to talk with one another. He continued by saying how great it was for him to find someone he could share his thoughts and feelings with without worrying about rejection. Jodi's interest was sparked by what she heard Marty say, and I saw her reach up and brush a small tear from her cheek. "There is still a spark," I thought.

When Marty finished I posed the same question to Jodi, and although she struggled to express the positive nature of their early relationship, once started she mentioned many of the same ideas Marty had expressed. She added how grateful she was for her feelings of safety when she was with Marty in their early years. Although Marty didn't cry, his face indicated an intense interest in what Jodi was sharing, and as she concluded her comments he reached over and touched her knee. She did not pull back or make any attempt to remove his hand. "Another positive connection," I thought.

This brief experience led us to a general discussion on how people fall in love in the first place—and how they fall out of love in the last place. I stressed with Marty and Jodi that in my opinion they had not "fallen out of love" but rather had become disconnected. I have found that to most people the phrase "falling out of love" is far more discouraging and permanent than the concept of "being disconnected," which seems to suggest a temporary condition.

We talked about how couples become connected while they are dating, and we came up with this list of what Marty and Jodi did:

They anticipated and prepared for each date.

They dressed to impress or at least to not depress their partner.

They provided surprises for their partner.

They talked and listened for hours together. (At least they told their parents that was what they were doing so late into the night.)

They tried to do things for each other.

They did things with each other.

They treated each other with courtesy, respect, and dignity.

They submitted their will to the will of their partner. (At least each of them felt they were doing so.)

They laughed at their partner's stories and jokes, even those that were not so funny.

They viewed their partner as a "whole" or "total" person, basically overlooking many of the minor flaws existing in most of us.

Defining how two people make the transition from a positive connection to a damaged connection is as easy as considering the opposites of the behaviors listed above. As we reviewed the opposite behaviors, Jodi and Marty were squirming in their chairs. In that dialogue, both were able to identify several behaviors that had worked to bring them together and that they were not presently doing. They each expressed a little embarrassment at the realization of their personal neglect of their marriage.

Our next challenge for this initial counseling session was to try to identify, other than the neglected behaviors noted, specific attitudes and actions that had helped lead to their disconnection. On the white board located in the office, we created two columns. Above the column on the left we wrote: *"That which makes a connection"* and above the column on the right we wrote: *"That which breaks a connection."* One by one, specific elements were written below the appropriate heading. We will identify these characteristics and offer a brief commentary after each addition.

That Which Makes a Connection	That Which Breaks a Connection
Edifying Communication	*Corrupt Communication*

There is an interesting scriptural challenge in Ephesians 4:29 relative to communication attitude and practices. It reads: "Let no corrupt communication proceed out of your mouth, but that which is good to the use of edifying, that it may minister grace unto the hearers." The message is clear. We should share thoughts, ideas, and feelings with one another only when they build or enhance our partner, and at the same time we should avoid saying anything that tends to corrupt or destroy the other. Marty and Jodi quickly admitted that, in recent years, the majority of their discussions were of the "corrupting" variety and that they had not recently been moved to share positive and helpful things with one another. Marty requested some examples of what might be labeled "corrupt communication," and I offered the following to help clarify.

It has been my experience that prolonged silence can create some very difficult problems, because the receiver is left with the responsibility of determining what the partner may be feeling or thinking. I suggested to Marty that sarcasm was another form of corrupt communication, because the recipient is never certain as to whether the words were spoken in jest or in seriousness. Deception is generally corrupting, and as a tool of the devil it is never edifying. Similarly, criticism, which is based on personal judgments, is generally disruptive and harmful. We can share frustrations and feelings with our mate without being critical of them or their values. Two additional examples of corrupt communication are profanity and angry outbursts. Each of these behaviors offends the Holy Spirit and insults or injures one's partner. Any intimidating threats we might make in an attempt to defend ourselves provide another example of corrupt communication. Such threats, whether referring to a person or to the relationship, will increase the distance between the couple. Threats never bring two people closer.

In my desire to help Marty and Jodi make their discussions more edifying than corrupting, I suggested that edifying communication contains words of encouragement and truth, helpful feedback, sincere compliments, words of support and comfort, and words containing timely information. Communication of this variety will make and maintain a positive connection.

The next points we listed on the board were:

That Which Makes a Connection	That Which Breaks a Connection
Edifying Communication	Corrupt Communication
Respect and Courtesy	*Disrespect and Rudeness*

We are challenged in 1 Corinthians 7:3 to "let the husband render unto the wife due benevolence: and likewise also the wife unto the husband." Benevolence has been defined as "a kindly disposition toward another." In our discussion about this element of their marriage, both Marty and Jodi agreed that they generally treated their friends and associates much more politely than they did one another. They were beginning to see more clearly why they had become so disconnected in their marriage.

I brought up a third variable to see if it played a role in their current problems, but both stated (rather emphatically, I might add) that this was not an issue in their marriage and never had been. I add it to our list for the sake of those who are reading this chapter.

That Which Makes a Connection	That Which Breaks a Connection
Edifying Communication	Corrupt Communication
Respect and Courtesy	Disrespect and Rudeness
Purity in Mind and Body	*Impurity of Thought and Action*

Even though this did not appear to be a problem within the Marty-Jodi relationship, I would like to share a thought or two about it. Relationships are disconnected when partners prove unfaithful and disloyal to one another. It has been my experience that one can demonstrate infidelity in a marriage without experiencing a physical and sexual affair. Emotional adultery is very real and usually has a major negative impact on the connectedness between the spouses. We live in a computer generation, and the World Wide Web has been blamed for many evil things, as well as lauded for countless contributions. Internet pornography has been instrumental in a host of marital breakups. While many males fall victim to the graphic displays available on the web, females often fall prey to what happens in "chat rooms" and the relationships that often result. Obviously, these two experiences are not exclusively male and female, but they occur primarily as we have noted.

The more Jodi and Marty shared about their life together, the clearer a major problem became. These two had been living "parallel" lives rather than truly joining in a marriage partnership. Individually, they were doing okay, but as a partnership they were failing. Rather than cooperating and supporting one another in various activities they had become vicious opponents and competitors, desiring to win at any cost. There was constant friction between them as each resisted the efforts of the other. Both had become extremely discouraged with the lack of support and understanding coming from the other, and

That Which Makes a Connection	That Which Breaks a Connection
Edifying Communication	Corrupt Communication
Respect and Courtesy	Disrespect and Rudeness
Purity in Mind and Body	Impurity of Thought and Action
Encouragement and Cooperation	*Discouragement and Resistance*

this neglect resulted in further weakening their connection. Even without obvious resistance, parallel lives place a heavy strain on the relationship. In relationships where each partner does his or her own thing with little consideration and concern for the partner, connections become very difficult to maintain. The Lord stated that it was "not good that the man should be alone" (Genesis 2:18) and the prophet Lehi added that "men are, that they might have joy" (2 Nephi 2:25), suggesting the necessity of there being more than one individual if true joy is to be experienced. One of the most poignant references suggesting the desirability of working together can be read in Ecclesiastes 4:9–12. It reads:

> Two are better than one; because they have a good reward for their labour.
>
> For if they fall, the one will lift up his fellow: but woe to him that is alone when he falleth; for he hath not another to help him up.
>
> Again, if two lie together, then they have heat: but how can one be warm alone?
>
> And if one prevail against him, two shall withstand him; and a threefold cord is not quickly broken.

Marty asked me to reread this reference and as I did, he took a deep breath, leaned back in the chair and lifted his eyes to the ceiling. After a couple of minutes, he lowered his head, looked straight at Jodi and said, "It's like we haven't even been married, isn't it?" Jodi nodded. They both knew they would have been happier and their connection stronger if they had chosen to work together more often.

At this point in our discussion I began to sense a change in their basic attitudes toward each other and their marriage. They were actually holding hands as they talked. I mentioned this to them and they glanced at one another without saying anything further about the topic.

I used their hand holding as a segue to another point I wanted to write on the white board and to which I wanted to call their attention. So far in our conversation, the topic of their physical relationship had not come up, and I wanted to ascertain its condition in the marriage. Many times a broad description of the physical relationship sheds valuable light on a couple's relationship in general. So we added it to our list.

That Which Makes a Connection	That Which Breaks a Connection
Edifying Communication	Corrupt Communication
Respect and Courtesy	Disrespect and Rudeness
Purity in Mind and Body	Impurity of Thought and Action
Encouragement and Cooperation	Discouragement and Resistance
Emotional and Physical Closeness	*Emotional and Physical Distance*

When I initially inquired about their physical relationship, assuring them I was not interested in any details, they looked at each other

219

and then Jodi blurted out, "What physical relationship?" Her point was made and I understood. I have often pondered which comes first, the absence of intimacy or the feeling of disconnectedness. Obviously, the ideas are twins and generally very closely related; but on the other hand, sharing physical intimacy is something a couple can do whether or not they "feel" like it. With this particular couple, it was interesting that the wife was the spouse feeling neglected in this area. Marty readily admitted that for the past several months he had had little motivation and desire for physical closeness with Jodi. In fact, he stated that he had purposefully avoided situations where intimacy may have been invited. Marty and Jodi both said that they had discussed this area of their marriage many times because it had been such a strong and positive part of their early marriage relationship.

Because they said they were interested in what the scriptures might say about their marriage relationship, I invited them to read and ponder 1 Corinthians 7:4–5, which they did. Here is what it says:

> The wife hath not power of her own body, but the husband: and likewise also the husband hath not power of his own body, but the wife.
>
> Defraud ye not one the other, except it be with consent for a time, that ye may give yourselves to fasting and prayer; and come together again, that Satan tempt you not for your incontinency.

They both expressed surprise at those words and seemed eager to determine what this might mean to their relationship. They said it was intriguing to learn that both the husband and the wife have the responsibility to do what they can to fulfill the sexual needs of the other. I explained that when we marry we covenant to not become involved in a sexual situation with anyone outside of marriage—and at the same time we promise to participate in a physical relationship with our spouse. I asked them to read the Joseph Smith translation of verse five at the bottom of the page, which changes the words "defraud ye not one the other" to "depart ye not one from the other"

220

for added clarity. Marty's wink and Jodi's slight smile were exciting to watch. Something we had just read had captured their attention.

To further foster emotional and physical closeness, I suggested they not confuse certain pairs of words, as so many couples have done and continue to do. For example, they should not confuse *proximity* with *togetherness*. These are not the same, and to assume they are will result in disappointment for both. Similarly, the words *listening* and *hearing* should not be confused. Many times we hear something, but we are not listening to what is being communicated. Along that same line, couples get into trouble when they confuse *talking* with *communicating*. To *communicate* suggests an exchange of information and feelings, while *talking* may mean just talking. Talking in and of itself does not necessarily lead to closeness, while communicating generally does. I asked Marty and Jodi if they had ever confused *intentions* (things we intend to do) with *actions* (actual behavior that is often left undone), and they laughed and said they had made this mistake far too many times. Finally, and in the context of our current topic of conversation, I mentioned the word pair of *sex* and *affection*. Marty looked down, then at Jodi, and said, "That is a mistake I used to make all the time, until I just backed away, completely." Jodi nodded in agreement. I thought my point was made and that we should move on.

Another point I wanted to share with Marty and Jodi relative to intimacy was that intimacy has a meaning much broader than physical affection. To help them more fully realize that they could be close in many areas of married life, I handed them a sheet of paper that described ten areas of potential intimacy and strongly suggested how each individual area tends to impact the other nine. These are the areas the sheet contained:

Physical intimacy: Enjoying the ultimate of physical closeness.
Emotional intimacy: Being on the same wavelength and feeling close.
Intellectual intimacy: Sharing thoughts and ideas.

Aesthetic intimacy: Sharing the beauties of the world.

Creative intimacy: Sharing acts of creating together.

Recreational intimacy: Playing together.

Work intimacy: Closeness in sharing common tasks.

Conflict intimacy: Facing and struggling with challenges and differences.

Crisis intimacy: Togetherness in coping with problems and pain.

Spiritual intimacy: Experiencing the "uniting of spirits."

Although we didn't spend much time on this exercise, Marty stated that he had not recognized the possibility of being close in so many different ways. He had thought of the physical and the spiritual intimacies but not of the others. Jodi didn't think they were all equally significant and mentioned, again, how much she missed the physical closeness the two of them had previously enjoyed. Marty nodded in agreement, and we were ready to move on.

When our counseling session was almost over, I simply wrote a final note on the board.

That Which Makes a Connection	That Which Breaks a Connection
Edifying Communication	Corrupt Communication
Respect and Courtesy	Disrespect and Rudeness
Purity in Mind and Body	Impurity of Thought and Action
Encouragement and Cooperation	Discouragement and Resistance
Emotional and Physical Closeness	Emotional and Physical Distance
Continued Courtship	*Neglect of Partner and Relationship*

In the classic book *Marriage,* President Spencer W. Kimball stated:

> Love is like a flower, and, like the body, it needs constant feeding. The mortal body would soon be emaciated and die if there were not frequent feedings. The tender flower would wither and die without food and water. And so love, also, cannot be expected to last forever unless it is continually fed with portions of love, the manifestation of esteem and admiration, the expressions of gratitude, and the consideration of unselfishness.[1]

He also made the statement that more marriages die from neglect than from sin. That is an interesting thought, isn't it? It has been my experience that when a spouse feels "taken for granted," whether or not the partner so intends, the connection is severely weakened, if not broken. Without continued courtship and frequent expressions of love and concern, a couple will not be able to maintain a positive connection, and with the disconnections comes a sense of a loss of love.

Although the phrase "love is a verb" has been used so often it may sound trite, it is nonetheless true. The fact is, love is an action verb, and when treated as one in a marriage relationship, the couple remains positively connected. This perspective need not take away the excitement and enchantment of "being in love." "Being in love" is a feeling and is generally the result of being loved and of loving another. In my experience with disconnected couples, this feeling of love comes *after* the action of loving and not before. I cannot count the number of times clients have informed me that the problem in their marriage is that they no longer love their spouse. They are shocked when I agree with them and then even more surprised when I suggest they go home and love their partner. They insist they don't love them, and I persist and tell them to go home and do so. It is sometimes difficult to help them understand that to *love* someone (action verb) has little to do with being *in love* with them. When the Savior commanded us to love our neighbors, he was not suggesting that we be in love with

223

them, but that we demonstrate love by our behaviors toward them. Staying connected in marriage is greatly facilitated by loving actions. We truly can "choose to love" our mates, and from my perspective this is what Marty and Jodi needed to do.

I knew I had really unloaded on this couple during this initial session, but I didn't know if I would get a second chance. Their behavior toward one another had changed during the session, and it was my impression that they were willing to try some things to reconnect. I continued with this thought in mind.

We talked about the wonderful "date a week" message that persists throughout the Church, and they agreed they would try it. To encourage them to get started, I suggested a simple exercise that had worked for many couples. Each of them was to take five small slips of paper and, on each slip, write an activity he or she would like to enjoy with his or her partner on a date night. There were a few basic ground rules for this exercise. One was that the activity had to be within the time and money budget available to the couple. Another was that it could not create a situation where one or the other would have to compromise his or her standards. Once the ten slips had been filled out, they were to be placed in a bowl or hat and then drawn out, one at a time, early enough so arrangements could be made for the coming date. I explained that planning the dating experience in advance allowed the couple to benefit twice—once by anticipating the date, and again by participating in the date. Marty and Jodi agreed to complete the exercise.

They were a little surprised when I informed them there was more I wanted them to do. If they were serious about reconnecting as a married couple, they would need to do more than go on a date once a week. I was, in fact, planning to give them daily assignments. I hoped I wasn't pushing them too hard. I proceeded to explain what they might do as they chose to demonstrate love to each other each day. Such a list could be unending, but I thought a few specific choices might take away any excuse for not trying. I reminded them that the overall objective of these suggestions was to help them reconnect with one another by expressing love. Doing so would help them regain their old love feelings.

Here are some of the things I suggested they might do with, for, and to each other each day:

Plan the day together, either prior to bedtime or before heading out of the house in the morning.

Review the day together prior to going to bed. This is a "return and report" exercise.

Provide *appropriate* touches, hugs, and kisses. (Emphasis on "appropriate.")

Touch good-bye and touch hello, meaning that when one leaves the home for an extended time, he or she should seek out the remaining spouse and "touch" good-bye. Similarly, when one arrives home after being gone, he or she should seek out the partner and "touch" hello.

Make a timely telephone call from time to time.

Say "I love you" to one another in a way that the partner can understand and appreciate. The "Golden Rule" says we are to treat others as we would like to be treated. I do not mean to sound sacrilegious or to suggest the "Golden Rule" is incomplete, but I would suggest a "Silver Rule" to apply as we interact and express love to our spouse. This rule reads: "Do unto others as they would like it done unto them."

Demonstrate interest in and support for what your spouse may be doing.

Pray together as a couple. Some couples take turns, with the husband praying on the even-numbered days and the wife on the odd-numbered days.

To summarize this "Daisy a Day" approach, I provided Marty and Jodi with some lyrics I had written some time earlier for a marriage workshop experience. The song goes like this:

Marriage Connections

The marriage road is not a breeze;
Most do not travel it with ease.
But when we walk it hand in hand,
And connections we expand.
Then united we will stand.
Then united we will stand.

Marriage is a duet song,
Not a tune to sing alone.
One that's rich with harmony,
Which makes life full for you and me.
Connected is what we will be.
Connected is what we will be.

If one should fall, the other's there,
To lift and help with loving care.
To give support when there's a need
Will help a marriage to succeed.
Connectedness will be our creed.
Connectedness will be our creed.

We'll talk and plan the day ahead,
Review it e'er we go to bed.
We will on each a kiss bestow,
We'll touch good-bye and touch hello.
Connecting as we come and go.
Connecting as we come and go.

A timely call will do so much,
When added to a gentle touch,
With tender words like "I love you,"
To keep our love alive and true.
These are connecting things we'll do.
These are connecting things we'll do.

If problems 'tween us should arise,
We'll look each other in the eyes
And say "I'm sorry" if we're wrong,
Or forgive and then move on,
Keeping our connections strong.
Keeping our connections strong.

We do not want to walk apart,
But hand in hand and heart in heart,
Making contact through each day,
Saying what we need to say.
In love, connected, we will stay.
In love, connected, we will stay.

Chorus:
Connections, connections,
Positive connections.
They keep our marriage glowing,
Our friendship ever growing.
As mates we've been selected,
Now we must stay connected.

I heard the outside door open and close and knew the next counseling appointment had arrived. As I mentioned to Jodi and Marty that our time was gone, Jodi asked if we were going to meet again. I said, "That is up to the two of you." They looked at each other, perhaps thinking back on their feelings toward one another a couple of hours earlier. It was Marty who said, "I can't speak for Jodi, but I would like to meet again." Jodi nodded in agreement. I expressed appreciation for their trust and thanked them for their willingness to try the things we had discussed and challenged them to do so. I also warned them that some of the old negative feelings would likely creep back into their minds, and if and when that happened they should not become discouraged but move forward. I also suggested that it would be a good idea if they were to look at this counseling experience as a new beginning for their marriage. They nodded and after shaking hands with me, took each other by the hand and left the office. At least tonight, they had connected and were still a couple.

Note

1. Spencer W. Kimball, *Marriage* (Salt Lake City: Deseret Book, 1978), 46.

12

The Plague of Pornography

Rory C. Reid

Pornography in our day has become part of a "plague of biblical proportion."[1] It is the catalyst for many individual and marital problems. Pornography promotes a fraudulent message about human sexuality that creates unrealistic expectations in the mind of the consumer. Use of pornography is often associated with isolation and secrecy, which diminishes the level of intimacy in marriage relationships. Other negative consequences from pornography use include a loss of companionship of the Spirit, diminished agency, a loss of spousal trust, employment difficulties, wasting time and money—and even loss of one's Church membership. Although such losses can be devastating, pornography itself is not the primary problem. More important than the existence of pornography is the underlying motivation for why individuals use pornography for such destructive behavior.

An increasing number of people are turning to the Internet for pornography and related activities, such as illicit chat rooms, cybersex, solicitation of prostitutes, or, worse, predatory behavior towards minors. In most cases, secrecy enables and perpetuates these problems. These behaviors have devastating effects on marriages. Unfortunately, most spouses do not know how to appropriately confront a partner who is indulging in these behaviors.

It is common for spouses to report, "I knew what was going on but I remained silent because I didn't know what to say," or "I really didn't want to face the pain of confronting him so I avoided the issue, even denying it was happening." These individuals claim that remaining silent reduces the potential for conflict. Some worry that confronting a spouse about their use of pornography may jeopardize the marriage, despite their own feelings of disappointment, hurt, or frustration. They choose to ignore the "elephant in the room" and instead tiptoe around pretending it doesn't exist or affect how they think or feel. Some discover a problem and immediately confront their spouse with inappropriate comments or actions that may unintentionally make the problem worse.

Ironically, many spouses who participate in these unhealthy activities desire to abandon their behavior and free themselves from a double life, but they do not know how to disclose their secrets to their partner. For them, disclosure is viewed as a frightening experience. They fear the adverse reaction or consequences they may encounter. A typical comment is, "If I told my spouse she would leave me." Although this may occur, the majority of spouses remain in the marriage. Other pornography users defiantly indulge themselves in their online sexual pursuits despite the disapproval of their spouses or other possible consequences. For healthy intimacy to exist, the problem must be confronted and mutually discussed.

Healthy intimacy requires confronting the problem and talking about it. This honesty is a necessary step in dissolving the secrecy and establishing a relationship built on trust. This openness will include awareness and acceptance of awkward or uncomfortable truths about oneself. Unfortunately, many want to avoid talking about such things because it's too painful. Although discussing sensitive issues may be difficult, it is a necessary part of achieving a healthier relationship.

Terminology

Although pornography issues are predominantly a male problem, there are a growing number of females who become involved in these matters. Yet for the purpose of simplifying the presentation of this chapter, the author has used the pronoun *he* to refer to a person with

229

a pornography problem and the pronoun *she* to refer to the non-participating spouse.

Why People Use Pornography

Although pornography use is a complex subject with no easy answers or solutions, we can safely say that people generally engage in behaviors because they *want something* or they *want to avoid something*. In the case of pornography it may be both. Individuals usually want to avoid some type of emotional pain and replace it with feelings of pleasure, as the following story illustrates.

John[2] was married, the father of three children. After graduating from a university, he secured excellent employment with flexible hours and a comfortable salary. He purchased a home in an affluent area, served in a Church leadership position, and was involved in the community. He was popular and enjoyed the praise of friends, neighbors, co-workers, and other Church members. Because of the image he created for himself, it was a particularly shocking revelation when he confessed to his wife that he was a pornography user. I asked her to write down a list of words to describe her thoughts and feelings. I have added to her list additional feelings from other women who found themselves in similar situations: anger, betrayal, rejection, confusion, depression, disappointment, fear, guilt, responsible, frustrated, unloved, filled with despair, abandonment, rage, disgust, indifference, denial, helplessness, hopelessness, bitterness, resentment, powerlessness, discouragement, loneliness, uncertainty, doubt, hesitancy, devastation, distrust, worthlessness, suspiciousness, alienation, victimized, humiliated, anguish, and even relief. Each of these thoughts or feelings is completely normal and understandable.

John's wife's biggest question was *why?* Why did he do this? How could John jeopardize their marriage relationship like this? She wondered if she was responsible. Was she no longer attractive or sexually pleasing to him? I assured her the problem had little, if anything, to do with her and that John would most likely be struggling with this behavior regardless of whom he married. I explained to her that wives are more empowered to help their husbands when they believe they are not responsible for and not to be blamed for the problem. I suggested some reasons for pornography use that may include any or all of the following:

Attempts to escape toxic shame (a negative self-image), possibly as a carryover from childhood experiences, including deprivation of needs, family dysfunction, or abuse.

A desire to be needed or validated without investing in a relationship.

A coping mechanism to deal with stress or a reward for accomplishments.

Inability to develop or fear of developing healthy intimacy.

Boredom and curiosity.

Escape into a fantasy world that pretends to meet unmet, unrealistic, and even unknown expectations.

John's problems with coping and self-esteem began long before his use of pornography. As a child, he developed a low sense of self-worth, perhaps, he thought, from a problem with bed-wetting. His family would criticize him with shaming statements like, "What's wrong with you?" or "Why can't you control yourself?" John reported that he must have internalized these comments, which contributed to a loss of self-confidence and self-worth. Every time he wet the bed it reinforced his belief that he was somehow flawed. Not only was this behavior bad, he came to believe, but *he* was bad! Making matters worse, John's problem interfered with attending Scout camps and other activities that required an overnight stay. Socially isolated and feeling helpless, John began engaging in masturbation. Although this behavior made him feel worse, he claimed it provided a temporary escape from the pain he felt. At least this was reliable and predictable, and it was something over which he had control.

John later added pornography to the picture. (Note: He could have easily developed other maladaptive coping behaviors, such as drug and alcohol use.) Although this form of self-medication never provided long-term relief, it was his way of avoiding his emotional pain. As John grew older, his secret became the bandage for the emotional cuts or bruises he experienced, even long after the bed-wetting stopped. Interestingly, he also began excelling in other areas of his life, seeking to compensate for the guilt he carried about his secret behavior. The result was a double life.

The example of John's situation is not intended to suggest that children who struggle with bed-wetting will grow up to use pornography. Furthermore, what John reported about family ridicule may not have been accurate, but what was important is how John perceived and felt about his childhood experiences. Each client has a unique story about how they became enmeshed in pornography, but the underlying issues are usually not unique. In fact, many similar patterns emerge as we work with individuals struggling with sexual impulsivity.

One common denominator is the toxic shame mentioned earlier. This shame, which says "I'm flawed" or "I'm a bad person," may develop from unresolved family-of-origin issues or from experiences unrelated to the family but perceived by the person to be traumatic. Pornography provides escape or avoidance from unpleasant, uncomfortable or painful emotions. For such individuals, negative feelings are translated from "I feel bad" to "I am bad." Over time, distorted views about the world and other people can develop. Experiences may be exaggerated or personalized beyond the norm, and situations are catastrophized in unrealistic ways (which may be an unconscious attempt to rationalize or justify the perpetuation of the unhealthy behavior).

Regardless of the motivation, the triggers for negative emotions are numerous and influence behavior that increases over time, until a terribly addictive habit is formed. Eventually, life becomes unbearable for the individual, or attempts to compensate for toxic shame or deprivation of their needs no longer work. As Dr. David Derezotes observed: "Attempts to avoid pain never ultimately lead to a painless life, and they are likely to create new problems and suffering . . . [that] may be worse than the initial suffering. For example, an addiction might be a substitute for pain. As John Bradshaw said, 'An addict is like a man on fire who jumps into the water and then begins to drown.'"[3]

Once we recognize that pornography problems are symptoms of other issues, we can focus our attention on resolving the concerns that contribute to a person's choice to use pornography to medicate personal pain.

Where There Is Smoke There Is Fire

Just as the old adage suggests, a fire may be located by following the smoke. There are several signs that indicate pornography use. Although such signs may be more subtle than smelling alcohol on someone's breath, they often indicate a pornography habit exists. Signs include the following:

Loss of interest in sexual relations or an insatiable sexual appetite.
Introduction of unusual sexual practices in the relationship.
Diminished emotional, physical, social, spiritual, and intellectual intimacy.
Neglect of social and religious responsibilities or obligations.
Increased isolation (late or long hours on the computer); withdrawal from family.
Irregular mood swings, irritability.
Unexplained absences.
Preference for masturbation instead of marital coitus.
Sexual relations that have become rigid, rushed, without passion, and detached.
Unexplained financial transactions.
Pornography sites on the computer.

Awareness of these signs is important in detecting a possible problem, and the subsequent absence of these signs during recovery becomes a measure of a person's success in abandoning a pornography habit.

How Is a Habit Developed?

There are various stages in the road to developing a compulsive habit with pornography. Some individuals may move through these stages in a matter of months or even weeks. For others, it may take years. Elder Richard G. Scott noted the following about pornography habits: "The tragic pattern is so familiar. It begins with a curiosity that is fueled by its stimulation and is justified by the false premise that when done privately, it does no harm to anyone else. Lulled by this lie, the experimentation goes deeper, with more powerful stimulations, until the web closes and a terribly immoral, addictive habit is formed."[4]

Dr. Kimberly Young and Dr. Victor Cline, both specializing in addiction therapy, have created slightly different variations of these stages in their respective publications. Understanding these stages can help determine the severity of the problem. These stages are not always sequential. Furthermore, it is possible that an individual can experience some of the stages and not others. For example, a person may go through the first three stages, fixate on a certain type of pornography, and remain there for an extended period of time, possibly years. To assume that the person will move automatically to the next stage may result in an inaccurate assessment of the problem.

1. *Discovery.* The thrill or arousal associated with the material is encountered during this stage. This can happen accidentally or through curiosity. This stage usually refers to initial exposure rather than exposure over a prolonged period of time. There can be a "rush" because the event represents entering an area that is taboo, forbidden, or simply sensually arousing.

2. *Experimentation and Exploration.* This stage is characterized by various cognitive distortions as one rationalizes exploring or experimenting with the material: "It's just harmless fun" or "This

isn't hurting anyone." Masturbation usually accompanies this stage, powerfully reinforcing the experience.

3. *Desensitization*. As exploration and experimentation continue, desensitization takes place. In this stage, what was once shocking now becomes "normal" or even routine, thus setting the stage for escalation.

4. *Escalation*. During this stage, pornographic material becomes rougher, kinkier, or more bizarre in order for the person to achieve the same level of arousal or emotional rush.

5. *Performance*. Frequent exposure to this material introduces many sexual behaviors that a person may want to act out. This stage is characterized by a person mimicking or insisting on behavior that is depicted in the pornography. In some cases, he may attempt to experiment and act out these behaviors with a spouse or even with someone outside the marriage.

No one starts using pornography with the intention of becoming hooked on it. The process is usually gradual, but it *can* occur in a relatively short period of time. Some individuals start using pornography and within a short period of time they've developed a habit. (Consequently, prophets have been very firm in denouncing pornography, warning us to "stay away from it.") Other individuals may dabble in it now and again over the course of several years and never really get hooked or follow the stages. Each case is different, of course.

We don't have concrete explanations as to why one person may see pornography and think to himself, "This is stupid," while another person views it and becomes entrapped. Research is unclear about why people choose specific habits and not others. For example, some people turn to alcohol rather than pornography. A third group may choose both alcohol and pornography. Professional literature suggests the third group should receive treatment for both habits simultaneously to avoid reducing one behavior only to discover the person has increased the frequency of the second habit.

In the gospel context, use of pornography for any reason is wrong.

Covenant obligations require complete fidelity to Christ and to one's spouse. Tragically, some have dismissed prophetic counsel and have become entangled in this salacious material. They have become enslaved to the lusts of the flesh through the adversary's "cunning plans which he hath devised to ensnare the hearts of men" (Alma 28:13). Those who have developed a habit discover that abandoning pornography is an extremely difficult task and usually requires outside intervention.

Confronting the Problem

If a loved one is found using pornography, you need to consider carefully how the issue should be addressed and avoid making assumptions or drawing conclusions prematurely about the severity of the problem.

A neighbor once discovered her teenager drinking alcohol. Although she was concerned about his behavior, she did not label him an alcoholic. Similarly, we should avoid labeling people with pornography problems. I seldom refer to people as *addicts* when they develop a habitual pattern of pornography use, because the word has such strong connotations and possible implications. The unwanted behavior we are trying to extinguish may inadvertently be reinforced through such categorizations as the individual plays out the expectations of the labeled identity: "I'm an addict; therefore, I can't help myself." It is often difficult to know how to react appropriately after discovering a problem and what consequences are appropriate for an offending spouse.

In the context of marriage, it is typical for a spouse to immediately confront her partner after discovering pornography use. However, if the confrontation is done while emotions are high, the offending partner may react to the emotions of the spouse rather than hearing what she is trying to communicate. If a spouse enlists the support of a Church leader or therapist, she will not have to go through the process alone. The following suggestions about confronting a spouse with a pornography problem are taken from a book by Dan Gray and myself titled *Discussing Pornography Problems with a Spouse*.

Don't Enable. Oftentimes a wife may react to the discovery of a husband's behavior with prolonged silence, which can be interpreted as indifference. Denial and avoidance can also manifest themselves through silence, which then becomes a form of enabling the behavior. Ignoring the problem, whether intentionally or not, is the same as condoning the behavior. Another example of enabling is a wife who makes excuses to her husband's employer by saying he is ill when in fact he spent the night on the computer viewing pornography. People do this because they are afraid of what might happen if they confront their spouse.

Don't Accommodate. Sometimes a wife may make excuses for her husband, thus accommodating the inappropriate behavior. She may think, "It's just a phase" or "He's under a lot of stress." Others report feeling like they are partially to blame. This misperception may inadvertently justify the behavior. Although he may use pornography to cope with stress or other emotional issues, as a wife you should not assume responsibility for his choices. Inappropriate behavior is not to be tolerated. This is one battle you must win. Pornography problems must be fought, not feared.

Establish and Maintain Healthy Boundaries. Sometimes when a spouse is confronted, he may become defensive or attempt to change the focus of the real issue. "How dare you snoop around on my computer!" one man yelled to his wife. This display of anger and outrage is a manipulative tactic. It may be true that inspecting his computer was a violation of privacy. This issue can be discussed at a later time, but for now the focus is on his behavior, not yours. This man's wife appropriately responded, "We can talk about my snooping later. Right now I want to talk about the pornography."

If a spouse's behavior becomes abusive or you fear personal harm, leave the house or call the police. If an aversive reaction is anticipated, choose a safe place for the initial confrontation, such as the office of a

Church leader or therapist. You are not on trial and do not need to feel guilty about wanting to extinguish this destructive behavior in your home and marriage. Recognize that your discovery may threaten the "good guy" image he has been working so hard to maintain, and any attempts to confront this will most likely be met with resistance.

Maintaining healthy boundaries also means saying "no" to any sexual requests you may feel are wrong or inappropriate. When individuals consume pornography they are often introduced to bizarre or abnormal forms of human sexual behavior. They may attempt to have you act out these inappropriate fantasies. By submitting to his demands for unusual or bizarre sex acts, you add fuel to his fantasies, which powerfully reinforces continued use of pornography. This is likely to exacerbate the problem and may increase the likelihood of further requests, which may become more bizarre or distorted.

Don't Reinforce Distorted Beliefs or Thoughts. People who use pornography to cope with life have numerous distorted thoughts and beliefs. This creates denial as a means of avoiding pain. It is important to show appropriate empathy for such people. However, reinforcing distorted thoughts and beliefs or showing misplaced sympathy may inadvertently justify the behavior in the offending spouse's mind. For example, the following statement indicates several thinking errors: "You haven't had sex with me for so long I had to have my needs met somehow." This expression is an *excuse* used to *rationalize* sexual behavior beyond the marriage relationship. It also attempts to *redefine* the real problem of the husband's misbehavior by attempting to deflect the *blame* to his spouse. This is *emotional manipulation*. His distorted belief is that with sufficient self-pity and *excuse making*, he will induce his wife to show compassion and excuse the inappropriate behavior. An appropriate response might be, "I'm sorry you feel frustrated about your lack of sex in our marriage, and we should talk about that later. Right now, I want to talk about your pornography and self-abuse." This response avoids reinforcing thinking errors while showing respect and validation for the husband's feelings about the lack of sex. It also keeps the conversation focused.

Show Understanding without Condoning Behavior. There are many possible explanations for why someone might use pornography. It is important to show understanding about your husband's pain—but remember that that is not the real problem. However, regardless of the root cause, childhood trauma notwithstanding, those who indulge in sexual improprieties remain responsible for their behavior. Shame and other psychological issues are possible explanations, not excuses. As Latter-day Saints, we believe that moral agency by mature adults supersedes what might be termed excuses or rationalization.

It is important to realize that expressions of empathy and validation of feelings do not mean acceptance, agreement, or approval of his behavior. In fact, while you show empathy it is also important to be assertive and clearly communicate feelings and disapproval of the behavior. For example, after listening to him discuss his pain, an appropriate response might be, "I'm sorry you feel so much hurt and pain. I can understand how unfair life may seem to you, and I want you to know that I love you. But I still feel disappointed and hurt by your behavior, and I will not tolerate it in our home."

Providing support to an offending spouse is a difficult endeavor. It should be done without taking responsibility for the offensive behavior. Women will often take responsibility by thinking they are to blame. This is erroneous, unhealthy thinking. A man with a sexual compulsion could be married to the most attractive woman alive, and he would still seek illicit sexual gratification. Recently, a supermodel's husband was the last man anyone thought would be unfaithful, and yet he was caught cheating with another woman while on a business trip. The problem is rarely about the nonoffending spouse.

Communicate Your Feelings, Thoughts, and Concerns. When addressing a spouse, it is important to clearly communicate how you feel and what you expect now. This can be done without attacking or shaming. Healthy confrontation is direct but nonthreatening. The focus should be on the problem behavior and the need to express thoughts and feelings. However, with uncontrollable crying, yelling, or screaming, the objectives of the confrontation may be undermined. The attention will focus too heavily on emotions, and the message may be lost. Waiting a few days, or in some cases longer, before confronting the problem may be helpful in order to reduce the intensity of emotions. Time may increase objectivity and appropriate responses for both parties. Care must be taken, however. Waiting can become avoidance. Avoidance can create denial and perpetuate secrecy. It is important that the nonoffending spouse not let too much time pass.

If you are concerned about your ability to control your emotions, perhaps the discussion can take place in the presence of a Church leader or therapist, where interactions can be moderated by a third person.

Anticipating a Spouse's Reaction

After being confronted about inappropriate behaviors, a spouse can react in a variety of ways. Reactions may include denial, anger, blame, guilt, shame, fear, defiance, rage, contrition and remorse, humility, relief, avoidance, withdrawal, humor, sarcasm, or ambivalence. Paying attention to the emotional reactions of a spouse will help you determine how to continue responding to the problem at hand. The following is again taken from the book *Discussing Pornography Problems with a Spouse,* by Dan Gray and myself:

Denial. A common reaction on the part of the user is denial. For example, one spouse claimed, "I haven't a clue how those images got on our computer," which constitutes a complete refusal to acknowledge that a problem exists. Another form of denial is minimizing. This form manifests itself when someone admits awareness but minimizes intent. A person may say, "I accidentally came upon a pornography site and that's why those images are on our computer," when in fact it wasn't an accident at all. Although both responses may at first sound legitimate, if many images are present or if an extensive history of adult web sites in the Internet browser exists, then the likelihood of it being an accident is remote.

If denial is the reaction, and there has been sufficient evidence to suspect or substantiate a serious problem, then it may be necessary to reaffirm your position more assertively. After listening to her husband adamantly deny any use of pornography, one wife responded, "I've stood at your office door on several occasions when you were staring at pornography on your computer. Each time, it was obvious to me that you were in no hurry to turn your monitor off. I wanted to give you the benefit of the doubt, but realized I could not." This spouse then communicated clearly how she felt about the problem. She also expressed her concern that her husband had attempted to lie in order to keep his behavior a secret. All of this was done in a nonthreatening way and her husband confessed to a problem, which they were then able to work through together.

Avoidance and Resistance. Avoiding responsibility or account-ability for a behavior enables a person to also avoid consequences. One form of avoidance is a dismissive response: "I don't want to talk about it." In this case, denial is replaced with a reluctance to talk about the problem. Another form of avoidance is being constantly unavailable to talk about the problem. "This isn't a good time right now—talk to me later," replied one spouse. When asked what would be a good time, the response was, "I don't know." This tactic is used to post-pone discussing the problem. If it is repeated often enough, some spouses become exhausted and eventually give up trying. An assertive person might respond by saying, "That's not acceptable to me. If you want to postpone this discussion I would appreciate your giving me a time when we can talk about it."

When this type of assertiveness is used, a common reaction is anger. It might be helpful to remember that anger is a secondary emo-tion and that primary emotions causing anger usually include embar-rassment, frustration, fear, or guilt. One spouse, recognizing this tactic, told her husband, "I know you're probably afraid to talk about this, but it's important to me. I love you and want to help, but I can't if you refuse to open up and have a discussion with me." This approach helped her husband feel safe, and he confided in her about his struggles.

Minimizing can also be used to avoid. "I *just* did it once," or "It *only* happened a few times." These expressions attempt to make behavior appear insignificant or unimportant. Minimizing often manifests itself with words such as "only," "just," or "once." Information provided is usually vague, unclear, or nonspecific, so the person listening is incapable of seeing the complete picture and is more likely to draw inaccurate conclusions.

Others avoid by redefining the issue, commonly known as "changing the subject." One husband told his wife, "I may have looked at a picture or two, but it isn't any worse than the romance novels you read or the soap operas you watch." This tactic attempts to take the focus off of his behavior and place it elsewhere. An appropriate response might be, "That might be a valid point that I would be willing to discuss later. Right now I want to talk about the matter of the pornography on the computer."

Another way to redefine the issue is to play the victim. When a person attempts to manipulate a situation through a "poor me" approach, the goal is to avoid responsibility by eliciting pity. If a wife feels sorry for her spouse, she may begin to caretake his emotions at the cost of processing her own. In this manner, the focus is changed and responsibility for behavior is avoided. One husband began to cry, and as he sobbed, he began to make excuses for his behavior because of all the stress he was feeling. His wife began to rescue him by expressing her sorrow for his situation. After the pattern repeated itself several times, she began to resent the fact that she was taken in by his self-pity. This trap could have been avoided had she been more assertive about her feelings from the beginning. This doesn't mean that appropriate empathy and compassion can't be expressed, but it's also important to avoid traps that prevent honestly communicating thoughts and feelings.

Defiance. One person became enraged when his spouse confronted him about the pornography that was discovered on their computer. The husband responded: "So what? I don't care. It's none of your business. Don't you dare go near my computer ever again. In fact, I'm going to put a password on it right now because I don't want you touching it!" Defiance, usually manifested through anger, can be a symptom of guilt, fear, embarrassment, or frustration.

In most cases, a person who leads a double life works very hard to maintain what some have called "image management." When all the work of maintaining his good-guy image is threatened by exposure of his embarrassing behavior, he may become very angry and defiant. Trying to communicate with someone who demonstrates this behavior will be difficult. It may be more helpful to postpone the discussion to a time when the person is less hostile. An ideal response might be, "I can see this is not a good time to talk with you. We will discuss this later. When would be the best time for you?" If this approach is met with additional defiance, it may be necessary to enlist the help of a therapist to formulate a strategy to address the spouse's resistance. If you can understand healthy boundaries, it will likely help you know how to respond to defiance.

Contrition and Remorse. "I'm sorry. I need help. I know it's wrong," responded one person after being confronted by his spouse. It's not uncommon for a spouse to express remorse, request forgiveness, and commit to abandon the behavior. Psychologist Dr. Kimberly Young notes:

> His promises at the time are probably sincere, and most loved ones want to believe the words. A honeymoon period may follow, including intense sexual activity between the couple. Since sex is often regarded as a sign of love, a spouse may be lulled into believing everything is really all right, offer forgiveness, and bind up her wounded spirit and go on. She

243

is later shattered to discover that the unaccounted time and secrecy has returned. If the core issues aren't addressed, relapse is bound to happen.[5]

Understanding the tendency for relapse can help put a contrite or remorseful reaction into perspective. Thus, when someone promises to abandon a problem with pornography, it is best to realize the magnitude of sex addiction problems. Even for those who show remorse, professional assistance is usually required to effectively address compulsive sexual behavior.

If a person appears contrite about his behavior, it is important to be patient in trying to understand him. This neither implies agreement with his behavior nor dismissal of your personal feelings. It does suggest receptivity to the offending spouse's feelings and perspective. Most people want to abandon their unhealthy habits because of the tremendous guilt and shame they feel.

Deception. Some individuals will admit wrongdoing with promises to abandon the behavior, yet they have no intention of doing so. The confrontation communicates to them that they need to take greater precautions to cover up their behavior. As a result, they agree to change, but instead they simply become more deceptive. The difference between this type of person and a person who is apologetic but relapses back to the behavior is that the contrite person actually intends to keep his commitment where a deceptive person does not. Furthermore, if a contrite person has a relapse, he will usually be more likely to disclose additional slips. This demonstrates a desire to break the cycle of secrecy, which a deceptive person is not interested in doing.

Ambivalence. Often ambivalence is at the heart of impulse-control disorders associated with pornography. It is a love-hate relationship between the user and his sexual compulsion. The love comes from the temporary relief he finds using sexual material to facilitate arousal, which creates his mood-altering experience. However, he feels shame and guilt afterwards and thus develops a hate for the pornography.

These coexisting, conflicting feelings create the dilemma about change and represent the core of the ambivalence.

Assessing the Reaction. A person who truly desires to change, but who has had numerous unsuccessful attempts at extinguishing the behavior, will not likely be successful on his own. These people tend to do better in a structured environment with a therapist and a support group.

Regardless of which reaction he demonstrates, it is important that he take responsibility for his own behavior. Letting a loved one own responsibility can be difficult. Some try to rescue the spouse, yet experience has shown that this can exacerbate problems rather than help.

Although a struggling spouse can be influenced, ultimately he must decide which path he will follow. What he cannot choose are the consequences that accompany those choices. Establishing what boundaries you will have is part of the process that applies consequences for his inappropriate and harmful choices.

Remember that the observable problem is not always the real problem. The purpose of confronting the pornography and also managing his response is to eventually open up the opportunity to address the underlying issues, whatever they may be. This will take time, but persistence can lead to increased intimacy as spouses begin to help meet each other's *real needs* in meaningful ways.

Receiving Help

Women often ask how they can help their husbands. My reply is always the same: "You can't until he is willing to take responsibility for his own behavior." This doesn't mean that women are helpless. They can work on establishing boundaries and addressing their own issues, but getting help for someone struggling with a pornography problem is contingent on that person wanting help! Of course, not everyone wants such help. Even when a person shows up in the office of a therapist, it doesn't mean he is ready to change.

Once an individual expresses a desire to change, it is essential that he receive proper help. One of the first steps is to assess the severity of the problem. Generally, if he has had a long history or high frequency of acting out, with numerous unsuccessful attempts to abandon the behavior, he will require therapy.

The first session with a therapist should always be a consultation, and neither you nor the therapist should expect to continue if either of you feels you will not be able to work together. Dealing with pornography issues can require several months of therapy, or even as much as a year. Your relationship with the therapist will be an essential part of your success, so choosing the right counselor is important.

Generally, most therapists will be willing to provide a free twenty-minute consultation with you to determine if the match is a good one. You are the consumer and have every right to shop carefully. Sadly, most people spend more time buying a car than choosing the right therapist.

Below is a list of questions you will want to explore during your consultation:

What are the therapist's credentials? Is the therapist in good standing professionally? Has anyone ever filed a complaint against him or her?

What is his educational training? How long has he been practicing? Does he have special training in the area of pornography and sexual problems? How many clients has he treated with issues similar to yours? Consider asking for some referrals.

Is the therapist currently accepting new clients? What are his hours of availability? Evenings, weekends? What does he charge for an initial consultation? Regular sessions? Cancellation fees? How long are sessions? Does the therapist offer a sliding scale to accommodate various income levels? Can third-party insurance companies be billed for services?

How far is his office from you? Where is the therapist located? Clinic, hospital, private agency?

Is the therapist married, single, old, or young? What is his ethnicity, sexual orientation?

What theoretical perspectives does he use? Psychodynamic, behavioral, cognitive, humanistic, existential, experiential, transpersonal. (Ask the therapist to explain the difference if you don't know.) Does he facilitate or offer any group therapy for pornography-related behaviors?

When speaking to the therapist, did you feel like he was genuinely interested in you? Did he take time to answer your questions? Do you believe he understood you? Is this someone you feel you could open up to and share your confidential issues? Do you believe he possesses values and beliefs consistent with your goals? Does he seem like the type of individual who will explore various options with you and help you recognize areas for improvement? Do you feel like you can trust him?

How does he deal with ambivalence?

Does he support your religious beliefs and values? Would he be willing to include your bishop as a religious advisor in helping you?

Will he include you as a spouse periodically as part of the therapeutic process?

After your initial discussion, ask yourself if you felt safe, if you felt like you were treated with respect, if you felt listened to and understood. Is the therapist the type of person you feel you could confide in? Do you feel like you can work together? Does the therapist demonstrate competency? You may decide to tell the therapist what you did not like or feel good about and see how you feel about the response you get. On the other hand, you may want to schedule a consultation with one or more therapists and then select the one you prefer.

The therapeutic relationship is different from many other professional relationships. We go to a medical doctor and expect him or her to fix the problem. We provide financial statements to accountants and expect our tax return to be completed. Lawyers advocate our cause and give us legal counsel. A therapist, however, does not always have the answers. In fact, some therapists believe that the answers to problems remain with the client, not the therapist. A therapist can make observations, interpret or challenge irrational thoughts and behaviors, assist the client in exploring his feelings, administer psychological tests, and much more. Still, it is not uncommon for a therapist to explore issues with a client and expect the client to develop solutions to his own problems. This can be frustrating for clients who have different expectations.

Therapists have different styles and approaches to therapy. Some are more directive than others. It is best to consider how you would like to interact with a therapist, and then shop around until you find someone with whom you feel you can work effectively.

Elements of Successful Change

People can successfully abandon pornography problems. There is hope for those who are willing to pay the price necessary to succeed. Increased levels of intimacy, self-awareness, and freedom await those who are willing to work hard. Although we do not take a cookie-cutter approach to helping people, several common denominators can be seen among clients who successfully abandon pornography. These elements also include those things necessary to address their underlying issues. Elements of successful change include the following:

Acceptance and recognition of the problem.
Education about the problem and the underlying causes.
Full disclosure to those who need to know.
A supportive network of friends, family, leaders, and peers.
Abolishment of secrecy and isolation.
A willingness to take risks, to be vulnerable, and to trust others to
    meet their needs.
A desire and motivation to change.

Reliance upon the atonement of Jesus Christ.

Patience with the process of incremental change.

A willingness to include a professional counselor if the problem is severe enough.

Confrontation with underlying problems. This may require an individual to revisit unresolved and painful parts of their past.

Recommitment and rededication to spirituality.

Creation of a maintenance or relapse-prevention program.

Development of healthy coping skills to deal with stress, tension, anxiety, emotional pain, and so forth.

Learning effective communication skills to share thoughts and feelings; learning to be more emotionally honest with self and others.

Reconnecting with one's inner self, including one's feelings and capacity for empathy; restoration of the authentic self.

Developing a pattern of replacing cognitive distortions with correct rational thoughts; this includes replacing personalizing and catastrophizing experiences that trigger awkward and uncomfortable feelings.

These skills are acquired over time, as part of a process. They take effort and practice. Letting go of old ways and adopting new coping strategies in life is a frightening endeavor, especially when you are exploring new territory that requires a leap of faith. The one thought that can give someone the strength to press forward is the recollection of the many things he has tried that haven't worked—so he has nothing to lose. Finding a support group to participate with can be very helpful. Friends who have already walked the path can offer encouragement and guidance along the way.

Suggestions for Mental Health Professionals: Treatment Strategies for Change

This section is for mental health professionals who may be exploring methods to effectively treat individuals with pornography problems. Several studies indicate the therapeutic relationship is of vital importance in helping facilitate change. An effective and trusting relationship will be paramount, as the client will be relearning to risk and be vulnerable. The following suggestions may be useful:

Use role induction to reduce anxiety about therapy and to communicate expectations clearly so clients do not feel frustrated with the process.

Educate the client about the root causes for the behavior. This will increase their awareness level, but it will usually be insufficient by itself to extinguish the behavior.

Understand that group therapy and individual therapy combined produce the best outcome results.

Try cognitive restructuring, where the client learns how to successfully challenge his own cognitive distortions and replace them with correct and rational thoughts.

Identify patterns of behavior, trends, or rituals, and develop strategies to interrupt such negative patterns. Develop new activities that are incompatible with the behaviors.

Implement a system of support, which includes accountability, to address appropriate disclosures, continuing disclosures, and a system of reporting, such as who to tell if there is a slip (may include bishop, spouse, therapist, group). The goal is to break the cycle of secrecy and isolation. This may include keeping a journal of thoughts and feelings.

Revisit painful parts of the client's past that remain unresolved issues, memories, and so forth. This may include reinterpretive work, reframing and reconnecting with the authentic self. This step should not be done prematurely, as it may retraumatize the client. The goal is catharsis.

Increase the congruence between affect and verbal expressions by developing skills in expression, self- and other validation, and empathetic responses. The goal is to learn to be vulnerable and to avoid personalizing or catastrophizing emotions.

Help the client learn to effectively communicate and express needs.

Work on helping the client to develop appropriate physical and emotional boundaries with himself and others. Lack of boundaries usually results from poor childhood attachment and insecurity, which confuses and distorts proper boundary development.

Redefine what healthy intimacy entails and how pornography hinders its development.

Address codependency issues if they are present in the client or his family system.

Recommit the client to use spirituality as a necessary component of his therapy, including a daily habit of personal prayer and scripture study.

Help the client develop emotional honesty with himself and others. This includes acceptance of awkward or uncomfortable feelings without having a need to react. Help a client learn to deal with life's challenges in a healthy way.

Develop a plan to help the client prevent relapse.

Address the impact of pornography on attitudes and beliefs about women.

Use experiential methods in therapy to help the client live in the here and now. The goal is to help the client abandon emotional avoidance through such means as fantasizing.

Periodically include the spouse. If the wife is not brought in and codependency issues exist, therapy may be sabotaged.

Use journal keeping, which has been an effective exercise in helping clients increase their self-awareness and allowing them to process on their own.

This list represents some of the ideas that mental health professionals have found effective in treating clients with pornography issues. It should not be considered exclusive, because new ideas and approaches are still being researched. It should also be noted that in some exceptional cases, clients have fairly healthy backgrounds with few underlying issues. In these cases, interruptions to routines and channeling the individual's energy into other areas of interest can be helpful. A web site located at www.confrontingpornography.com has been established as a resource for therapists and others wanting additional information on this subject.

Conclusion

Once we recognize that problems with pornography are symptomatic, we can begin to focus on the underlying issues that contribute to its use. If you struggle with a pornography habit, there is hope! However, just as the habit was most likely developed over time, abandoning it may also require time. It is a battle that will require commitment, strength, and perseverance. Some battles will be fought "within the silent chambers of the soul,"[6] where only you will know of your small victories along the road to recovery. Regardless of the type of struggle, the desire to abandon pornography is a worthy endeavor, one that will bless your life and the lives of those you love.

Notes

1. Boyd K. Packer, "Our Moral Environment," *Ensign,* May 1992, 66.
2. Names and identifying information have been changed to maintain anonymity.
3. David S. Derezotes, *Advanced Generalist Social Work Practice* (Thousand Oaks, Calif.: Sage Publications, 2000), 210.
4. Richard G. Scott, "The Sanctity of Womanhood," *Ensign,* May 2000, 37.
5. Kimberly S. Young, *Tangled in the Web* (n.p.: 1st Books Library, 2001), 83.
6. David O. McKay, in Conference Report, April 1969, 95.

13

"It Is Not Good That the Man Should Be Alone"

Sherrie Mills Johnson

After speaking at a fireside on the subject of chastity, I noticed a young man waiting to talk with me and watched from the corner of my eye as he neared the front of the line. He was excited about something—almost buoyant—and I found myself eager to know what was on his mind. "Thank you so much," he began. "All my life people have been telling me to be chaste, but you are the first person to tell me why I should be. After tonight I won't even think about breaking the law of chastity."

Indeed, there is something about knowing *why* that helps all of us to keep the commandments more completely. But the surprising thing about the law of chastity is that once we understand it, we not only know that we should abstain from sexual relations before marriage, but we understand the significance of marriage and why sexual relations are such a sacred part of that companionship.

Adam and Eve

To understand the importance of chastity before and after marriage, I like to turn to the very first man and woman.[1] From the scriptures we learn that after Eden was created, God placed Adam in the garden and instructed him "to dress it and to keep it" (Genesis 2:15). He told Adam to eat of any of the fruit of the garden except for that grown on "the tree of the knowledge of good and evil" (Genesis 2:17). Then God explained, "It is not good that the man should be alone; I will make him an help meet for him" (Genesis 2:18). In conjunction with this divine pronouncement, sociological research has found that "marriage appears to have a softening and tempering effect on men, changing them most significantly in the intrinsic aspects of religious devotion."[2] But this tempering effect is not the only reason it is not good for the man to be alone.

Most modern writers combine the words *help* and *meet* to make the word *helpmeet,* which means "companion" and is the same as helpmate or spouse. However, in all places in scripture two words are used (*help meet*), and while the meaning "companion" is still implied, there is something more being conveyed by the two words. In English, this usage of *meet* is an antiquated adjective that means "fitting, adequate, proper, or necessary." In footnote 18b to Genesis 2:18, we learn that the phrase *help meet* means "a helper suited to, worthy of, or corresponding to him."

The original Hebrew word that is translated as *help* in this verse is *ezer. Ezer* is used by Old Testament writers twenty-one times, and in sixteen of these occurrences the word refers to God. "Our soul waiteth for the Lord: he is our help and our shield" (Psalm 33:20) and "Behold, God is mine helper" (Psalm 54:4) are examples of this usage. In English, the word *help* can mean a servant or subordinate, and thus some interpret that verse to claim that woman is a subordinate of man. However, that is not the meaning of the Hebrew word. God is not our subordinate or our servant. He is our help in the sense that through the Atonement he provided a way to alleviate our sins and to remedy the effects of the Fall. He is our *help* because he is our cure.

But does this apply to the man and the woman? It does because woman was the remedy for man's incompleteness. She was literally his necessary cure, his restoration. Alone, he was limited. He needed help to be completed in the image of God. Alone, he could not have children, nor could he fully use his priesthood because there was no one to use it on. As Elder Boyd K. Packer observed:

> The plan of happiness requires the righteous union of male and female, man and woman, husband and wife. . . .

A body patterned after the image of God was created for Adam, and he was introduced into the Garden. At first, Adam was alone. He held the priesthood, but alone, he could not fulfill the purposes of his creation.

No other man would do. Neither alone nor with other men could Adam progress. Nor could Eve with another woman. It was so then. It is so today.

Eve, an help meet, was created. Marriage was instituted, for Adam was commanded to cleave unto his *wife* [not just to a *woman*] and "to none else."[3]

The Hebrew word for *bride* exemplifies this. The word is *kallah,* which is derived from the primary root *kalal,* which means "to complete or to make perfect."

In two of the three narratives of the creation—Genesis and Moses—what follows further exemplifies this principle. After explaining that it is not good that the man be alone, you would think that God would then create woman. But instead the "Lord God formed every beast of the field, and every fowl of the air; and brought them unto Adam to see what he would call them: and whatsoever Adam called every living creature, that was the name thereof. And Adam gave names to all cattle, and to the fowl of the air, and to every beast of the field" (Genesis 2:19–20).

Think about this for a minute. *Every* beast of the field and *every* fowl of the air! This was not a small task. It was monumental. It must have taken months if not years to accomplish, and it meant an even longer period of time during which the man would be alone—after God had just acknowledged that it is not good for the man to be alone. Obviously there was something very important that the Lord wanted Adam and all of us to understand before he created woman.

As Adam viewed all the creatures of the earth and named them, he was seeing them in pairs. He saw the cow and the bull and named them. He saw the hen and the rooster and named them. He saw the mare and the stallion and named them. In this process, Adam saw that every living creature had a counterpart—except for himself. "And Adam gave names to all cattle, and to the fowl of the air, and to every beast of the field; but for Adam there was not found an help meet for him" (Genesis 2:20). Reading this verse in context, and considering the time involved, the pathos of those last words digs deep into the heart. "But for Adam there was not found an help meet for him."

We are only two chapters into the Bible when God says it is not good for man to be alone. He then provided a lesson for Adam to teach this point. It was only after Adam came to the realization that something was missing in his existence, that he was alone and incomplete, that the Lord created woman. Though the Genesis account of woman being formed from a rib is figurative, that symbolism is important enough that it is found in three different books of scripture.

In the figurative sense, God caused a deep sleep to come upon Adam, and as he slept God removed one of Adam's ribs and created from it a woman. What was Adam's reaction? "This is now bone of my bones, and flesh of my flesh: she shall be called Woman, because she was taken out of Man" (Genesis 2:23). Because of his experience with naming the animals, Adam recognized that Eve was the necessary remedy for his incompleteness. Likewise, Eve was only part and not whole herself without the man. Sealed together, they were completed in the image of God. And what is the image of God? In Moses we read, "In the image of his own body, male and female, created he them" (6:9) and in Genesis 1:27 we find, "So God created man in his own image, in the image of God created he him; male and female created he them" (see also Moses 2:27). When quoting a similar verse found in Moses 2:26, President Spencer W. Kimball inserted words to help us understand. He said, "Let us make man [not a separate man, but a complete man, which is husband and wife] in our image, after our likeness; and it was so."[4] President Kimball also explained: "God made man in his own image and certainly he made woman in the image of his wife-partner. You [women] are daughters of God. You are precious. You are made in the image of our heavenly Mother."[5]

Here again, we learn more about this from the Hebrew construct. The Hebrew word that is translated as God is *elohim*. "Im" is the Hebrew plural ending, and the word literally means "divine beings." A man alone cannot be a god and a woman alone cannot be a god (see D&C 132:18–20). Only after being sealed together by the proper priesthood authority can a man and a woman attain godhood.

It is interesting to consider the symbolism employed by the figurative use of Adam's rib as the material from which the woman was formed. Symbolically, Adam was made from dust of the earth, and the woman was made from bone. They were made of different materials and for different purposes. It seems the woman was not made of Adam's muscle to move him or to be moved by him. She was not taken from his heart so she would feel exactly as he felt, or from his mind so she would think the same way that he thought. Instead the woman was made of Adam's bone, the part of the body that gives structure and stature and where the marrow, which produces the life-giving element of mortality—blood—is found. Sealed together eternally, they complement one another. What one lacks the other has. Where one is weak the other is strong. When united by covenant and righteousness, a synergy takes place that transforms an ordinary man and woman into a divine unity—God.

This concept of understanding husband and wife as one—and yet different—is so important to marriage and family that some of Satan's most insidious and subtle efforts have been aimed at causing our misunderstanding. When men or women go into a marriage relationship defining the spouse as "other," problems occur. The basic assumption of "other" is that there is a hierarchy, and that one is better than the other; that one is subordinate and one is superordinate. It doesn't matter which is considered subordinate and which is superordinate. The attitude causes a stratification, a differentiation that will always stand in the way of oneness and unity and thus happiness.

The Genesis, Moses, and Abraham accounts all make it clear that

257

this is not what was intended. We are different, yes. We have different purposes and earthly assignments, yes. But we are the same.

A good way to illustrate this concept is to compare it to water. Hot water is not better than cold water. Hot and cold water are the same—they are both water—and yet they serve different purposes. When water is needed, the situation at hand determines which water is right for that moment. On a summer day when sweat pours even while you sit in the shade, you don't want a glass of hot water. You want ice water. On a freezing day when snow is three feet deep and the wind is adding its chill factor to air that penetrates windows and the cracks under doors, you don't want a cold bath. But there is not a hierarchy of hot and cold. One is not better than the other. Likewise as men and women, as husbands and wives, we are all children of God who are striving to come back into his presence with different duties to perform to accomplish his purposes.

One Flesh

If one does not understand the context of the Genesis account, the next verse almost seems like an editorial comment thrown into the narrative. But when we properly understand, the verse stands as a powerful capstone. The verse begins "Therefore," or in other words, *because* a man and a woman separately are incomplete, *because* man and woman need to be completed in the image of God, "shall a man leave his father and his mother, and shall cleave unto his wife: and they shall be one flesh" (Genesis 2:24).

After quoting this verse, Elder LeGrand Richards wrote:

> It is evident that the Lord did not have in mind that they should be one in purpose and desire, for he makes himself clear as to what this oneness should consist of: "one flesh."
>
> Jesus understood this principle fully, as we learn from his statement: "For this cause shall a man leave his father and mother, and cleave to his wife; And they twain shall be one flesh; so then they are no more twain, but one flesh. What

therefore God hath joined together, let not man put asunder." (Mark 10:7–9.)

Thus Jesus gave us to understand that both man and wife should be "one flesh."⁶

When God made Adam and Eve husband and wife, there was no death upon the earth. Hence their union was meant to be forever, and the word *cleave* takes on added significance. They are to "adhere, cling, or stick fast" to one another forever. In the eyes of God they are no longer two separate beings but are intended to be one flesh or one unit eternally. This unity is emphasized again in Moses 6:9, where we are told that in the beginning they shared even the same name. "In the image of his own body, male and female, created he them, and blessed them, and called their name Adam, in the day when they were created and became living souls in the land upon the footstool of God."

As Elder Richards explained, being one flesh is not simply about being one in purpose or desire; it is about being one entity. This unity should begin with legal marriage vows. To be eternal, these vows need to take place in a temple wherein the man and the woman are *sealed* together by the priesthood keys restored by Elijah. Symbolically the temple ceremony is extremely insightful. The man and woman kneel at an altar—known throughout scripture as a place of sacrifice. At the marriage altar they sacrifice their singleness, their separateness, their self-centeredness. No longer will problems be "my problems" or "your problems"; they will be "our problems." No longer will it be "my money," but it will be "our money." No longer will it be "my goals" and "my dreams" and "my joys" and "my worries," but life will consist of "our goals," "our dreams," "our joys," and "our worries." With this unity in mind, it is interesting to look into the eyes of your husband or wife so that you see yourself reflected there. In a very real sense, when you see yourself reflected in the very being of your spouse, you are seeing the real you. When you hurt or abuse or neglect your spouse, you are literally hurting, abusing, and neglecting yourself.

But there is something else. This unity involves more than just the man and the woman. Gospel covenants are made with God, not with mortals. As Elder Bruce R. McConkie explained, "In the gospel sense, a *covenant* is a binding and solemn compact, agreement, contract, or mutual promise between God and a single person or a group of chosen persons."[7] Therefore, the marriage covenant is not a covenant between a man and a woman, but a covenant between the man and God and between the woman and God. Part of the covenant with God is that each will sacrifice selfish desires and receive the spouse as their own flesh. God, therefore, is an integral part of a temple marriage. The oneness intended is not simply a relationship between the man and the woman. The oneness intended is a triangular relationship between God, the man, and the woman. In the marriage ceremony, an officiator, a holder of God's holy priesthood, stands in proxy for God to perform the marriage. Thus in the ceremony itself there is a symbolic representation of the three parties involved in the relationship.

Authority

After being married, the couple now has the authority to perform the rites that belong to marriage. As a unit, they are now entitled to a relationship of physical, emotional, intellectual, and spiritual intimacy that is capable of bringing not only joy but exaltation to both man and woman. This relationship has the potential of being more rewarding than any other relationship in this world. However, since there is "opposition in all things" (2 Nephi 2:11), this relationship also has the potential for bringing more pain and sorrow than any other relationship.

The symbolism doesn't end with the formal wedding ceremony; instead, it just begins. Once given the authority, the couple is entitled to a physical relationship. This relationship can be looked upon as a renewal of the covenant the couple made at the altar. In this way it is similar to the sacrament, a renewal of the baptismal covenant. As Elder Jeffrey R. Holland explains, "Sexual intimacy is not only a symbolic union between a man and a woman—the uniting of their very souls—but it is also symbolic of a union between mortals and deity, between otherwise ordinary and fallible humans uniting for a rare and special moment with God Himself and all the powers by which He gives life in this wide universe of ours. In this latter sense, human intimacy is a kind of sacrament, a very special symbol."[8]

One of the main purposes of a sacrament is to bind us to God by reminding us of our covenants. Sacraments are holy ordinances. They are meant to further the work of the Lord and to establish his kingdom. In addition, all covenants and sacraments teach principles through the symbolism found in the action of the ritual. For example, when we partake of the sacrament of the Lord's Supper we ingest emblems—bread and water—that represent the body and blood of Christ. Literally the things we eat become part of us. Food is used not only for energy, but literally becomes hair, skin, blood, and fingernails. When we eat the bread and water of the sacrament of the Lord's Supper, we are symbolically taking Christ into our bodies and making him part of us.

As Elder Jeffrey R. Holland explains:

An act of love between a man and a woman is—or certainly was ordained to be—a symbol of total union: union of their hearts, their hopes, their lives, their love, their family, their future, their everything. . . .

Physiologically we are created as men and women to form such a union. In this ultimate physical expression of one man and one woman, they are as nearly and as literally one as two separate physical bodies can ever be. It is in that act of ultimate physical intimacy we most nearly fulfill the commandment of the Lord given to Adam and Eve, living symbols for all married couples, when He invited them to cleave unto one another only, and thus become "one flesh" (Genesis 2:24).[9]

There is much in the gospel of Jesus Christ that we do not completely understand; and the importance and sacredness of physical intimacy seems to be one of these things. The act of physical union is part of what makes a man and a woman one flesh. Paul asked the Corinthians, "Know ye not that he which is joined to an harlot is one body? for two, saith he, shall be one flesh" (1 Corinthians 6:16). Somehow two souls are conjoined to be one through physical intimacy, and therefore a promiscuous giving of self to others outside of marriage is the very giving away of body and spirit—the soul. That is why sexual relations with our spouse enhance and expand and exhilarate—they add to us. They are holy. However, if entered into without the authority to do so, they damn and damage and destroy, because they diminish us.

A Sacred Union

In Elder Holland's book *Of Souls, Symbols, and Sacraments,* he explains what these sacramental experiences should be like. "These are moments when we quite literally unite our will with God's will, our spirit with His Spirit, where communion through the veil becomes very real. At such moments we not only acknowledge His divinity, but we also quite literally take something of that divinity to ourselves. Such are the holy sacraments."[10]

In accordance with this, President Joseph F. Smith said, "Sexual union is lawful in wedlock, and, if participated in with right intent, is honorable *and sanctifying.*"[11] Elder Boyd K. Packer said: "Within your body is the power to beget life, to share in creation. The only legitimate expression of that power is within the covenant of marriage. *The worthy use of it is the very key to your happiness.*"[12]

The happiness Elder Packer refers to is not just earthly, mortal happiness. In their book *Between Husband and Wife,* Stephen E. Lamb and Douglas E. Brinley explain that "our sexual nature is not a temporary power limited to a brief period of mortality. If we receive exaltation, our resurrected bodies, like those of our heavenly parents, will be capable of procreation." [13]

This is one of the major differences between those who inherit the celestial kingdom and those who don't. President Joseph Fielding Smith taught, "Some of the functions in the celestial body will not appear in the terrestrial body, neither in the telestial body, and the power of procreation will be removed."[14] The ability to carry on the marital relationship in the next world is actually one of the rewards for righteousness.

But intimacy is not only a reward for the future. Physical intimacy plays a very important part in making a marriage celestial. Lamb and Brinley point out that there are at least four purposes for sexual intimacy in marriage: "1. To provide a profound expression of love. 2. To bring emotional and physical closeness. 3. To fulfill God's commandment to have children. 4. To experience pleasure and joy."[15] Each of these purposes increases the bond and the closeness between spouses. As one woman expressed it: "Sometimes I look at my husband—at odd times like when he's sitting on the stand at church or he's filling the car with gas—and a delightfully warm sensation tickles my spirit while I watch him. I realize that the feeling at those times comes from the memories of other times. He is the only person in this whole world who has ever made physical feelings well up in me with so much intensity. He is the only person in this world that has given me such pleasure. He is the only person who shares my very being."

In her book *Purity and Passion,* Wendy Watson writes: "Marital intimacy is an act of love, ordained by God, that offers access to His power in order to co-create life and love. Sadly, far too many couples live far beneath their privileges because they look to the world for their standards of sexually appropriate behavior."[16] It is this looking to the world that keeps us from obtaining the true joy the Lord intends. If instead we seek the Spirit and draw closer to our Father in Heaven and our Savior Jesus Christ, all aspects of our marital relationship will improve and we will find joy therein.

Joy grows exponentially—unlike pleasure, which happens in an instant and passes. Joy not only lingers, but it seeps into everything we do and are. It influences our future and even tempers our past. When we understand the sacredness of physical intimacy and that we are one flesh in the eyes of God, our attitudes change not only concerning our spouse and marriage, but concerning how we deal with life, for we know that even adversity can weld us tighter together. We know that the flashy romance portrayed by the media isn't love at all—it's selfishness in the pursuit of pleasure. We understand that even within marriage there are impure practices that should be avoided. We know that as we struggle to work through the inevitable problems in our relationships, we have everything to gain by being patient and persistent.

Conclusion

For one of our wedding anniversaries, I wrote a poem for my husband in an attempt to express what I'd learned over the years about what it means to be one flesh. I think it summarizes more than my editorializing can.

Thirty Years

They sat across from me
  on the bus today.
He clasped both her hands in his lap.
  She laid her head
upon his shoulder.
  Their legs,
Thigh to knee, pressing
  so that anyone could see
the yearning to be flesh
  of each other's flesh.

Years ago we wished
  to breathe one breath,

cleave bone to bone,
  flesh to flesh,
thought we could
  touch it into being.

Tears later
  we've buried one daughter,
fought out differences
  during dark nights,
survived an infection
  that wanted me dead,
an ulcer that bled you
  to an ashen gray,
paid the taxes of '89
  that surprised us both,
worked so hard we didn't
  know each other anymore,
and started over again.

You go on reading your newspaper
  not knowing that I
am thinking about lovers.
  You turn the page.
I pick at gravy
  Dried on the tablecloth.

Me at one end of the table
  you at the other,
bone of bone,
  flesh of flesh,
without touching.

Adam needed time to ponder and come to understand that "it is not good that the man should be alone." We also need time to ponder. No wonder the Lord wants us to attend the temple. We must be familiar with the account of Adam and Eve, to correct the misconceptions so prevalent about the marriage relationship, to remember that God is part of our partnership and that physical intimacy is meant to be a sacred and holy experience. As we do this, we, like my young friend, will feel an excitement that will motivate us to be better. As our understanding increases, life will become more holy and our marriage relationships more ennobling.

Notes

1. I am building here upon concepts first taught to me by Gerald N. Lund that can be found in "The Book of Mormon—Keystone of a Happy Marriage" in *Selected Writings of Gerald N. Lund* (Salt Lake City: Deseret Book, 1999), 99.
2. James T. Duke and Barry L. Johnson, "The Religiosity of Mormon Men and Women through the Life Cycle" in *Latter-day Saint Social Life: Social Research on the LDS Church and its Members,* ed. James T. Duke (Provo, Utah: Religious Studies Center, 1998), 331.
3. Boyd K. Packer, "For Time and All Eternity," *Ensign,* November 1993, 21; emphasis in original.
4. Spencer W. Kimball, "The Blessings and Responsibilities of Womanhood," *Ensign,* March 1976, 71.
5. *The Teachings of Spencer W. Kimball,* ed. Edward L. Kimball (Salt Lake City: Bookcraft, 1982), 25.
6. LeGrand Richards, "The Eternal Companionship: Husband and Wife," in *Woman* (Salt Lake City: Deseret Book, 1979), 41.
7. Bruce R. McConkie, *Mormon Doctrine,* 2d ed. (Salt Lake City: Bookcraft, 1966), 166.
8. Jeffrey R. Holland, *Of Souls, Symbols, and Sacraments* (Salt Lake City: Deseret Book, 2001), 27.
9. Ibid., 17–18.
10. Ibid., 28.
11. Joseph F. Smith, "Unchastity the Dominant Evil of the Age," *Improvement Era* 20, no. 8 (June 1917): 739; emphasis added.
12. Boyd K. Packer, "To Young Women and Men," *Ensign,* May 1989, 54; emphasis added.
13. Stephen E. Lamb and Douglas E. Brinley, *Between Husband and Wife* (Salt Lake City: Covenant, 2000), 12.
14. Joseph Fielding Smith, *Doctrines of Salvation,* comp. Bruce R. McConkie, 3 vols. (Salt Lake City: Bookcraft, 1954–56), 2:288.
15. Lamb and Brinley, *Between Husband and Wife,* 18.
16. Wendy L. Watson, *Purity and Passion* (Salt Lake City: Deseret Book, 2001), 139.

14

Marital Intimacy:
A Sacred Key to a Successful Marriage

Douglas E. Brinley

As I visit with married couples, it becomes apparent that the quality of their sexual relationship is an important component in their overall rating of marital happiness. What takes place in the intimate exchange between a husband and wife is a fairly reliable barometer of the condition of their marital state, because such private acts between them take place in a context of vulnerability, trust, and genuine feelings about each other. There is little to hide in the way of feelings and attitudes during lovemaking episodes. Consider this wife's comments:

> Marital intimacy is a very important and valuable aspect to a marriage. It is very sacred and should be reserved for marriage. I remember right after my husband and I were married, we were driving to our reception talking about some things. We both commented on how we really didn't feel married yet. It wasn't until after making love for the first time that we felt we were actually married. It was a neat experience for both of us.
>
> Later, as we thought about things, we realized how important it is and why it is stressed so much in the gospel to wait until you are married. It put things into perspective on how sacred intimacy can and should be. I realized how damaging it could be to someone if they were not married.
>
> I think that like a lot of newlyweds, we were kind of naive when it came to intimacy. It was very difficult for me to share myself with my husband. It was embarrassing for me the first

few weeks. But, as it turned out, what better way to build trust and closeness between us?

Intimacy has really been a good strengthening aspect in our marriage. It really does work as a form of therapy for both of us. It is a way for us to kind of forget about all our troubles and focus on each other. It seems like whenever we would have a fight, big or small, after we would make amends, we would find ourselves wanting to be intimate. It has become a way for us to show our love for one another. It relieves stress that might be hurting our marriage. I love being close to my husband. It is so amazing how much it strengthens the bond between us. My husband and I are pretty open about discussing intimacy. I think that helps us to talk about other things also. I trust my husband that he's not going to blab to a friend about our intimacy. It is sacred, and should be kept between the two of us.

Contrast that young wife's expression with this one:

Serious problems have arisen in our marriage and it makes intimacy that much more difficult. I don't feel loved, respected, or appreciated by him, and then he wants to have sex. That just doesn't work for me. We still participate a couple of times a week, because I know that if I refused it would only make things worse for us. But I end up feeling a little used. I also know that my husband wishes I would lose weight. This is one of the more serious problems in our marriage, since he can't promise me that, if I gain more weight, he'll still love me!

The problems are serious enough in our marriage that I am deathly afraid of getting pregnant. I don't want to add children to this mix, and, therefore, any intimacy is dangerous. This relationship is becoming such a frustrating experience that I'm losing interest rapidly.

My husband, however, is not. He is very impatient. And since the only time he compliments me spontaneously is when he wants to have sex, it simply doesn't hold the same attraction that it used to. Overall, intimacy has been frustrating, and an emotionally draining experience for me. I know that if or when our marriage improves, so will the intimacy. I just don't see that happening in the near future, though, and the thought of continuing to be intimate with my husband is depressing and frustrating. I end up feeling used, unfulfilled, and unappreciated. For now, I put if off as much as I can, and give in now and then to keep my husband satisfied. I look forward to the day when I'll be able to enjoy an emotional, validating, joyous experience.

Marital Intimacy As a Barometer of the Marriage

At the time of marriage, each individual feels that exploring masculine and feminine natures together is a natural and expected part of the new union. However, when either spouse is upset or angry or contention arises, both emotional and physical intimacy are negatively affected. It is clear that happily married couples anticipate this time together, while unhappily married couples consistently find this area difficult to negotiate. Though all married couples have challenges in their sexual compatibility at some time during their lives together (during and after pregnancy, differences in desired frequency, aging and related health issues), couples who rate their marriages as satisfactory find ways to adjust to the various physical and emotional aspects of sexual relations over their life cycle. It is in this most intimate contact between a husband and wife that confidence, pleasure, self-worth, and feelings of love and appreciation are transparent.

"When was the last time you two were intimate?" I recently asked a couple.

"A month ago," responded the husband.

"And the time before that?" I followed up.

269

The answer was the same—more than thirty days had passed.

"Is that frequency meeting your personal needs for companionship, therapy, and love?" I asked.

Both responded almost in unison, "No."

It was hardly a surprise. Having intimate relations once a month is an abnormally low amount for two healthy spouses in their thirties. But this couple seemed unable to break this negative cycle, not because they were physically incapable, but because their feelings for each other would not allow it. With their marriage hurting them both, their intimacy also suffered.

The Purpose of Marital Intimacy

The Lord provided married couples—those dealing with clunky cars, financial challenges, children (two-year-olds and teens!), health issues—with a way to renew their marriage vows and recommit themselves to each other. The sexual union provides a way for them to express to each other profound feelings of love and appreciation. "Honey," a husband basically says to his wife, "I just want you to know how much I love you and how much I appreciate all you do for me and the children." A wife is free to initiate or reciprocate a similar message to her husband: "Sweetheart, I'm so glad we are married; I appreciate all you do for me and our family; I love being close to you and look forward to this time together." Physically, emotionally, mentally, and even spiritually, couples, in this special way, exchange genuine feelings of love that provide comfort and consolation to each other in a world where forces tear at their unity, commitments, and covenants.

Besides its procreative power, sexual intimacy was designed by our Creator to be a positive expression of caring between covenant spouses. Contention and argument, on the other hand, destroy feelings of love and stifle any desire to participate in what Elder Jeffrey R. Holland refers to as a marital "sacrament."[1] Physical and emotional intimacy provide security and wholesomeness to happily married couples.

In sexual relations we express our highest and most noble feelings of kindness, caring, and mutual appreciation. Caressing each other's body in ways that arouse and stimulate, each one feeling free and confident to trust their physical and emotional natures to the care of a spouse, allows us to experience some of the most poignant, satisfying, and powerful emotions known to mortals. On the other hand, nothing is more hypocritical and deceptive than the desire to use another's body for selfish gratification without regard for the feelings of the spouse. No husband or wife would want to share their heart and soul with someone who does not appreciate the most intimate gift we share with each other.

Enriching Marital Intimacy

For married couples, I want to remind you of a few guidelines that will improve and enhance your sexual relationship.

First, no matter the number of years together—whether newly married or experienced sweethearts—it is clear to both of you by now that intimacy requires the highest form of charity in the form of patience, kindness, gentleness, and, importantly, a willingness to talk to each other about this important dimension of marriage. Only you two know what is needed in the way of sexual arousal and fulfillment. I recall listening to a woman who said to me: "I can't stand it when my husband does . . . to me," meaning a particular sexual arousal technique. Another one said: "I wish my husband would just not . . ." referring to his way of loving her. I always wondered what either of these women thought I could do about their problem! The person who needs to hear such concerns and feelings is the husband, not me. I repeat: There must be a willingness to talk and share this important aspect of marriage with each other.

Marital intimacy requires frequent monitoring by both spouses. Your best source of help and learning about passion, passionate embraces, emotions, desires, and physical responses is your sweetheart. You two must be your own therapists in this dynamic area of marriage.

Marital intimacy is designed to produce a wonderful bonding process between spouses and is a new adventure for newlyweds. As Latter-day Saints we come into marriage from a culture of abstinence. It is at this time in our existence that we participate in such intimate exchanges with a spouse for the very first times. Our mutual task, therefore, is to help each other to an arousal of passion by providing each other with clear instructions on how we want to be loved and caressed. In this sacred inner sanctum we must be exceptional teachers and eager students, for we have much to learn from each other regarding our part in this sacred union. Because we are so open and vulnerable in this setting, feelings can be easily hurt by rude, insensitive, or inappropriate comments.

As we grow older and our lives become more complex because of children, work, and Church assignments, physical changes also affect the intensity of our sexual responses. Emotions and reactions differ, for example, during pregnancy, following childbirth, as we move into the "golden" years, and so forth. Sexual interest never remains constant. Aging affects our libido in such a way that we may require more time for sexual arousal or more physical stimulation to achieve arousal goals pleasing to each other. The advantage we have by that time in our lives is that we are usually more comfortable with each other in terms of vocabulary and an ability to risk with each other. We have seen each other undressed many times by that point, and we are less inclined to be bashful and shy about bringing up the topic. We have taught each other what feels good and what is enjoyable and fulfilling for us over the years. And the good news is that healthy individuals should be able to find satisfaction in their intimate relations most of their lives, unless severe health factors interfere. Medications exist that enable couples to enjoy sexual intimacy well into their advanced years.

Second, it is apparent that sexual fulfillment is closely allied with the quality of life in the *nonsexual areas* of marriage. Because the frequency and quality of sexual expression mirrors the marriage relationship, it is difficult for either spouse to give freely and fully to the other without fear of being hurt when one is easily irritated, harsh, sarcastic, angry, or moody. One of my favorite books is titled *Sex Begins in the Kitchen*.[2] Its theme is that sexual desire and interest, especially for women, are closely tied to what takes place in the nonbedroom arenas. It is difficult, in other words, for a wife to give herself to a husband who is unromantic, uncharitable, or critical of her role performances. A wife, to enjoy intimate relations, must feel that her husband cares about her personally and that he functions as an able companion in both marriage and parenting responsibilities. Likewise, it is difficult for a husband to want intimate contact with a wife who is carping, critical, and emotionally insensitive.

Dating and courting within marriage should be part of a lifelong effort to convey feelings of love and appreciation and a sense that you do want and need your companion to be an intimate part of your life. In marriage, dating and courting include the privilege of being touched by a "spouse-lover" in sensitive and caring ways. Frequent positive exchanges of ideas and feelings set the stage for heightened sexual pleasure in intimate marital contact.

Third, generally, men have a greater sexual interest because orgasm (ejaculation) is more predictable for them, and therefore it probably has a greater psycho-physical connection for them. Human beings seek pleasure and avoid pain, and sexual relations are enjoyable and pleasurable for the male portion of the species. On the other hand, in many marriages these days, it is the wife who desires more intimate contact than the husband. Perhaps it was with this in mind that Elder Richard G. Scott counseled men: "There are times, brethren, when you need to restrain those feelings. *There are times when you need to allow their full expression.* Let the Lord guide you in ways that will enrich your marriage."[3]

As an illustration of how we must be careful about stereotyping, consider what one wife reported:

I must fall into the minority of women who enjoy sex at least as much as her husband, if not more. In fact my husband tells me that he usually doesn't want sex as much as I do. We can discuss intimacy openly. I frequently ask my husband about my technique and give him feedback about his.

Things have definitely changed since the honeymoon. I enjoy sex more now than my husband does.

Couples must adjust to the frequency desires of each other. When a husband seeks intimacy on a more frequent basis than is desirable for the wife, both may need to seek mutual understanding and a willingness to be sensitive to each other's needs. It may require a frank discussion on what intimacy means to both spouses. Just because a husband desires sex more than his wife doesn't mean that is right or proper, given her health and desires. Further, there are times when a husband needs to exercise self-control and restraint as he observes his wife's involvement in parenting and other stress-filled responsibilities. Sexual relations are not always therapeutic for a busy or exhausted wife. On the other hand, sexual relations may be therapeutic to a husband whose wife initiates intimate relations because she has learned that her husband doesn't differentiate between love and sex. Charity must be the overarching virtue for both spouses, as mutual consideration allows each spouse to be comfortable in initiating or declining a sexual episode. Each must realize that there are times when sexual relations are not preferable, comfortable, or even desirable for the spouse.

It is important for each spouse to understand that husbands are typically aroused by visual or erotic themes and messages and that wives generally enjoy a more romantic approach (flowers, a call from work, helping with housework or children). Gentle and sensitive holding and touching, coupled with genuine expressions of love and endearment, are important for both spouses to experience if they are to be good sweethearts.

Fourth, certain factors hinder sexual satisfaction and functioning.

For example, if either spouse is unaware of or insensitive to the other's work or Church schedules, employment pressures, or physical and health challenges, or if physical factors such as weight problems, lack of cleanliness, or irritating techniques interfere, the enjoyment of one or both partners may be negatively affected. There are times when neither spouse will feel "sexy" or sexually aroused, particularly after a stressful day with children or career. Both spouses need to be wise enough and sufficiently mature to realize that the only performance standards in marriage are yours; you need not send in statistics to Church headquarters or the government! Your only desire should be to please each other. That requires an honest sharing of feelings about what is enjoyable and pleasurable, knowing that respect and love for each other will override personal preferences at times.

Fifth, as Latter-day Saints, we come from a background of strong premarital standards and abstinence. That means we are not likely to know how to fulfill our sexual roles when we first marry. At that point, our vocabulary is rather limited in discussing sex matters together. The best source of help and information in this area is the spouse. It is from his wife, and her only, that a husband obtains feedback and instruction on how to be her lover. Only she knows what techniques and touching are most helpful in reaching a state of emotional passion. And only the husband can best provide information and help to his wife on how to be his lover; only he can teach her what is pleasurable and stimulating for him.

I have seen couples live together for years without knowing how to or helping each other to reach a climax or orgasm level. It takes time and information for each of us to learn the intricacies of sexual relations, because of the newness and novelty of the experience. Satisfaction in the sexual arena requires a sincere desire to please each other and must be coupled with a sense of humor where neither one embarrasses the other on the way to greater sexual fulfillment. I underscore a sense of humor, because for most couples honeymoon ignorance is quite humorous when compared with what both partners know and prefer at a later time. Both spouses must help each other to an arousal of sexual passion that culminates as both might wish.

Marriage is not just for sexual activity, of course, but this union provides a profound way for each spouse to express love and commitment. Sexual intercourse was designed by Deity to be a physical, emotional, and spiritual union that fulfills our deepest desires for intimacy within the context of marriage. Just as a good marriage increases sexual libido, so also do satisfactory sexual relations confer soul-strengthening emotions on both spouses. A couple in this physical embrace shuts out worldly interference, renews marriage commitments, and thereby increases their love and commitment to each other and to their marriage goals. In this union they demonstrate a willingness to cooperate and share in the joys and challenges unique to marriage and parenthood. This acceptance of each other's efforts of mutual service acts as a therapeutic dimension for each spouse, for it is centered in charitable feelings, coupled with an eternal perspective. Both partners therefore raise each other to a level of spirituality by an act of love that expresses their strongest emotional feelings.

Sometimes couples go years without sharing in this intimate emotional and physical exchange. What a tremendous loss it is to their souls and to their own happiness! How therapeutic, refreshing, consoling, relaxing, and wholesome physical intimacy is for married couples who live in a world of stress and who seek frequent reassurance from the most important person in their world that they are desirable, lovable, and attractive.

It is through meeting each other's sexual needs that trust is enhanced and a couple's commitment to work together to avoid or resolve marital and family disagreements is strengthened. With an eternal perspective of marriage, we can understand that sexual intimacy is not limited to this brief mortal sphere, and we can be patient with our sexual progress as a couple.

We live in a time of media myths; one says, for example, that both partners should reach orgasm together. The truth is that it often takes time for a couple to establish the psychological and emotional climate where this expression of love ripens and fully blossoms. We live in a day when so much stress is put on the mechanics, techniques, and skills of sex that we can easily lose sight of our goal to strengthen marriage and recommit ourselves to each other and our family goals.

A gentle reminder: when one member of the partnership has a sexual problem, both should work on it together. Neither spouse has a problem in a vacuum. A husband troubled with premature ejaculation, for example, requires an interested and attentive wife for its resolution. If a wife cannot respond well physically, it is an issue for both spouses, because the sexual relationship is an integral part of the total marriage relationship.

Here are a few simple suggestions:

1. Acquire a vocabulary early in marriage that enables you to discuss intimacy. It is true that most of us grow up without talking about male or female anatomy with members of the opposite sex. When we marry we are often hesitant to talk to each other until we have been married long enough to relax our timidity and shyness.

2. As you discover what is pleasing and pleasurable to you, teach or provide feedback to your spouse. It is your responsibility to assist your spouse in learning how to be your lover, for who else but you knows what is most stimulating and enjoyable to you? Of course, it usually takes some time and experience before we ourselves learn what is stimulating and enjoyable.

3. You have the responsibility to learn what constitutes a good experience for your spouse. You must learn from him or her what is relaxing, stimulating, refreshing, and pleasurable. Being able to answer these questions might be helpful to both of you:

    (a) What situations or conditions make lovemaking the best experience for me? for my spouse?

   (b) What is needed and wanted in the way of stimulation and therapeutic technique for me? for my spouse?

   (c) What aspects of lovemaking are the most pleasurable for me? for my spouse?

   (d) What are my needs for frequency? my spouse's needs? (This answer needs joint input.)

4. The way to teach each other how to enjoy intimate times together can be as simple as sharing these statements: "I really become aroused when you . . . " or "How do you feel about . . . ?" or "What can I do to help you reach a level of arousal that is enjoyable for you?" "How can I help you reach an orgasm or climax more easily?"

5. For more experienced married couples, it is important to remember that a series of steps or stages exist between the first physical touch and the most passionate embrace. What those steps once were, and what those steps are now, are questions that we all ought to ask ourselves periodically. It is not uncommon for couples to skip these initial steps after they have been married for awhile and focus only on the final stages of sexual expression, to the detriment of one or both spouses—particularly the wife. The greatest tenderness and romance are often expressed before or after a lovemaking episode.

Summary

The Lord designed that intimate expressions of love and appreciation within the marriage covenant should be rewarding and fulfilling. This profound way of sharing body and soul with a spouse in the bonds of marriage is one of the highlights of married life. Latter-day Saints are unique among Christians in their belief that sexual relations are not limited to this mortal sphere. In the resurrection we continue to procreate children—spirit children—who will be to us then as we were to our Heavenly Parents in our premortal life. An earlier First Presidency taught this principle:

> So far as the stages of eternal progression and attainment have been made known through divine revelation, we are to understand that only resurrected and glorified beings can become parents of spirit offspring. Only such exalted souls have reached maturity in the appointed course of eternal life; and the spirits born to them in the eternal worlds will pass in due sequence through the several stages or estates by which the glorified parents have attained exaltation.[4]

This mortal probation allows married couples to apprentice in marital intimacies. If we are faithful in keeping the commandments regarding the law of chastity, intimate expressions of love and procreation will continue in the highest degree of glory in the celestial kingdom (see D&C 131:1–4). This marital privilege allows us to recommit ourselves to each other and our marital goals through an act of love that enhances and enriches our marriage relationship in "time" as we prepare for eternity.

Hopefully you will feel about your intimacy as this married student does:

> For us intimacy is very much an expression of love and a renewal of our marriage covenants. We can't help but feel close after the fact, and we find that our desire to serve and bless each other increases. Intimacy brings much pleasure and joy, as well as relaxation and therapy. It is amazing how we are able to shut out the world and our troubles and focus entirely on each other at these times. This has really helped ease the burden of life's various stresses. We both feel that our intimacy is a reflection of the quality of our marriage, and we feel that this is an appropriate gauge of our marriage. It is difficult to be intimate or especially enjoy intimacy when there exist bitter feelings or feelings of contention between the two of us.

Generally we enjoy intimacy the most after various experiences throughout the day have brought us closer. This is particularly true for my wife, who has difficulty if she has had a really difficult, stressful day. What goes on during the day does affect intimacy later. We have never been shy about expressing our feelings or concerns relating to intimacy. We have been very open and honest about our likes, dislikes, and preferences. This level of open communication has, for us, helped bridge the gap between the twenty-plus years of virginity and marriage.

Notes

1. See Jeffrey R. Holland, *Of Souls, Symbols, and Sacraments* (Salt Lake City: Deseret Book, 2001), 27.
2. See Kevin Leman, *Sex Begins in the Kitchen: Because Love Is an All-Day Affair* (Grand Rapids, Mich.: Fleming H. Revell, 1999).
3. Richard G. Scott, "The Sanctity of Womanhood," *Ensign*, May 2000, 37; emphasis added.
4. James R. Clark, comp., *Messages of the First Presidency of The Church of Jesus Christ of Latter-day Saints*, 6 vols. (Salt Lake City: Bookcraft, 1965–75), 5:34.

15

Marriage and the
New and Everlasting Covenant

Guy L. Dorius

Years ago I had an interesting and enlightening experience while I was serving as an elders quorum president. In my ward were a lot of young couples who were just starting their lives together. The economy was a little down at the time, and many couples were working two or three jobs in order to make ends meet. Generally, they had two or three children, a mortgage, car payments, and a dog—fairly representative of middle-class America and Church-membership North America. The thing that disturbed me was their church attendance, which was less than stellar. I was also alarmed at the lack of stability in their marriages. Though married in the temple, some had been divorced, and I was anxious to know what problems they faced and how I could be of help to them.

I decided to visit them in their homes. It was a wonderful experience to meet all of these fine people, and they were quite open and willing to talk with me. I eventually got around to asking them why they weren't coming out to their Sunday meetings to renew their covenants and meet with the Saints. They shared their concerns with me about trying to keep bread on the table. It appeared, on the surface, to be a financial issue. In their minds, they were working so much during the week that they viewed Sunday as the only day they had to spend time together to strengthen their relationship. In their minds, they couldn't afford the hours to go to church because they were so busy trying to make ends meet.

Over the years, I have come to realize that their devotion to each other and to their marriage at the expense of their worship on the

Sabbath was one of the very things dragging their marriages down. Their priorities, which sounded good—earning income and improving their relationship—were backwards. They were making the mistake that is so frequently seen in our modern society: *flip-flopping the first two commandments*. Love of God was taking a back seat to loving their neighbor. (Even though a spouse is an important neighbor, he or she is still a neighbor!) Elder Neal A. Maxwell explained the risk of this type of rearranging:

"Mankind has not had much success in keeping the second commandment by loving our neighbors as ourselves, without also keeping the first great commandment, loving God with all of our heart, might, mind, and strength. Try as mankind may to achieve the brotherhood of man without the Fatherhood of God, it is cosmetic and does not last!"[1]

The motivation of these young couples to love each other and spend time together was not wrong; it was simply a matter of misplaced priorities. I have come to realize that most of these choices came from not understanding the doctrines of the kingdom and the covenants that prepare us for exaltation. We seem to want to fix marriages by focusing on behavior rather than the doctrines of marriage and the covenants that tie us to God and each other. Elder Boyd K. Packer taught this principle:

> True doctrine, understood, changes attitudes and behavior.
>
> The study of the doctrines of the gospel will improve behavior quicker than a study of behavior will improve behavior. Preoccupation with unworthy behavior can lead to unworthy behavior. That is why we stress so forcefully the study of the doctrines of the gospel.
>
> The laws of God on marriage, birth, and nurturing of little children may seem rigid, but they are very practical.[2]

This chapter was written with the intent of solidifying testimonies of the restoration of the doctrine of eternal marriage and families. A reminder of God's restored law and its meaning in marriage will bless the reader with renewed testimony and insights that can alter behavior for the better.

Early in this dispensation it became obvious to the Prophet Joseph Smith that along with the restoration of the true church came the restoration of the true ordinances. It was also clear to the Prophet that keys were necessary to perform ordinances. The Lord revealed that the keys of baptism were needed in order for the ordinance of baptism to be recognized by God (see D&C 13). Joseph Smith and Oliver Cowdery learned while translating the Book of Mormon plates that authority to perform baptisms was necessary. After they sincerely prayed, inquiring about baptism, John the Baptist appeared to them and restored the keys of the Aaronic Priesthood, including the keys of baptism. Not only was this the restoration of the keys to perform the ordinance of baptism, but it was the beginning of the restoration of the new and everlasting covenant, which includes all of the ordinances leading to exaltation (see D&C 22).

The idea of marriage as an ordinance was suggested early in the Restoration, through a revelation intended for the Shakers. The Shakers taught that in order to receive a higher degree of salvation, one had to be celibate. The Lord gave a revelation to be read to the Shaker community (see D&C 49). Within this revelation he refuted the Shaker doctrine that taught against marriage. The Lord stated: "And again, verily I say unto you, that whoso forbiddeth to marry is not ordained of God, for marriage is ordained of God unto man" (D&C 49:15). Therefore, in the early days of the Restoration the doctrine of marriage was firmly established as a God-ordained ordinance. Additionally, the Lord addressed the objection the Shakers had to the intimate relations between a husband and wife in bringing children into the world. The revelation continued: "Wherefore, it is lawful that he should have one wife, and they twain shall be one flesh, and all this that the earth might answer the end of its creation; and that it might be filled with the measure of man, according to his creation before the world was made" (D&C 49:16–17). Therefore, not only marriage or the companionship of a husband and wife was revealed to be ordained of God, but also the bringing of children into the world was revealed as an essential part of God's plan in the very creation of the earth.

During this same time period, Joseph was instructed more specifically concerning future laws and keys that would seal a husband and wife in the covenant of marriage after the resurrection. B. H. Roberts taught that there is evidence to believe that Joseph received the information contained in section 132 of the Doctrine and Covenants, the section on eternal marriage, as early as 1831.[3] Why was the revelation not written down until twelve years later? One obvious answer is that the keys or authorization needed to seal marriages for eternity had not yet been revealed when he first learned of the doctrine. That which was revealed to Joseph at such an early date placed emphasis on the keys of the priesthood necessary to perform marriage.

On 3 April 1836, in the Kirtland Temple, Joseph Smith received important keys that would enable him to officiate in the fulness of priesthood ordinances. After the appearances of the Savior and Moses, and before the appearance of Elijah, "Elias appeared, and committed the dispensation of the gospel of Abraham, saying that in us and our seed all generations after us should be blessed" (D&C 110:12). Though often overlooked, this was an important event in the unveiling of eternal or celestial marriage. Elder Bruce R. McConkie taught:

> Now what was the *gospel of Abraham*? Obviously it was the commission, the mission, the endowment and power, the message of salvation, given to Abraham. And what was this? It was a divine promise that both in the world and out of the world his seed should continue "as innumerable as the stars; or, if ye were to count the sand upon the seashore ye could not number them" (D&C 132:30; Gen. 17; Abr. 2:1-12).
>
> Thus the gospel of Abraham was one of celestial marriage; . . . it was a gospel or commission to provide a lineage for the

elect portion of the pre-existent spirits, a gospel to provide a household in eternity for those who live the fulness of the celestial law. This power and commission is what Elias restored, and as a consequence, the righteous among all future generations were assured of the blessings of a continuation of the seeds forever, even as it was with Abraham of old.[4]

Elias restored the dispensation of the Abrahamic covenant, thus restoring the doctrine of celestial marriage. This restoration was still not sufficient for celestial marriage to last beyond death. It was necessary for Elijah to return with keys of the priesthood. Why was Elijah's return so necessary? Joseph Smith answered: "Why send Elijah? Because he holds the keys of the authority to administer in all the ordinances of the Priesthood; and without the authority is given, the ordinances could not be administered in righteousness."[5]

It was through these keys and authority that Joseph was finally able to officiate in all of the ordinances necessary for the salvation and exaltation of men and women. Elijah restored the keys that seal all blessings to us for time and all eternity.

Joseph then was prepared to instruct the Saints in celestial marriage. In 1843 he issued the revelations that teach the doctrine of celestial marriage. Joseph gave the following instructions to the Church: "In the celestial glory there are three heavens or degrees; and in order to obtain the highest, a man must enter into this order of the priesthood [meaning the new and everlasting covenant of marriage]; and if he does not, he cannot obtain it. He may enter into the other, but that is the end of his kingdom; he cannot have an increase" (D&C 131:1–4). This section introduces to the Church the need to have the new and everlasting covenant of marriage sealed upon a couple in order for them to qualify for exaltation. It also defines what is meant by exaltation—those who do not receive this covenant will not have an increase. This sounds much like the promise made to Abraham that his seed would be innumerable, not only in this life but throughout all eternity. Therefore, the restoration of the blessings of Abraham enables men in this dispensation to enjoy a continuation of the promises made to him.

In Doctrine and Covenants 132, the Lord continued to clarify the doctrine of marriage. The revelation first exhorts those reading it to "prepare thy heart to receive and obey the instructions which I am about to give unto you; for all those who have this law revealed unto them must obey the same" (D&C 132:3). Why prepare our hearts? With increasing divorce rates, it is understandable that the Lord teaches that successful marriages take a prepared heart. He is also about to reveal that not only do certain marriages continue through eternity, but that some will not.

The revelation then gives the law of marriage and the conditions of the law:

> For behold, I reveal unto you a new and an everlasting covenant; and if ye abide not that covenant, then are ye damned; for no one can reject this covenant and be permitted to enter into my glory.
>
> For all who will have a blessing at my hands shall abide the law which was appointed for that blessing, and the conditions thereof, as were instituted from before the foundation of the world.
>
> And as pertaining to the new and everlasting covenant, it was instituted for the fulness of my glory; and he that receiveth a fulness thereof must and shall abide the law, or he shall be damned, saith the Lord God (D&C 132:4–6).

The idea of a "new and everlasting covenant" was familiar doctrine for the Saints. In Doctrine and Covenants 22 they learned of the new and everlasting covenant of baptism. The covenant of baptism initiates our salvation and exaltation, but in order to enter into God's glory one must accept the new and everlasting covenant of marriage. Those who do not will be damned, or in other words, denied eternal increase.

The revelation then teaches the conditions that make this law binding:

> And verily I say unto you, that the conditions of this law are these: All covenants, contracts, bonds, obligations, oaths, vows, performances, connections, associations, or expectations, that are not made and entered into and sealed by the Holy Spirit of promise, of him who is anointed, both as well for time and for all eternity, and that too most holy, by revelation and commandment through the medium of mine anointed, whom I have appointed on the earth to hold this power (and I have appointed unto my servant Joseph to hold this power in the last days, and there is never but one on the earth at a time on whom this power and the keys of this priesthood are conferred), are of no efficacy, virtue, or force in and after the resurrection from the dead; for all contracts that are not made unto this end have an end when men are dead (D&C 132:7).

Stated simply, covenants made in this life must be sealed by the Holy Spirit of Promise to be recognized in the next life. At the time of the revelation Joseph held the keys, or in other words the power that Elijah had committed to him, to initiate covenants that would be valid after death. This included the new and everlasting covenant of marriage, or celestial marriage. In the Church today, we sustain the present prophet as the only one authorized to exercise these keys. Though the keys may be delegated to others, such as sealers in the temple, they are always used under the direction of the living prophet.

The Lord reiterates this point by reminding us that anything of this world, "whether it be ordained of men, by thrones, or principalities, or powers, or things of name, whatsoever they may be, that are not by me or by my word, saith the Lord, shall be thrown down, and shall not remain after men are dead, neither in nor after the resurrection, saith the Lord your God" (D&C 132:13).

The revelation clarifies which marriages do not endure through eternity and provides two examples of marriage that do not fall under the eternal nature of the new and everlasting covenant of marriage. The first of these involves a man who marries a woman "not by me nor by my word" (D&C 132:15). This marriage union is not of force after they are dead. These marriages are what we call civil marriages, in which the participants do not pretend their marriage will have eternal consequence.

The second example of marriage is discussed in verse 18, which speaks of a situation where a man may "make a covenant with her for time and for all eternity," using in the ceremony some of the language the Lord has approved, but doing so without the proper authority. In such cases, the marriage will not continue beyond death. These marriages may be those performed by well-meaning individuals who believe in eternal marriage but do not understand the necessity of keys and authority. These may also include marriages where a couple may write their own vows and include eternal language. Regardless, neither of these civil marriages are valid when men are dead. As the Lord has stated:

> Therefore, when they are out of the world they neither marry nor are given in marriage; but are appointed angels in heaven, which angels are ministering servants, to minister for those who are worthy of a far more, and an exceeding, and an eternal weight of glory.
>
> For these angels did not abide my law; therefore, they cannot be enlarged, but remain separately and singly, without exaltation, in their saved condition, to all eternity; and from henceforth are not gods, but are angels of God forever and ever (D&C 132:16–17).

Finally, the Lord teaches us of the only marriage that will exist beyond death. He states:

> And again, verily I say unto you, if a man marry a wife by

my word, which is my law, and by the new and everlasting covenant, and it is sealed unto them by the Holy Spirit of promise, by him who is anointed, unto whom I have appointed this power and the keys of this priesthood; and it shall be said unto them—Ye shall come forth in the first resurrection; and if it be after the first resurrection, in the next resurrection; and shall inherit thrones, kingdoms, principalities, and powers, dominions, all heights and depths—then shall it be written in the Lamb's Book of Life, that he shall commit no murder whereby to shed innocent blood, and if ye abide in my covenant, and commit no murder whereby to shed innocent blood, it shall be done unto them in all things whatsoever my servant hath put upon them, in time, and through all eternity; and shall be of full force when they are out of the world; and they shall pass by the angels, and the gods, which are set there, to their exaltation and glory in all things, as hath been sealed upon their heads, which glory shall be a fulness and a continuation of the seeds forever and ever (D&C 132:19).

It is interesting that in both sections 131 and 132, after teaching the new and everlasting covenant of marriage, the Lord speaks of having one's calling and election made sure. This gives added emphasis to the doctrine of marriage as a major step towards exaltation. Indeed, exaltation can be enjoyed only by those who are married and sealed as man and wife, to live together eternally.

It is also important to consider the language of the Lord as he discusses the civil marriage in contrast to celestial marriage. As he taught us of civil marriage, in both instances he refers to a man making a "covenant with her" (D&C 132:15, 18), meaning his wife. In verse 19, the idea of a man covenanting with a woman is conspicuously missing. In other words, in eternal marriage, the covenant is made with God. This covenant includes a man and a woman and involves promises to each other, but eventually it comes back to a covenant relationship between us and God. In all forms of civil marriage, the vows are made to another person. We know from sad experience that covenants between men are easily negotiated and broken. We also know that covenants with God are not negotiable. In referring to teachings of Heber C. Kimball, Hugh Nibley stated:

> As Heber C. Kimball reminded the saints, there are no covenants made between individuals in the church. All promises and agreements are between the individual and our Father in Heaven; all other parties, including the angels, are present only as witnesses. Therefore whether anybody else observes and keeps the promise is not my concern, but if I do not do what I have promised, what blessings can I expect?[6]

This reminds us that when we break our marriage covenant, we are not just breaking covenants with man or woman, but we are breaking covenants with God. It is ironic that people would hold carefully to their baptismal covenant, but the idea of breaking a marriage covenant does not hold the same fear. I remember a young man who was toying with the idea of divorce. He had been married for only six months, and he and his wife just weren't getting along. There was not any evidence of abuse, and they were both striving to live the gospel. The young man was fairly insistent that divorce was his best option. In an attempt to catch his attention, the bishop suggested that they entertain the idea of divorce. At the same time, he suggested that they have the young man's name removed from the records of the Church. Of course, the young man was shocked at the suggestion. When asked why, he stated that he held his baptismal covenants sacred and would never turn away from them. At that point the bishop pointed out how tenaciously the young man held to that Aaronic Priesthood ordinance but was willing to dismiss the higher Melchizedek Priesthood ordinance of marriage. This observation caused a priority shift and some serious thought for the young man.

Some of us may also be guilty of the general acceptance of divorce as a solution. We may even counsel friends about divorce. I've frequently pointed out to missionaries that their new converts will often come up against barriers soon after their baptism. Maybe people aren't accepting them at their ward. Maybe their previous faith or friends have a strong pull upon them. When new converts come questioning their baptism, no faithful member would ever suggest they leave the Church and deny the covenant they have made with God. The member would likely teach them to hold that covenant sacred, despite the sacrifices involved and the challenges faced.

What does this mean in the day-to-day struggle that exists among mortal beings, especially those who have entered into the marriage covenant? Some observations may help in the application of this doctrine. The first observation comes in the context of keeping covenants. All covenants and ordinances that are part of the new and everlasting covenant are contingent upon the previous covenants made in the ordinance chain. Like the families mentioned earlier in this chapter, sometimes we neglect previous covenants in the attempt to strengthen the marriage covenant. This has the opposite effect. Keeping covenants and commandments gives us the strength to do what must be done to have strong marriages.

A man came seeking advice in his marriage. He and his sweetheart had been sealed in the temple, but soon afterward she decided the Church was not for her. She stopped attending and spoke of her desire to not have their future children brainwashed in Primary. This man was desperate, for he loved his wife but also had a testimony of the gospel. After many discussions about the inactivity of his wife, it occurred to me that we had never spoken of him. In the context of our close relationship, he gave me permission to ask some pointed questions about his worthiness. It became apparent that he was not going to the temple, did not have a current temple recommend, did not pay his tithing, and was not attending church to renew his covenants through the sacrament. When I asked him why, he said that his wife would be unhappy if he did those things and might leave him.

He hadn't even considered the blessings that could come to him if he kept his covenants. As he kept his promises, the Lord could bless him and possibly touch his wife's heart. I could make no promises other than the fact that the Lord is bound when we do what he says (see D&C 82:10).

What are the promises made to those who keep covenants? They are numerous and far-reaching. As we seek to be one as husband and wife, we are seeking to do something that is countercultural. As the natural man is an enemy to God, so he is likely an enemy to other natural men or women. To overcome this enmity, we need a power beyond us. That power is the Atonement, which is magnified and delivered through the covenant. As Elder Henry B. Eyring taught:

> We see in His words the way families will be made one, as will all the children of our Heavenly Father who follow the Savior and His servants:
>
> "As thou hast sent me into the world, even so have I also sent them into the world.
>
> "And for their sakes I sanctify myself, that they also might be sanctified through the truth.
>
> "Neither pray I for these alone, but for them also which shall believe on me through their word;
>
> "That they all may be one; as thou, Father, art in me, and I in thee, that they also may be one in us: that the world may believe that thou hast sent me" (John 17:18–21).
>
> In those few words He made clear how the gospel of Jesus Christ can allow hearts to be made one. Those who would believe the truth He taught could accept the ordinances and the covenants offered by His authorized servants. Then, through obedience to those ordinances and covenants, their natures would be changed. The Savior's Atonement in that way makes it possible for us to be sanctified. We can then live in unity, as we must to have peace in this life and to dwell with the Father and His Son in eternity.[7]

The change to our natures must be vitally important to us. When we go seeking help in our marriages, our minds are usually on how we can get along better with each other. In effect, we are seeking a change in our natures. I was often interested at the perplexed look on a couples' faces when they came seeking advice about communicating with each other, yet I would discuss with them the idea of communicating more effectively with God. True changes of nature and disposition come only from him. I have witnessed many couples who have taken the counsel and increased their commitment to God and their covenants. Slowly, I have watched their natures change and the love in their relationship increase. It takes time and sacrifice. The Lord stated:

> Verily I say unto you, all among them who know their hearts are honest, and are broken, and their spirits contrite, and are willing to observe their covenants by sacrifice—yea, every sacrifice which I, the Lord, shall command—they are accepted of me.
>
> For I, the Lord, will cause them to bring forth as a very fruitful tree which is planted in a goodly land, by a pure stream, that yieldeth much precious fruit.
>
> Verily I say unto you, that it is my will that a house should be built unto me in the land of Zion, like unto the pattern which I have given you (D&C 97:8–10).

These verses were given in the historical context of the commandment to the Saints to build the temple. If we liken the building of the Lord's house to the building of our own homes and families, we gain much insight into the power available to us in the effort. In an earlier command the Lord stated:

> Verily I say unto you, it is my will that you should build a house. If you keep my commandments you shall have power to build it.
>
> If you keep not my commandments, the love of the Father

293

shall not continue with you, therefore you shall walk in darkness.

Now here is wisdom, and the mind of the Lord—let the house be built, not after the manner of the world, for I give not unto you that ye shall live after the manner of the world (D&C 95:11–13).

If we desire to build a marriage with all the desired blessings, we must do it after the manner the Lord has shown us. It is interesting to note that when we don't keep the commandments, the love of the Father is absent and our life is comparable to walking in darkness. That is what so many couples feel when their marriages deteriorate. The love of the Father is the love we must have for our spouse. It is of light and comes from obedience to the commandments and covenants. Once we have entered into the new and everlasting covenant of marriage, our success in that relationship is absolutely contingent upon our relationship with God. Speaking of those who have entered this covenant, Elder Matthew Cowley stated:

We . . . have entered an eternal triangle, not a companionship of two, but of three—the husband, the wife, and God—the most sacred triangle man and woman can become a part of. But my heart sinks in despair when I witness so many who have and are withdrawing that hand from one another. They don't do that until they first divorce God from that triangle, and after divorcing God, it is practically impossible for them to stay together side by side.[8]

The divorce from God occurs when we fail to keep our promises to him and love him first through obedience.

Finally, the exalting power of the new and everlasting covenant of marriage must not be overlooked. The Lord invites us to consider this as he continues in section 132 by teaching that as we accept this covenant and abide in it:

Then shall they be gods, because they have no end; therefore shall they be from everlasting to everlasting, because they
continue; then shall they be above all, because all things are
subject unto them. Then shall they be gods, because they have
all power, and the angels are subject unto them.

Verily, verily, I say unto you, except ye abide my law ye
cannot attain to this glory.

For strait is the gate, and narrow the way that leadeth
unto the exaltation and continuation of the lives, and few
there be that find it, because ye receive me not in the world
neither do ye know me.

But if ye receive me in the world, then shall ye know me,
and shall receive your exaltation; that where I am ye shall be
also.

This is eternal lives—to know the only wise and true God,
and Jesus Christ, whom he hath sent. I am he. Receive ye,
therefore, my law (D&C 132:20–24).

The Lord directly ties our exaltation to our willingness to receive
his law and abide in it. The law eventually includes this sacred order of
marriage. It is interesting that the scriptures here invite us to think of
"eternal lives" in contrast with "eternal life" (see John 17:3).
Exaltation is experienced as couples and families, not as individuals.
We also learn that to receive this law is to receive the Savior. It may
be concluded that in order to truly know Christ, we must experience
marriage under the new and everlasting covenant.

When we look at marriage as an ordinance and part of the new
and everlasting covenant, it alters our priorities. We establish appropriate attitudes of worship and covenant renewal that allow God's
blessings to flow to us. Included in those blessings are his *love,* his
light, and his *power* to become one with him and with each other. We
eventually gain exaltation, or his *life,* in eternal families. All of these
blessings come to us as we live in the new and everlasting covenant.

Notes

1. Neal A. Maxwell, "This Is a Special Institution," Inaugural Address at BYU–Hawaii, 1 July 1997, BYU–Hawaii President's Page, retrieved from http://www.byuh.edu/about/president/inaguration/maxwell.jsp.
2. Boyd K. Packer, "Little Children," *Ensign*, November 1986, 17.
3. See B. H. Roberts, "Introduction," in Joseph Smith, *History of The Church of Jesus Christ of Latter-day Saints,* ed. B. H. Roberts, 2d ed. rev., 7 vols. (Salt Lake City: The Church of Jesus Christ of Latter-day Saints, 1932–51), 5:xxix-xxx).
4. Bruce R. McConkie, *Mormon Doctrine,* 2d ed. (Salt Lake City: Bookcraft, 1966), 219–20.
5. Joseph Smith, *Teachings of the Prophet Joseph Smith,* sel. Joseph Fielding Smith (Salt Lake City: Deseret Book, 1976), 172.
6. Hugh Nibley, *Approaching Zion,* ed. Don E. Norton (Salt Lake City: Deseret Book and Provo: Foundation for Ancient Research and Mormon Studies, 1989), 385.
7. Henry B. Eyring, "That We May Be One," *Ensign*, May 1998, 66.
8. Matthew Cowley, in Conference Report, October 1952, 27.

About the Authors

Elder Bruce C. Hafen was sustained as a member of the First Quorum of the Seventy of The Church of Jesus Christ of Latter-day Saints on April 6, 1996. Elder Hafen is married to Marie K. Hafen, and they are the parents of seven children. Elder Hafen served as president of Ricks College in Rexburg, Idaho, for seven years, dean of the Brigham Young University Law School from 1985 to 1989, and from then until the time of his call as a General Authority, he served as the provost of the university. As a law professor, he became an internationally recognized scholar in the fields of family law, educational law, and constitutional law, with particular interests in the legal rights and needs of children and the legal status of marriage.

Douglas E. Brinley is an author or co-author of six books on marriage and family topics, including *Between Husband and Wife: Gospel Perspectives on Marital Intimacy* and *First Comes Love*. He is a professor of Church History and Doctrine at Brigham Young University. He teaches at BYU Education Week and Know Your Religion series. He and his wife, Geri, are the parents of six children.

Daniel K Judd is an associate professor and department chair of Ancient Scripture at Brigham Young University. He has a Ph.D. in counseling psychology and a master's degree in family science, both from BYU. His research interests have focused on the relationship of religion and mental health, although his most recent book, *Taking Sides: Clashing Views on Controversial Issues in Religion* (McGraw-Hill/Dushkin, 2003), is concerned with both doctrinal and philosophical issues. Dan and his wife, Kaye, are the parents of four children and live in Orem, Utah, where he serves as a stake president.

Marleen S. Williams is president of AMCAP (Association of Mormon Counselors and Psychotherapists) for the period from 2003 to 2005. She is a licensed clinical psychologist and associate clinical professor of counseling psychology in the Counseling and Career Center at Brigham Young University. Her research focuses on work with women's issues, spirituality, and eating disorders. She is married to Dr. Robert F. Willliams and they are the parents of nine children.

Kent R. Brooks is an associate professor of Church History and Doctrine at Brigham Young University. He formerly taught at BYU–Idaho. He is a popular speaker and writer. He and his wife, Camille, are the parents of five children.

Terrance Olson is a professor in the School of Family Life at Brigham Young University. He obtained a Ph.D. in marriage and family from Florida State University. He has served on Church writing committees. He was appointed to serve on a sixteen-member federal panel in the mid-1980s to address problems of adolescent pregnancy. He was an editor for the *Encyclopedia of Mormonism*. He has presented papers to the National Council on Family Relations and the International Association for Moral Education. He and his wife, Karen, are the parents of six children.

Brent A. Barlow teaches in the School of Family Life at Brigham Young University. He is a clinical member of the American Association for Marriage and Family Therapy. He is the author of many books and articles, including *Dealing with Differences in Marriage, What Wives Expect of Husbands, What Husbands Expect of Wives, Twelve Traps in Today's Marriage—and How to Avoid Them,* and *Just for Newlyweds.* Brent is a popular speaker in the BYU Education Week program as well as the Know Your Religion series. He and his wife, Susan, are the parents of seven children.

Kenneth W. Matheson received his doctorate in social work from the University of Utah. He was employed with LDS Family Services for nineteen years and currently is a clinical professor at Brigham Young University in the School of Social Work. He is a licensed clinical social worker and marriage and family therapist. He teaches at BYU Education Week. He and his wife, Marlene, are the parents of six children.

John Livingstone hails from Canada. He has been an associate professor of Church History and Doctrine at Brigham Young University since 1998, after serving as president of the Michigan Detroit Mission from 1995 to 1998. He has been in the Church Educational System as an institute director in Calgary, Canada, where he was a licensed psychologist. He is presently a board member of AMCAP (Association of Mormon Counselors and Psychotherapists). He and his wife, Linda, are the parents of six daughters and one son.

Charles B. Beckert is now retired from the Church Educational System, where he served as an institute instructor in Arizona and Ogden, Utah. He is a licensed marriage and family counselor, having obtained his Ph.D. from Brigham Young University. He and his wife, Olga, have four sons.

Rory C. Reid has a master's degree in social work from the University of Utah and is a licensed psychotherapist who works with clients at the Salt Lake Counseling Center and also at the Gathering Place in Orem, Utah, where he coordinates the Sexual Addiction Program. He has previously worked as a therapist with LDS Family Services, the Utah State Prison Sex Offender Program, and the Monarch Treatment Assessment Center. His graduate research focused on impulse-control disorders with pornography and cybersex on the Internet. In addition to treating individuals with problematic sexual behaviors, he has presented papers at many conferences and workshops, including BYU Education Week. He is actively involved with continuing research on the treatment of pornography problems and teaches part time at BYU. He is the coauthor of *Discussing Pornography Problems with a Spouse* and one of three editors of *Confronting Pornography: A Guide to Prevention and Recovery for*

Individuals, Loved Ones, and Leaders. He lives with his wife, Renee, and their son, Craig, in Lehi, Utah.

Sherrie Mills Johnson has a Ph.D. in sociology from Brigham Young University. Her dissertation is entitled "Religiosity and Life Satisfaction of LDS Women." She currently teaches Book of Mormon classes in the Department of Ancient Scripture at BYU. She has published *Man, Woman, and Deity; Spiritually-Centered Motherhood;* and several books for children based on stories from the Book of Mormon and the Bible. She and her husband, Carl, are the parents of ten children and live in Orem, Utah.

Guy L. Dorius is an associate professor of Church History and Doctrine at Brigham Young University; he also teaches LDS marriage and family relations there. His Ph.D. is in family studies. He is a specialist in marriage and parenting issues. He served as a bishop in both his home ward and in a campus married student ward. He and his wife, Vicki, are the parents of seven children.

Index

Abel, 194

Ability, role of, in relationships, 118

Abinadi, missionary work of, 33–34

Abraham: receiving blessings of, 38; significance of covenant of, 45; gospel of, 284–85

Abstinence, premarital, 275

Abuse: seriousness of offense, 23; of spouse or child, 46, 152, 183; victim of sexual, 79; as reason for divorce, 179; lasting consequences of, 231

Accomplishments, praising spouse's, 113–14

Accountability: as element of happy marriage, 77; refusal of pornography user to accept, 241–42

Accusations, 181

Actions: influenced by perceptions, 119–20; as elements of marital connection, 214–25; purity in, 217; considering meaning and implications of, 221; effect of loving, 224

Adam: naming of animals by, 255–56; symbolism of rib in story of, 256–58; learned by experience, 265

Adam and Eve: Atonement received by, 2; Fall of, 35, 38; perspective of, after Fall, 104–5; creation of, 253–57; oneness of, 259

Addiction, sexual, 79, 233; receiving professional help for, 9, 236–38, 245–52; reasons for, 235; labeling, 236. *See also* Pornography

Administering, ministering and, 90

Adultery: as manifestation of selfishness, 13; as reason for divorce, 61, 179. *See also* Divorce

Adversity, 3–4; togetherness in facing, 87, 264; overcoming, 104; refusal to blame God for, 121; attitudes toward, 123–24; enduring, 137, 140; as part of mortality, 139; hoping to avoid, 139–40

Advice, 118

Affection: physical signs of, 177–78; considering meaning and implications of, 221

Afflictions: physical, 91; helping spouse bear, 105

Agency, 119; improper use of, 51, 59–60; of others, 126–27, 129–30; wise use of, 126–30; accepting principles of, 142–43; unwise use of, through pornography, 239

Aging, sex and, 272

Agnosticism, 21

Alcohol addiction, 235

Alienation: reasons for family, 133; in marriage, 210

Alma the Elder: change of heart experienced by, 33–34; on having hearts knit together, 125–26

Altar, temple, significance of, 259

Ambition, 138

Ambivalence, of pornography user, 244–45

Ammon, on faith in God, 73

Amulek, on blessings of coming unto Christ, 66

Dunn, Loren C., on mutual respect, 174

Education, secular, not a substitute for inspiration, 20–21
Efforts, praising spouse's, 177–78
Ejaculation, premature, 277
Elias, appearance of, in Kirtland Temple, 284
Elijah, appearance of, in Kirtland Temple, 284
Elohim, Hebrew meaning of, 257
Embarrassment, 197
Emery, Robert E., on effects of divorce on children, 153
Emotional intimacy: definition of, 79; development of, 79–82; attitudes that discourage, 80; perfectionism as enemy to, 81. *See also* Intimacy
Emotions: victims of own, 132–36; assuming control of own, 135–36, 182–83, 208–9; vs. feelings, 196–201; using pornography to escape, 232; when confronting spouse regarding pornography use, 239–40; learning to express, 250–51
Enabling, as hindrance to resolving pornography problem, 237
"Encounter groups," 206
Encouragement: words of, 113–14; role of, in marital connectedness, 217–19
Endowment, temple, 2, 37–39; scriptural elements of, 44–45
Enduring trials, 98, 137, 140
Enoch, 100
Entertainment(s): life as series of, 13, 98; inappropriate, 46
Entitlement, attitude of, 78
Errors, 175–76
Escalation, as stage in pornography addiction, 235
Eternal life: mortality as preparation for, 23–24, 50–51, 56; marriage as preparation for, 76

Eternity, marriage for time and, 288–89
Ethics, secular, 21
Eve, symbolism in story of creation of, 256–58. *See also* Adam and Eve
Evil, returning good for, 207–8
Exaltation, 42–43, 289; not hindered by spouse's unrighteous actions, 12; marriage essential to, 35; marriage as practice for, 38; power of procreation as element of, 43–44, 278–79; significance of, 285; conditions for, 295
Example, of Jesus Christ, 36. *See also* Jesus Christ
Excuses: for unwillingness to build relationship, 118; for pornography use, 237–38
Exercise(s): for resolution of problems, 173–74; for regaining marital closeness, 211; for assessing marital closeness, 212; for date night, 224
Expectations: unrealistic, 13, 78, 107, 139–40; meeting spouse's, 50; regarding marriage therapy, 145–48; essential and nonessential, 170; sexual, 228
Experience: learning from, 9–10, 105–6, 137; mortal, 97–106
Eyring, Henry B.: on the first commandment, 74; on keeping covenants, 292

Fagan, Patrick F., on effects of divorce on children, 152–53
Failure: as normal part of life, 8, 98; marital differences not evidence of, 172
Faith, 122, 143; marriage as leap of, 2; as element of successful marriage, 48, 56; in Jesus Christ, 62; essential to growth, 86–87; responding to challenges with, 95, 122, 124, 135–36; required of us in mortality, 97–98; trials of, 99; miracles in marriage accomplished through,

194; not indication of superiority, 257–58

Gladness, voice of, 112

Goals, realistic, 118

God: marriage ordained by, 4, 15, 283–84; justice of, 12; seeking guidance from, in marital problems, 16, 176–77; wisdom of, 18; loss of faith in, 21; relationship with, 32, 65–66, 73, 97; interested in success of each marriage, 34–35, 190; use of agency by, 35; and covenants, 38, 289–90; offended by spouse or child abuse, 46; slow to hearken to prayers of unrighteous, 67; commandment to love, 72, 282; submission to, 109; reliance on, 137; seeking kingdom of, 138; Adam and Eve made in image of, 256–57; Hebrew word for, 257; increased commitment to, 293; loss of obedience to, 294

Godhead: ordinances performed in name of, 34; our accountability to, 37

Godhood, prerequisites for, 257, 295

Golden Rule, 14–15, 137

Good: intentions, 83–84; all things work together for, 126

"Good guy" image, of pornography user, 243

Gospel: as remedy for marital problems, 9, 13, 17–20; basing therapy on, 15; living the, 22, 34, 37, 121, 125, 292; dispensations of, 45; principles, family strengthened by, 52–53, 95; as foundation, 56, 68–69; clinging to, during difficult times, 63–64; attitudes regarding, 118, 119; study of, as catalyst to change, 282; loss of obedience to principles of, 294

Gottman, John, on positive communication, 186–87

Gratification, instant, 8

Gratitude, expressions of, 41, 87, 187; through marital intimacy, 270

Gray, Dan, 240; on pornography addiction, 237

Greed, 13

Grief, 3, 99

Growing apart, as insufficient reason for divorce, 61–62

Growth, 209; challenges lead to, 9; through marriage and family experiences, 40; marital climate necessary for, 81–82; spiritual, 94; resolving differences as key to, 175–76; through controlling anger, 205

Grudges, 133

Guidance, regarding marital challenges, 41, 66

Habits, bad: breaking, 107–8; choosing to overlook, 172; of pornography user, 244

Hafen, Marie, 4–5

Hales, Robert D., on building family relationships, 55

Hand, touch of Master's, 114

Hanks, Marion D., on forgiveness, 111

Happiness: righteousness as basis of marital, 12, 14, 35; marital, 18, 119, 170, 174; assessment of marital, 22–23; gospel as basis of family, 30n. 12, 56; through Jesus Christ, 95; working to ensure spouse's, 104; children's, 154; plan of, 254–55

Hard-heartedness, 139

Harmony, marital: as realistic goal, 119; creation of, 136–39

Hatred: attempting to justify, 131; choosing to feel, 201

Havel, Václav, on following conscience, 129–30

Healer, Jesus Christ as, 110, 114

Healing: spouse as minister of, 109–10; undermined by unforgiving spouse, 111

Health: professionals, excessive reliance on, 7–9; mental, 9; professionals,

Principles, gospel: worldly attitude
regarding, 119; abandonment of, in
adversity, 124; living, 125
Priorities, 13; correct, 64–65, 295;
spiritual, 67–68; mistaken, 281–82,
291–92
Problem(s): emotional, receiving
counseling for, 8; financial, 13, 181;
mental and emotional, 30n. 2;
attitude toward, 82–83; blaming
spouse for, 84, 181–82; "owning"
responsibility for, 85–86, 188;
behavioral, 173; resolving, 173–74,
185–86, 277; running from, 177,
228–29; divorce not always solution
to, 178–79; differences in men's
and women's approaches to,
184–85; sharing spouse's, 185,
259–60. See also Problems, marital
Problems, marital: spiritual basis of, 12;
seeking God's help with, 16, 41;
seeking bishop's help with, 17, 160;
seeking instant solutions to, 19;
gospel as remedy for, 19–20, 24;
ineffectiveness of communication
alone in resolving, 25–29; sharing
responsibility for, 50, 185;
resolution of, 104; list of most
common, 148; intimacy destroyed
by, 268–69
Proclamation, Family. See "Family, The:
A Proclamation to the World"
Procreation, power of, 39, 262–63; as
element of exaltation, 43, 278–79,
286, 289
Profanity, as element in marital
unhappiness, 215
Progression, eternal, 37, 279; not
hindered by spouse's unrighteous
actions, 12; limitations to, 288–89
Promiscuity, 262
Promises, to those who keep
covenants, 292
Promptings, willingness to heed, 36
Prophet(s): counsel of, regarding
marriage, 45–47; priesthood keys
held by, 287

Prostitution, on Internet, 228
Proximity, meaning and implications
of, 221
Psychiatrists, secular, 17
Psychology, mistaken ideas in, 24–26
Purity and Passion, 263

Quarreling: as result of negative
communication, 25; marriage
destroyed by, 171; lessons learned
from, 192; children's perception of
adult, 195; avoidance of, 205;
physical intimacy lessened by, 270

Rage: spirituality lost due to, 171–72;
choosing to feel, 201
Rationalization, by pornography user,
234–35, 238
Reaction, of pornography user, to
confrontation, 240, 245
Reciprocation, in marriage, 50
Recreation, as element of successful
marriage, 49
Rector, Robert, on effects of divorce
on children, 152–53
Regret, post-divorce statistics
regarding, 155
Rejection, fear of spouse's, 79
Relapse, in pornography use, 244;
prevention of, 249, 251
Relationship: praying to improve
marital, 40; irredeemable, 61, 147,
180; with God and Christ, 65–66;
key to maintaining, 118; pride and
selfishness damaging to, 187–88;
troubled, God as healer of, 190;
reducing fearfulness in, 205;
assessing success in, 212; physical,
219–20, 260–62; neglecting,
222–24; of therapist and clients,
245–48
Relief Society, 52
Remorse, of pornography user, 242–44
Repentance: as element of successful
marriage, 13, 48; as taught in
temple, 37–38; need for, 38, 56,